The Complete Divorce Guide

The Complete Divorce Guide

By Brette Sember, JD

Published by Sember Resources

ISBN 978-0-9995942-9-2

This publication is designed to provide accurate and authoritative information in regard to the subject matter covered. It is sold with the understanding that the publisher is not engaged in rendering legal, accounting, or other professional service. If legal advice or other expert assistance is required, the services of a competent professional person should be sought.

From a Declaration of Principles Jointly Adopted by a Committee of the American Bar Association and a Committee of Publishers and Associations

This product is not a substitute for legal advice.

Disclaimer required by Texas statutes.

Contents

Contents

Contents

Contents

Contents

Contents

Contents

Contents

Contents

Contents

Introduction

Divorce can be one of the most difficult times in your life. You are going through a total upheaval that affects nearly every part of your day-to-day existence. It's disorienting to have everything suddenly uncertain. It can be hard to think clearly, understand how things will affect you in the long run, and know what questions to ask in order to get the information you need. Sometimes you need someone to help point out those things you should be considering. *The Complete Divorce Handbook* is designed to be your companion through all of this and to help you think through issues and concerns that may affect you. If you are handling the divorce on your own, this book will help you understand the issues you need to work out and provide guidance as to how to manage the case yourself. If you have an attorney (or plan to get one), this book will arm you with knowledge so you can ask intelligent questions and have a framework on which to base your decisions. Most importantly, this book is meant to offer you information so you have a sense of the path your divorce will take and the issues you need to deal with.

Divorce is emotional. Whether you want the divorce, are opposed to it, or really don't know what you want right now (which is not unusual), you're probably worried about your financial security, your children, and your entire life plan. A divorce is a major change and has the added double whammy of being not only a complicated emotional transition, but also a detailed legal proceeding. It's natural to feel a bit lost, confused, angry, hurt, and sad all at once as you try to come to grips with your situation and work through everything that must be done.

This book is here to offer you a roadmap, so you can take the time and energy you need to begin to heal from the emotional turmoil. Divorce is a process and it's important to establish a support network to assist you, including friends and family to lean on, and perhaps a therapist to help you cope with your feelings. You also need an attorney because this book is not a substitute for legal advice. Laws are always changing, and every state has its own particular rules, procedures, and statutes. No book can provide everything you need to know. It is essential that you get personal legal advice from an attorney who can explain the laws of your state to you and help you make decisions that are right for you in your situation.

Throughout the book, and in the appendix, you will find links to helpful information. These links are as up to date as possible, but web sites do change. If a link is not working, try typing in the main part of the link (for example, if the link is www.courts.state.ny.us/litigants/ and it does not work, try typing in www.courts.state.ny.us). This will take you to the home page of the site and from there you may be able to find the information you are seeking. If not, you should do a search for the information using a search engine such as Google.

It can be tempting to sit down at the computer and read a lot about divorce. You need to be careful about the information you are getting online, however. What is true in one state is not necessarily true in another. Information people share on bulletin boards or in chat rooms is not always reliable. The only way to be certain you are getting solid information is to talk with an attorney in your own state. The Internet is great for getting some basic facts, but never rely on something you read there unless you check with an expert.

The Complete Divorce Handbook is broken down into thirteen chapters that correspond to the issues you will be dealing with in the divorce. You will also find a resource guide (Appendix A) at the end of the book. This contains some recommended books and lists web sites where you can get more information. Note that there are links to state bar associations, state mediation associations, state collaborative law associations, and state court web sites, which will help you access state-specific information. Some sample forms have been included in Appendix B so you can see what they look like. However, every state requires that you use its own specific forms, so these are for information purposes only. In Appendix C, you will find a section of frequently asked questions. These are questions I've been asked by clients when I was a practicing divorce attorney and mediator, as well as questions I've been asked while serving as an expert for a divorce web site. Hopefully these answers will help address some of your own questions and will help you know that you are not alone in your concerns.

It may seem now as if there are millions of things to decide, all of them complicated. As you work through your divorce you will probably find, however, that a lot of the decisions make themselves. For example, for many families, custody is easily worked out. Once that's agreed on, it can be simple to determine what to do about the marital home and child support. In addition, most divorces settle—rather than going to trial, the spouses agree to a compromise. It's very likely your divorce will settle as well. Try to stay relaxed and calm as you work through the choices and situations ahead. While divorce might seem like a huge upheaval, you will come out on the other side, able to move forward with your life in a positive way.

I hope that this book will help you gather some basic information and point you in the right direction as you make the important decisions in front of you. You will undoubtedly experience a lot as you progress through your divorce; however, this is also an opportunity for a new beginning. I wish you the best as you move forward with your life.

Chapter 1

━━━━━ ❦ ━━━━━

Do You Want or Need a Divorce?

Contemplating divorce can be an overwhelming and frightening feeling. The thought of your life completely changing and the fear of the unknown are powerful reasons to stay frozen in place in your marriage. In many situations though, living in a relationship that is damaging, painful, unfulfilling, or just wrong can be a strong reason to begin to take steps toward making a change. Divorce is not always the answer though. Many couples are able to fix what is wrong in their relationship through counseling. Others make changes on their own that allow them to stay married. Other people choose to live with their marriage as it is. You might fall into one of these categories. But for many people, divorce is the choice that is right for them when they are faced with an unhappy marriage.

Divorce is not a decision to make lightly or on the spur of the moment. It has important implications that will resonate in all aspects of your life. In fact, divorce is considered to be the second most stressful life event, second only to the death of a spouse or close family member. If you are thinking about or wondering about divorce, it is important that you get some information first about how the process works and what your rights would be before you take any big steps toward a divorce.

Reasons for Divorce

There are many reasons people consider divorce. One of the most common situations is that the two people have grown apart. Sometimes this can happen gently and calmly. Other times it is associated with a lot of resentment, anger, and hurt. Fighting is the biggest reason people say they want a divorce. People fight for many reasons—a different life view, parenting disagreements, money, wanting different things, or even individual changes. Some marriages include mental, emotional, or physical abuse, which can be a dangerous situation for everyone involved. Living in a home where there is anger and blame is not usually a comfortable situation. It's possible to reconnect if you've become strangers to each other or to find ways to solve some of the things you disagree about. Marriage therapy can be helpful in getting to the root of what you fight about and in helping you find new ways to relate to each other.

Adultery is usually considered a common reason for divorce, but in most cases, adultery happens when there is something wrong in the marriage. That is not to say the person who has been cheated on is at fault; however, there is often a breakdown of the relationship (or at least a breakdown from one person's point of view) when one spouse chooses to go outside the marriage. Adultery causes major trust issues that may be able to be addressed in therapy if you want to save the marriage. Many couples do manage to repair their marriage after an affair.

Money is another big factor in divorce. Couples fight about money more than anything else. If you and your spouse have differing ideas about how to use money (save versus spend) it can create a huge rift in your marriage. Additionally, couples in financial trouble often find that they lash out at each other because the stress of money problems can really disrupt a relationship. Financial and marriage counseling can both be useful in this kind of situation.

Substance abuse is a situation that can easily harm a marriage. If one partner is not in control of himself, it is nearly impossible to have a real and healthy relationship. Substance abuse treatment can be the first step to repairing the marriage. Trust can be rebuilt once recovery is begun.

How to Decide

Deciding whether or not you want a divorce is one of the hardest decisions you will ever make. No matter what kind of a state your marriage is in right now, there was likely a time when you loved your spouse. Those feelings don't go away quickly or easily. In fact, even if you do decide you want a divorce, there will likely be times when you question what you're doing, long for your spouse, miss the good times, and possibly even try again. Some people even continue to love (in a different way) their ex after a divorce, even though they have decided they cannot be married to each other.

Ups and Downs

The road to divorce is a long one and, for many people, it is not a straight path. From the time you first start considering divorce to the point of a final divorce decree (should you reach that point), you'll probably change your mind a hundred times. This is normal. No matter what your marriage is like, it is nearly impossible to suddenly turn around and decide it is over without looking back. The most important thing you need to do throughout this process is to give yourself time to work through it and be patient with yourself. Divorce is a process in many ways—legally and emotionally. It simply takes time to make the decision and move through the many steps. Many people go through this rollercoaster ride and eventually reach a turning point where they know for certain that divorce is the answer—or decide that it isn't.

Things to Consider

No one can decide for you whether a divorce is the right option for you. When thinking about divorce, you should consider what your marriage is like now and how, or if, it could be fixed. Think about how your marriage and spouse makes you feel and how you would feel if you were no longer married.

Factors to Look at When Considering Divorce

Following are some issues to consider when weighing divorce. Think through each of these categories and use them to question how divorce might affect you.

- Your happiness and what you want for your life. If you aren't happy in your marriage, this is a major consideration for you. What kind of a life are you living if you are not happy? You need to consider whether you are truly unhappy with the marriage, or if there are only certain aspects of it (which may be repairable) that bother you. You must also consider whether you are unhappy with other things in your life (career, finances, your health and so on) and if this could be spilling over onto your marriage, causing discord. You need to spend time thinking about where you want to go in your life, and who you want to spend it with.

- The financial implications of a divorce (they are often huge and are more far-reaching than you might expect). Think about how you will live on one income and how you will afford to pay child support or alimony should you be ordered to do so. Consider how your assets and debts will be divided and what that will mean for your financial security. Lifestyle change you would face. You may no longer be able to live in your home. You would be a single person on holidays and may face fears of "growing old alone."

- How a divorce would affect your children. There have been important studies about the impact of divorce on children you might want to consider. Divorce is always hard for children, no matter how friendly it is, so you will want to think about the potential impact.

- What it would take to make your marriage one you would like to stay in, and how likely that kind of change is to happen.

- If you are seeing someone new (and many marriages end because one spouse has found someone new), think about how important that relationship is to you and how likely it is to become a long-term relationship.

- If you have been divorced before, you know how expensive and difficult divorce is. Weigh your experience against the situation you are in to help you decide if you want to go through another divorce.

Some therapists, when helping patients who are considering a divorce, recommend that they take a week and live as if they are getting a divorce and then live a week as if they are staying in their marriage. It might sound like this is something you must do as a couple (and sometimes that is the recommendation), but it really is about a mental shift you personally make. Really living with the choices and honestly trying them on for a full week gives you a good sense of how comfortable you are with the choices and which one may be right for you in your situation. Realizing you want a divorce is usually a gradual process and one that often takes many months to work through.

Marriage and Family Therapy

If you are unhappy in your marriage, it makes sense to try therapy before choosing to get a divorce. Marriage and family therapy may be able to help you and your spouse (and possibly your children) work through some of the issues that are making you feel unhappy. Marriage and family are two important aspects of your life. Think of all the other things in your life you try to repair before throwing them away. If your dishwasher breaks, you call a repair man. Even if a button falls off a shirt you probably sew it back on instead of tossing the shirt. It took years to create your marriage. You've invested a lot of effort into it and it makes sense to take some time to find out if it can be fixed. It also makes financial sense to try therapy. Marriage therapy is much less expensive than divorce. And if you do end up deciding to go ahead with the divorce, it is likely you will want to find a counselor to help you and you will already have started to explore many of the issues of your marriage.

It may take some work to find a therapist who is right for you and your spouse. Each has a unique personality and there are various approaches. It's a good idea to call a therapist and ask some questions over the phone to get an idea if you would be comfortable with this person. There are also a variety of types of therapists to consider. Some options include:

1. Marriage and family therapists (MFTs): psychotherapists with a master's or doctorate
2. Social worker (MSW or LCSW): social workers with a master's degree and varying amounts of experience
3. Mental health counselor: usually holds a bachelors or master's degree
4. Psychologist: an expert with a doctorate in psychology
5. Psychiatrist: medical doctor who specializes in mental health
6. Clergy: a clergy member who offers counseling to members of his or her church or temple, or who offers religious-based counseling to anyone

To find a marriage or family counselor, you could ask your family physician for a referral. Family or friends may have names they can offer you. If you have a therapist of your own, you could ask him or her for a referral. You can also contact the national or state organizations for therapists and request a referral. These include:

- American Psychiatric Association www.healthyminds.org
- American Psychological Association www.apahelpcenter.org
- National Association of Social Workers www.naswdc.org
- American Psychoanalytic Association www.apsa.org
- American Association for Marriage and Family Therapy www.aamft.org

When choosing a counselor or therapist, be sure to ask about his or her education, experience, professional licensing, and professional memberships. Another important factor may be cost. Check with your health insurance company to find out if there is mental health coverage available for your counseling. Find out what your co-pay would be and how many sessions per year are paid for (there is usually a limit). If you do have insurance coverage, be sure you obtain a list of the counselors who are on the approved list for your insurance company. If you have no insurance coverage, ask the counselor about the cost of the treatment, how many sessions could be needed (26 weeks is often considered about average for marriage therapy), and if any payment plans are available.

You will also want to talk with the counselor about what his or her approach to the counseling is. There are many new approaches to marriage counseling. Some types of therapy considered effective include:

- integrative behavioral therapy (which focuses on making arguments less hurtful)
- marriage education programs (workshops teaching couples how to get along)
- behavioral marriage therapy (helps couples be nicer to each other)
- insight-oriented therapy (focuses on understanding the reasons behind your problems), and
- emotionally focused therapy (focuses on breaking free of destructive cycles)

While some marriages can't be saved (a recent article in the *New York Times* says 38 percent of couples who enter marriage therapy are divorced within four years), it is probably worth the effort to find out if yours could be. At the very least, if you try counseling you will know you have done everything possible to save your marriage. If you do decide to go ahead with the divorce, some counselors will work with you through the beginning stages of the divorce so that you can both approach it in a fair and reasonable way.

Individual Therapy

You may find that individual therapy can help you as you wrestle with the decision whether or not to divorce. Some couples each see separate counselors to help them through marital problems. If your spouse refuses to go to marital counseling, seeing a counselor on your own may be very helpful for you. Should you decide to go forward with a divorce, having a counselor who can help you deal with the emotional fallout is important. Whether you reconcile or end your marriage, you are facing some very difficult issues and having professional help coping with them is essential. For many people, divorce is a time of fresh starts and big changes. A mental health professional can offer you help as you make choices and rethink things. A counselor can also provide much needed support if you do end up going through with the divorce.

Domestic Violence

Domestic violence is emotional, physical, or sexual abuse or control by a person who at some point had an intimate relationship with you. Abuse creates fear and involves coercion—physically, mentally, emotionally, economically, or sexually. Nearly one-third of American women (31 percent) report being physically or sexually abused by a husband or boyfriend at some point in their lives, according to a 1998 Commonwealth Fund survey. In the year 2001, more than half a million American women (588,490 women) were victims of nonfatal violence committed by an intimate partner. The Bureau of Justice Statistics Crime Data Brief reports that more than three women are murdered by their husbands or boyfriends in this country every day.

Domestic violence is a very serious issue for women (although it does happen to men as well), and can be a major reason for divorce. If you are the victim of domestic violence, the first thing you must do is get out. It is not safe to remain with your abuser. You must either call the police while you are being harmed or in danger of being harmed, or get away from the situation to a safe location. You may also be able to get to family court and file for an immediate order of protection which will remove your batterer from your home. Look in the phone book or online for the phone number of your local domestic violence shelter. Call them and ask them for advice. You can also call the National Domestic Violence Hotline at 1-800-799-SAFE (7233). For information on how to plan to leave, visit their web site at http://www.ndvh.org/help/planning.html.

If your children are the subject of abuse or neglect by your spouse, they need to be protected immediately. Call the police or the local social or children's services office to file a report. You might also wish to get in touch with Justice for Children www.jfcadvocacy.org, an organization that provides resources to help children who are abused receive fair treatment in court. If you know your children are being abused by your spouse and you do nothing to stop it, you could be found guilty of abuse or neglect. You cannot ignore a situation like this.

Once you have gotten yourself or your children to safety, it is important that you find an attorney who has experience working with domestic violence. Your attorney will need to make sure there is always an order of protection in place throughout the process, and can help you understand what your rights are and how to enforce them. If you contact your local domestic violence shelter, they can put you in touch with an attorney who can help you. Some attorneys volunteer their services to these shelters to help women obtain orders of protection.

Telling Your Spouse

Telling your spouse you want a divorce may be a difficult conversation. Some couples talk about their relationship and reach the conclusion together that a divorce is where they are going, but most of the time, one person confronts the other about divorce.

If you aren't in a position to talk with your spouse about where your marriage is headed, you may end up just announcing you want a divorce. This could fly out of your mouth, unplanned in the middle of an argument, or be something you present in a thought-out way. If you are able to plan this, think about what you will say. Do you want to get into the reasons? Or would you be more comfortable cutting to the chase and trying to talk about where things will go from here? You might be prepared to ask your spouse to move out, or you might be packed and ready to go. Regardless of the situation, it is a good idea to think it over in advance if possible so that you can decide what you want to say and what information you want to convey.

You can expect your spouse to react with shock, sadness, anger, and suspicion (that there is someone else). If you are in a volatile situation and are afraid for your safety, you need to make sure you are in a secure environment when you give the news. Some people talk to a lawyer before they talk to their spouse. This can be helpful if there is going to be a big blow-up with someone locked out of the house.

If you are seriously considering divorce, but are not certain that is what you want, you should talk this over with your spouse as well if possible. There are a lot of options available to you, such as marital therapy, individual therapy, or a trial separation.

You will probably have many more conversations with your spouse about the divorce and both of you will consider various outcomes and options. The good news is that once you've made the announcement, it is out in the open and you can both begin to deal with the situation and find your way through it.

Trial Separation

A trial separation is a non-legal, informal decision to spend some time apart. Many couples decide to separate on a temporary basis to see how it feels and to get some space. Sometimes taking time apart from each other can bring clarity and it can certainly cut down on conflict in the short term. Having some time apart can help you really think about what you want and what will work for you. Some couples find that a trial separation makes it clear to them that they are much happier apart. Others find that the separation makes them miss things about each other.

Couples often try a trial separation before seeing an attorney or taking any steps toward a divorce. A trial separation is simply a decision the two of your make about your living arrangements. There are no legal documents involved and you do not need an attorney.

While taking a break may be a good idea, it can also raise questions about how you will share time with your children, who will support the children, who will pay the bills at the marital home, and if one of you needs financial assistance from the other. At any time while you are legally married, you can go to family court and obtain orders of custody, visitation, child support, and spousal support (see chapter 3 for more information about this) which will help sort out your situation while you are separated. You can hire an attorney or you can handle this on your own (family court is very user friendly).

During a trial separation, it is important that neither one of you use up or spend marital assets in an unfair way. For example, if you move out and decide to buy a waterfront estate, using up all available cash in the marriage and taking on a huge mortgage, this will be considered to be dissipating marital assets. Likewise, selling the home for below market value would be an act detrimental to the marital assets. It is also a good idea to note the date of separation because, should you divorce, assets are usually divided as of their value on the date of separation.

Should you decide to separate and it looks like you will be staying that way, it is a good idea to consult an attorney so that you can get some basic information about your state laws regarding things such as changing the locks, withdrawing funds from marital accounts, using marital credit cards, and the basics of custody and support.

Understanding What Divorce Really Means

Although most people are aware of what a divorce is and how it works, you can't really understand it completely until you have gone through it. There are several parts to the divorce.

Physical Divorce

First is the physical divorce, and this usually happens when you physically separate. Making this decision can be difficult. It is not uncommon for couples to separate and then reunite several times, while trying to work things out. Additionally, many couples may take what they see as a break or trial separation and find that it turns into a permanent physical separation. Some couples don't physically separate until much later, often due to financial reasons, or because of the children.

Legal Divorce

Another component is the legal divorce—when the court declares your marriage to be legally over. It takes many months to get a divorce in even the simplest of cases. Courts are often backlogged. The legal process of divorce can be frustrating since it moves slowly and is very paperwork oriented. It is important that it be done correctly, however, so you have to have patience with the process.

Emotional Divorce

The other three components of the divorce are more difficult. The emotional divorce, in which you make the emotional split, takes a long time to work through. You may not completely resolve this until months after your divorce is legal. There are many stages to emotional healing and they can include anger, denial, bewilderment, reunification (if only temporary), fear, regret, joy, resignation, depression, and acceptance.

Financial Divorce

The financial divorce involves the separation of your financial lives. Unraveling years of joint finances is complicated and painful. What many people don't realize is that divorce is going to negatively impact your life financially, no matter what the settlement. You go from having X amount of dollars that supports one household to suddenly having the same X amount of income but which must suddenly support two separate households. Your property and debts will be divided and there may be payments between you for alimony or child support. No one ever comes out financially ahead in a divorce. In addition to the separation of assets and debts, there will be legal expenses, which can take a big bite out of your available cash. The financial part of the divorce often causes a lot of emotional distress because you are reducing your marriage to numbers on a piece of paper. Arguments over money can be very nasty and very cutthroat.

Parenting Divorce

A divorce is a complete end to your joint venture as spouses. If, however, you are parents together, divorce does not end your partnership as parents. For the rest of your lives, you will still be parents together. Divorce simply changes your perspective on your parenting relationship. You are no longer a couple with children; however, you are still a family in which the parents must function as partners for the good of the children. The parenting divorce is a tough one in the same way that diets are hard. You can't just stop eating like you can stop smoking. In the same way, you can't just stop parenting together. You will always have children together, so you have to re-order your relationship as parents as part of the divorce process and learn how to work together in your new roles.

The Effects of Divorce

Divorce completely changes every aspect of your life, even those that you think should remain untouched. You will likely experience financial repercussions, a change in lifestyle, a reworking of who you are, changes in how you parent your children, and possibly changes in your living arrangements. Although it might seem like divorce should not affect things like your career, friends, or extended family, it has far-reaching effects on these parts of your life as well. See chapter 12 for more information on these issues.

Career

You may find you need to change jobs because you need to earn more after a divorce in order to pay legal bills or survive the changes to your financial situation. You will also find that the appointments you need to keep (such as meetings with your attorney or mediator, court appearances, and sessions with a therapist) will impact your work schedule.

Friends

Friendships are also affected by divorce. You may find that you want to spend more time with people who are single and may feel uncomfortable around married friends. There is also the issue of loyalty—some friends may feel closer to your spouse and may just disappear from your life. Some friends may not be understanding and supportive through your divorce and you may phase them out of your life. Additionally, you may make new friends who have experience with what you are going through.

Family

Your extended family is impacted by the divorce as well. Your parents will no longer have a son or daughter-in-law. You will suddenly come alone to family gatherings. If you have children, you will likely be sharing time with them with your spouse, which may make it more difficult for the children to go to all extended family gatherings.

Children

Divorce has a tremendous impact upon children. No matter what their age, they are affected by the tension and stress between their parents as well as the change in living arrangements. There has been much media coverage about the impact of divorce on children, and certainly when weighing whether to get a divorce, the effect it will have on the children is a primary consideration. However, it is the opinion and experience of the author that children are much better off being raised in two homes by two happy parents rather than in one home with parents who are miserable. It's easy to pile guilt on top of yourself about what the divorce could do to your kids, but the fact is there are plenty of happy and well-adjusted children whose parents are divorced. You will not be ruining your child's life by getting a divorce. And if getting a divorce means you can be a more fulfilled and happy person, and in turn be a more engaged and better parent, then you must make the choice that is right for you.

You might read all of the information here about the changes that divorce brings and be frightened, but one important point to remember is that if you are in a marriage that is already falling apart and which is unhappy or painful, then you have already started to go through some of the changes described here. You are likely already somewhere on the pathway of emotional divorce.

You may already be experiencing financial difficulties if your spouse is withholding or separating funds. Your children are well aware of the marital difficulties you are experiencing. Whether you choose to continue along the divorce continuum is something you must decide.

Positive Effects of Divorce

While a divorce might seem like a very difficult situation, it can end up having a lot of positive effects in your life. Some of these can include:

- The freedom to chart your own life course. The rest of your life stretches out ahead of you with only you making the call as to where it will go.
- An end to fighting and disagreements in your home. Arguments can be very upsetting and distracting. Peace and quiet (relative, if you have kids!) can be quite a relief.
- Financial independence. You will be in charge of your own money and handle it in your own way.
- A healthier environment for your children. A house filled with loud arguments may not be a comforting place. Two separate homes with two happy parents is a much better environment.
- A chance to learn new things. You could take up hiking, learn Spanish, or travel the globe.
- The opportunity to meet new people. At some point you will probably start dating and may meet someone special with whom to share your life.
- A big decrease in the stress in your life. Getting through the divorce and moving on with things will eventually be a huge relief to you. Getting a toxic person out of your life will make you feel much happier and very relieved.
- The opportunity to do some self-discovery. You might find out things about yourself that will surprise you.

The Costs of Divorce

As previously mentioned, divorce has significant financial implications for both parties. Dividing property and debt, and negotiating alimony and child support are difficult matters. Taking on the cost of moving or replacing items your spouse took from the home (or furnishing a new home of your own), and figuring out how to make it on your income alone are serious financial concerns. The actual divorce itself is a significant cost on its own. Attorneys fees, mediator costs, court fees, therapy costs, in addition to possibly having to miss time at work to meet all of your appointments add up to large costs.

It is difficult to offer an average cost for attorney's fees. How much it costs will depend entirely on how much time your attorney has to spend on the case. The time spent on the case is determined by how complicated it is. If you and your spouse agree on everything and simply need someone to put together papers and file them, your attorney costs could be one or two thousand dollars. There are attorneys who advertise lower rates, but you want to be sure that whoever you hire takes the time to discuss all of your rights with you and go over every detail.

If you and your spouse agree on nothing and spend months (or years) arguing, going to court, and making each other's lives difficult, you will easily spend tens of thousands of dollars. Attorneys usually request a retainer, which is a sum of money you pay up front. You then pay by the hour. Most attorneys charge a higher hourly rate for in-court work. Your attorney's hourly rate may average $200 to $500 per hour. You pay for time your attorney spends on the case, whether it is in court, in meetings, on the phone, researching, or reviewing the file. In addition to your attorney's time, you will be responsible for expenses, such as photocopying, service (having papers formally served), consultations with experts, paralegal time, postage, and investigatory costs.

You and/or your spouse will also be responsible for court costs. These vary by state but generally total several hundred dollars. There are filing fees for almost everything filed with the court, as well as costs for transcripts, certified copies, and so on. Your attorney can give you a complete breakdown of these costs, or you can Google them for your state.

If you and your spouse choose to work with a mediator instead of pursuing a traditional divorce, you will still each need to retain an attorney for legal information and advice and will pay the mediator an hourly rate for his or her services. Mediation does end up being much less expensive than a traditional divorce (see Chapter 6 for more information).

Depending on your financial situation, the court could order one spouse to pay some or all of the other's attorney and court costs. Usually if one spouse is in a significantly better financial position, this is considered. It is also possible to negotiate responsibility for the costs of the divorce as part of a settlement you reach with your spouse. It is also possible for just one of you to retain an attorney who will handle the divorce in an uncontested way—one spouse files papers that the other has already agreed to. This is a very simple, streamlined process, but it works only if you can agree without having to use a mediator or negotiate through your attorneys.

Divorce versus Separation

Some people wonder about whether they should seek a legal separation instead of a divorce. There are benefits and detriments to each option. For some people a separation sounds less contentious than a divorce. It doesn't seem as serious or to have as many negative consequences in some people's minds.

A legal separation is a declaration by the court that you and your spouse will live separate and apart. Just as in a divorce, a separation usually entails the division of property and debts, alimony, custody, and child support. You and your spouse get all of these issued resolved and can then go about your lives separately. You do, however, remain legally married to each other and cannot remarry and must list your status as married on your tax returns. Some couples prefer to have a legal separation so that they can move forward with their lives while they consider whether they do want a divorce, which will completely end their marriage. Other couples do not believe in divorce and choose separation as a way to remain married while living separate lives. Additionally, in some states, a legal separation is a pathway to a divorce (instead of pointing a finger of blame at each other, the spouses agree to separate and that separation is then converted to a divorce after a set period of time).

A legal separation can be as agreeable or contentious as you and your spouse make it. You can both agree to the terms of the separation and smoothly part ways or you can have drawn out battles over custody or finances. In this sense, a separation is not a cost saver. Because you have to pay for legal representation and court costs for both the separation and the divorce, should you later decide to do it, a separation may in fact end up costing you more.

A divorce is a final resolution to your marriage and all the issues surrounding it. A separation can be a first step towards a divorce. Some people feel that divorce is too fast and furious a path for them and prefer to first experience a separation and then go from there.

If you are weighing a divorce against a separation, consult with an attorney and find out:

- the cost of divorce and separation
- whether a separation provides any legal advantages in your state
- if it is possible to convert a legal separation into a divorce with a simple proceeding in your state
- what the attorney recommends for you in your particular situation.
- We'll discuss legal separation in more detail in chapter 2.

Divorce versus Annulment

There is a lot of confusion about the difference between a divorce and an annulment. There is also confusion between a legal annulment and a religious annulment.

A divorce is a legal end to the marriage—deciding all issues involved in the closure of the marriage and often assigning fault to one of the parties for the end of the marriage. The end result of a divorce is a dissolution of the marriage. An annulment is also an end to the marriage and involves all the decisions a divorce involves if needed—property and debt division, custody, child support, and alimony. However, an annulment is a legal determination that the marriage was never valid in the first place.

Reasons for Annulment

Each state has its own requirements for granting an annulment, but they usually include:

- One spouse was underage at the time of the marriage
- One spouse misrepresented him or herself to the other in some significant way (this often involves fraud of some kind)
- One spouse was mentally ill at the time of the marriage
- One spouse is unable or unwilling to consummate the marriage
- The parties are related to each other in a way that prevents marriage in that state
- One spouse was already married to someone else at the time of the marriage
- One spouse concealed or withheld important facts, such as having a disease, having previous children, being infertile, and so on.

An annulment determines that the marriage was not legal or valid when it was entered into and therefore never truly legally existed. The annulment legally erases the marriage, as if it never was. One important thing to note is that if you had children together during the marriage, the children are still considered to be legitimate—conceived in and born into a legal marriage and legal child of both of you. Annulments are more common with very short marriages, where one or both parties realizes rather quickly that a mistake was made, but it is certainly not unheard of for a much longer marriage to end in annulment. Alimony cannot be awarded in a judgment of annulment, since the court is deciding there was no legal marriage to begin with.

Annulments are not available because you've changed your mind, aren't happy, feel you made a bad decision, are abused by your spouse, or feel you've been treated unfairly. There has to be a legal basis for determining the marriage was not valid. In most states, the legal process for an annulment is very similar to that for a divorce. Similar papers are filed and similar hearings are held. An annulment can be contested, just as with a divorce. However, annulments are often agreed upon by both parties and since they usually happen very early in a marriage, the process is generally quick and easy. Annulments are not very common, but a lot of people seem to think they ought to be able to get one. In fact, an annulment is really the exception to the rule and very few people actually do get them.

Religious Annulment

A legal annulment is one granted by the court. It decides that legally, there is no marriage. Once the marriage is annulled, you are a single person who has never technically been married. A religious annulment is entirely different. Religious annulments are granted by your religious institution. They have separate requirements and processes. Some people get a legal divorce and then seek a religious annulment, so that they will be able to marry again in their church or temple. It is not always possible to obtain a religious annulment, so it is best to consult with your priest, rabbi, or other religious authority to learn what the requirements and steps are.

Perhaps the most important thing to understand about an annulment is that it can't undo the pain or hurt you have suffered. Even if your marriage is decided to have been legally or religiously void, it was real while you lived it and the only way to deal with the pain is to cope with it directly.

Divorce and Common Law Marriage

A common law marriage exists where a couple lives together and holds themselves out as being married and are granted the same privileges as a married couple under the state law. Holding yourself out as married can include introducing each other as husband and wife, filing joint tax returns, or taking the other partner's last name. Some states require an actual intention to hold yourselves out as married (instead of people just assuming you're married because you live together).

Some states also recognize putative spouses—those who believe they are married, when technically they are not (such as if there was some glitch in filing the marriage license or in the ceremony, or if one spouse knew the marriage was not legal but the other had no idea). If you believe you are legally married, then you may be entitled to a divorce in your state.

If You Do Not Want a Divorce

If you are reading this book because your spouse has come to you and said she wants a divorce, you probably feel very upset and disoriented. If you do not want a divorce, you should first suggest counseling. Marital therapy can help the two of your talk about what is happening in your marriage and consider how you might fix it.

Learning your spouse wants a divorce can be a very shocking discovery, so it is important that you take some time to deal with the situation. If your spouse already has an attorney, you should get one for yourself, so that you can get some basic information and have someone to turn to should your spouse begin legal proceedings.

Many marriages go through difficult periods, so the announcement by your spouse is by no means a guarantee that you will end up divorced. It is, however, something you should pay attention to because it is a sign that your marriage needs to be repaired.

States Where Common Law Marriages Exist
- Alabama
- Colorado
- District of Columbia

- Georgia (before January 1, 1997)
- Idaho o(before January 1, 1997)
- Iowa
- Kansas
- Montana
- New Hampshire
- Ohio (before October 10, 1990)
- Oklahoma
- Pennsylvania (before 2004)
- Rhode Island
- South Carolina
- Texas
- Utah

If you live in one of these states and meet the test for common law in that state, you are legally married in the eyes of your state. You are entitled to use the divorce courts of your state to obtain a divorce.

Chapter 2

Legal Separation

A legal separation is one option available to you as you consider whether or not you want a divorce. Some couples choose this avenue while others find that moving forward to divorce best suits their needs. A legal separation can give you time apart, while also putting in place a financial plan that will allow you to live independent from each other. Some couples get separated and never get divorced. Often this is because of religious beliefs, while other couples want to remain married, but just find they cannot live together. In some states, a separation can be a pathway to divorce.

Legal versus Non-Legal Separation

Any couple can decide to live separate and apart. You don't need a court's permission to do this. Sometimes a couple decides to separate on a temporary basis to get some time to think things through. Other times, a separation happens on the spur of the moment, out of anger or upset. In other instances, you may wish to separate on a long-term or permanent basis. No matter how it happens, you're allowed to make that choice as adults.

The difference between a legal separation and a non-legal one is that a legal separation involves either a settlement being filed with the court, or an order or judgment being issued by the court declaring you to be living separate and apart. There are some benefits to a legal separation. First of all, it resolves all the issues you're facing about custody, visitation, child support, spousal support, and how to divide your assets and debts. These are the same decisions that must be made in a divorce, but when you seek a legal separation, they are decided now.

Reasons to Get a Separation When You Don't Want a Divorce

- You want to send a wake-up call to your spouse
- You want to compel your spouse to seek alcohol or drug treatment, or other counseling
- You can't afford to get divorced, but cannot go on the way things are currently in your marriage
- You are not physically safe—or your children are not safe—and you need to get out
- Your spouse wants a divorce, but you don't and a separation is a reasonable compromise
- You need time to assess where your marriage is going and if it can continue
- You don't feel you can make any permanent decisions and need time to get your head together
- You don't want to stay married, but need to continue to get health insurance through your spouse
- You do not believe in divorce or your religion prohibits it

The second benefit to getting a legal separation is that getting one starts the clock ticking towards any required period for which you must be separated before converting that legal separation into a divorce. In some states, after you are legally separated for one or two years, you can automatically convert your separation into a divorce (see page TK for more information). Making your separation legal begins that official countdown.

If you simply separate without a legal agreement, this can open you to a charge of abandonment (a legal term which means you have left your spouse for a certain period of time and not come back), which can work against you in the divorce proceeding in some states by giving your spouse a grounds for divorce and even affecting your right to the marital assets. A legal separation ensures this cannot happen.

A benefit of legal or non-legal separation that many people may not be aware of is that it can decrease the couple's total income tax. When you are separated, you file your taxes separately (married filing separately). This may lead to you each being in different tax brackets which can impact how much you will pay total as a couple in taxes.

How to Get a Legal Separation

Legal separations are available in all states except Delaware, Florida, Georgia, Mississippi, and Pennsylvania. In these states, you can live apart from each at any point, for as long as you wish, but you cannot make it a legal separation. You can, however, go to family court for assistance with issues of custody, visitation, child support, and spousal support while you are married, whether you live together or apart. What you don't have access to is a court that will divide assets and debts during the course of your separation. Should you choose to separate in one of these states, you can go to a mediator and work out how to divide your assets and debts on your own. Your mediator can make this into a legal document—a post-nuptial agreement.

Another important point is that in some of these states where legal separations are not recognized, living separate and apart from your spouse can be used a grounds (reason) for divorce. So you can't get a legal paper saying you are separated, but you may be able to seek a divorce based on the fact that you've been physically separated.

In states where legal separations are permitted, there are several paths you can take to become legally separated.

Self-Help

You and your spouse can decide between yourselves what the terms of your separation are and then file a separation agreement with the court. You can purchase sample separation agreements or forms through online paralegal sites, or by hiring a local paralegal. You should also check your state court Web site to locate any packets or information pamphlets about your state laws and requirements.

Mediation

A mediator can help you and your spouse create a separation agreement that resolves all of the issues between you. If you use a mediator who is an attorney, she may also be able to file the agreement with the court for you, or tell you how to do it yourselves. For more information on mediation, see Chapter 6.

Attorneys

You and your spouse can each hire an attorney to help you work out a separation agreement. You have to hire two attorneys, because it is considered unethical for an attorney to represent two parties in a divorce case (although some will do it anyhow). The attorneys will negotiate and hammer out a separation agreement that fulfills all of your needs and requirements. Plan on it costing several thousand dollars to have a separation agreement negotiated. It can cost more if lengthy negotiations are needed. The separation agreement is filed with the court and it becomes a legally binding agreement.

If you and your spouse are unable to reach an agreement, your attorneys can represent you in court. You can begin a separation proceeding, seeking to have the court decide all the issues between you and issue a decree of separation. This option is just as expensive as seeking a divorce, so if you find yourself in this position, it is often just better to go ahead with the divorce (unless you have religious objections). A separation proceeding is almost identical to a divorce proceeding, with similar papers filed.

Reasons for a Legal Separation

In most states you need to provide a reason that is acceptable under your state statutes for why you are getting a legal separation. This can be as simple as incompatibility or as complicated as adultery. Each state has differently worded statutes, so do a search for your state and "legal separation" and you will find the law, or talk to your attorney. Be aware that the real reason for your separation—what has compelled you to make this decision—may not fit exactly within your state's requirements, so it is very important to always find out what the wording requirements are in your state and choose the one that best suits your circumstances. For example, you might want a separation because you believe your spouse had an affair. In most states, adultery is difficult to prove and your gut feeling that there has been one would not be enough. So in a situation like this, you would need to rely on another legal reason for the separation. An attorney can explain these to you and also point out the legal reason that is most commonly used in your state—usually the one that is simplest to prove. While your spouse may have committed adultery, using that as a legal reason is an entirely different matter. See chapter 5 for more information on grounds.

The Separation Agreement

A separation agreement is a binding contract entered into by both spouses. This is the most common way to become separated (it is less common to go to court and have a judge issue a separation decree). Before you can sign a separation agreement, you and your spouse have to make complete financial disclosure to each other and most likely to the court as well. This means completing a financial affidavit. The reason for this is to be certain that you both have the complete information about the financial situation and are able to make an educated decision based upon this information.

The agreement also may include information about maintaining insurance policies. You should always get legal advice before signing a separation agreement. Everyone's situation is different and each state's laws are different.

Items Covered by a Separation Agreement

- Custody
- Child support
- Spousal support
- Division of property
- Division of debt
- Payment of attorney fees by one spouse for the other
- Who will file the separation agreement and convert it to a divorce, if one will be sought

Separation agreements are binding the entire time you are separated and if you convert your separation to a divorce, the terms of the agreement automatically become the terms of the divorce, unless you ask otherwise. It is possible to determine that the terms of the agreement do not work for you, and to ask that the divorce have different terms. If you both agree to a change, it is simple. If you do not agree, you will end up in court and the judge will decide. Judges are unlikely to alter the terms of a separation agreement, however, because you voluntarily entered into it. If the circumstances have changed though (such as losing your job, your spouse getting a big raise, your child having emotional problems, and so on), then you have a good basis to ask for a change.

See the sample settlement agreement in Appendix B.

What a Legal Separation Means

Once you obtain a legal separation, you are still legally married to each other. You cannot legally marry another person. You are still entitled to all the benefits of being married, which include being able to file wrongful death suits should your spouse die, collect Social Security as a surviving spouse, inherit from your spouse, obtain health insurance through him or her (however, be sure to check with your insurance plan—some consider a legal separation to be the same as divorce and will discontinue coverage), and many more benefits. You must enter a legal separation with the intention to remain separated and not to resume marital relations. This means that you do not plan to re-unite as a couple or have sex again.

You are still required to list yourself as a married person on all legal forms, including tax returns. Additionally, legal separations usually require that you and your spouse live separate and apart. This may mean not sharing a bedroom or bed, or not sharing a residence. Because you are still married, technically it is adultery to have sexual relations with someone else during your legal separation.

How to Live Under a Separation Agreement

It can be confusing to know how to live your life once you are legally separated. You've taken a major step towards dissolving your marriage, yet you are still legally bound together. Making sense of it and figuring out how to move forward from this point is not always easy. The agreement (or separation decree issued by the court) directs that you will live separate and apart and will not engage in marital relations.

If you have separated as a stepping stone to divorce, the separation is a good opportunity for you to experience what life as a single person will be like. You're now in charge of your own budget, income, expenses, and household. Your time is your own to manage as well and this may be a good time for you to learn how to go out with friends again or do the things singles do. It will take you some time to adjust to living alone in your home. While you're adjusting to the big changes in your life, you are also getting ready for your divorce to become final. Although the actual separation is tremendously difficult, the finality of the divorce itself can be unexpectedly hard for some people, so it is important to take the time now to heal and prepare yourself for that final step. The waiting period also allows you to be absolutely certain that a divorce is what you want and need. For many people, it gives them piece of mind because they are able to live separately and come to the conclusion that a divorce is absolutely the best path.

In this situation, the separation period also allows you to work out any kinks in your custody, child support, and spousal support plan. You know that your separation has not been finalized into a divorce yet and if you need to make changes, you can do so before it becomes final.

If you have separated on a permanent basis and do not intend to divorce, this is the beginning of your new life. The separation was the big decision and the big event and you aren't gearing up for an actual divorce. The biggest challenge may be feeling out what your relationship with your spouse will be like from now on. You're still married, but you've made a decision not to live together as partners anymore. That is a big change. You need to determine how involved with each other you will be and what kind of contact you will have with each other from here on out.

At any time during your separation, you are free to reunite, move back in together, or resume your marriage (see later in this chapter for information on undoing your separation). You should not feel as if you are unable to do these things just because you are legally separated. However, if you do so, your legal separation could become invalid.

If you wish to date other people during your separation, that is a choice you must make for yourself, but it is a good to first consult with your attorney. Doing so could give your spouse additional ammunition when you go to finalize your divorce because you are technically still married and any sex you have is legally considered adultery. Dating someone else is not adultery, but having sex with someone else is. You need to be clear about what the repercussions are in your state about dating other people. You also need to think about how your divorce is progressing. Is your spouse looking for any reason to make things difficult and expensive for you? If so, you might consider being careful. Most people who are separated, however, feel that they are practically divorced and free to get on with their lives and see other people.

Separation Drawbacks

A separation has many drawbacks that you may not fully understand until you live through it. Some of them include:

- It is more expensive to live as a separated couple than as a couple under one roof. Y\will find it is more financially difficult to support your expenses and way of life.
- A separation may just drag out the end of your marriage. A divorce offers a relatively quick solution, whereas a separation usually takes at least a year by itself, and then you must handle the divorce proceeding after that.
- A separation may be hard for children to understand. It does not have the finality of a divorce and offers the ongoing hope that the parents will reunite, even if that is not your intention.
- Although you are living separately, you are still legally married, which means you're legally responsible for debts your spouse incurs until a separation agreement or divorce decree says otherwise. Even if your agreement or decree specifies who is responsible for certain debts, the problem is the court has no jurisdiction over your creditors, so your only recourse is to sue your spouse if he doesn't pay something he is supposed to.
- Because you are still legally married, your spouse's failure to pay marital debts can negatively affect your credit rating, which may make it harder for you to get on your feet financially once you are divorced.

Separation as a Prelude to No-Fault Divorce

As mentioned previously in this chapter, in many states, you can get a legal separation and then use the separation itself as the grounds for a no-fault divorce. A no-fault divorce means that neither spouse is to blame (such as blaming the divorce on adultery or cruel and inhuman treatment). It is important to note that there are many states where you can get a no-fault divorce without separating first (see chapter 5 for information about this).

In order to convert the separation to a divorce, you need to follow your state procedure. Because you will be seeking a no-fault divorce, it is a simplified procedure, which does not involve a trial. Instead, you or your attorney will file many documents with the court, which essentially ask that a divorce be granted based on the separation agreement. The terms of the separation agreement then become the terms of the divorce decree and your divorce is finalized. Note that if for some reason, things change and you no longer agree to the terms of the separation agreement, you can go ahead and have a contested divorce.

States that Require Separation for a No-Fault Divorce

Below is a list of the states that require a separation in order to receive a no-fault divorce, and the length of time required for the separation. (See chapter 5 for a full list of states that permit no-fault divorce.)

- Alabama – 2 years
- Arkansas – 18 months
- Connecticut – 18 months
- District of Columbia – 6 months
- Hawaii – 2 years
- Idaho – 5 years
- Illinois – 2 years
- Illinois – 2 years (if both parties consent it can be reduced to 6 months)
- Louisiana – 180 days
- Maryland – 1 year
- Minnesota – 180 days
- Nevada – 1 year
- New Jersey – 18 months
- New York – 1 year
- North Carolina – 1 year
- Ohio – 1 year
- Pennsylvania – 2 years
- Rhode Island – 3 years
- South Carolina – 1 year

- Tennessee – 2 years (permitted only if there are no children)
- Texas – 3 years
- Utah – 3 years
- Vermont – 6 months
- Virginia – 1 year (can be reduced to 6 months if no children)
- West Virginia – 1 year

Undoing a Separation

You and your spouse can choose at any time to reunite, even if you are legally separated. You don't need court permission to do so. Should you decide that your reunion is permanent and you would like to remain married, you can ask the court to dismiss the separation case, essentially undoing the separation.

Should you think you are getting back together, but then decide it isn't going to work, you need to understand that you may need to restart the clock on the time of your separation, since some states require that you have lived separate and apart for a certain time period without engaging in marital relations.

Chapter 3

Family Court

Many people assume that if they are having family legal problems that they have to wait to address them in a divorce. There is a faster, more accessible solution. Family court exists in every county of every state and is available to help families in crisis. Although you may be contemplating a divorce, family court can be of great help to you as you make decisions or face problems with your spouse.

Family Court Basics

Family court handles paternity, child support, custody, visitation, spousal support, and orders of protection in domestic disputes (in addition, child abuse neglect cases as well as juvenile delinquency cases are heard). In some states family courts also handle divorce, but in many states, divorce is handled in a separate court. Family court is for anyone who has a child together or is married. Most family courts are very user friendly. Many people come to court for help without an attorney. The court employees assist them in completing necessary paperwork and the judge moves the case forward, while helping them to understand the procedure.

How Family Court Can Help You

Family court can be a good way to work out problems you are having with custody or finances while you are deciding if you want a divorce or who will file for divorce. It can sometimes take many months to reach a final decision about your marriage, and during that time you and your spouse may not be able to agree about how to handle the temporary arrangements. Family court can provide orders of custody and visitation to help resolve your parenting disputes. You can also go to family court and obtain child support and spousal support. If you are in danger from your spouse, you can obtain an order of protection and may also be able to get an order directing that you will have exclusive residency in the home, due to domestic violence concerns.

Family court is usually very easy to access. If you file papers, you will likely get a preliminary court date within a week or two, depending on the volume in your area. This is very fast relief, compared with waiting months for a matrimonial court appearance. You can also get a same-day or next-day hearing if you are in an emergency situation, such as in the case of domestic violence

You don't need an attorney in family court, and this makes it accessible to those with low incomes, as well as those who want to be in charge of their own case. If you retain an attorney, family court is usually cheaper than divorce court in terms of time spent on the case; however, if you go to family court and then to divorce court, you will likely end up spending more than if you had just gone to divorce court directly.

Family Court versus Divorce Court

If family court can provide all of this help, you may wonder why you even need to go to divorce court. There are several key differences between the two courts. Family court looks only at the one issue that is before it—such as child support or custody. It does not consider the big picture at all. So, if you go to family court for spousal support, the court is only going to consider monthly support, and won't think about a property division.

Family court cannot divide property or debts or dissolve your marriage. Once you have gotten a divorce, you may be able to return to family court to iron out future problems with custody or support, or your divorce court may retain jurisdiction and require you to come back there for any future problems.

There can be some strategy involved in choosing whether you will go to family court or directly to divorce court. One trick that many divorce attorneys employ is using family court to set the stage for divorce court. If you go to family court and file for an order of protection and get exclusive residency of the home, when you do go to divorce court you've already created legal documentation of the other spouse as the bad guy. Already living alone in the home is likely to give you a leg up on getting the house in the property settlement. Going to family court and getting residential custody of your children creates a situation that the divorce court will want to leave intact. If you win temporary custody of your children, you are already miles ahead in the battle to win permanent custody. So, in this sense, family court is sometimes used as a way to manipulate what will happen in divorce court.

How to Access Family Court

To find out where your local family court is, check your state court system Web site or the government guide section of your phone book. In most cases, there is a family court in every county, usually located in the county seat. Small (in population) counties may share a judge with other counties or may have traveling courts.

To begin a family court case, you usually need to file a petition, which states what you're asking for and offers some basic information about your family. The petition is filed with the court, which opens a file for your family. Usually the court then handles making sure your spouse is served. If you are responsible for service, find out what the requirements are by asking a court employee.

If you are served with family court papers, read them carefully so you understand when you are required to appear. You may be able to file a response or answer to the petition you've been served with or you may need to appear on a certain date—check with the court.

Preparing Family Court Documents

Your family court has particular forms that it requires you to use. It is not acceptable to write a letter to the court or type up lists and submit those. You may be able to download family court forms from your state court Web site. Your family court may have its own individual web page with its own forms. If there are forms specifically for your county, always be sure to use those instead of generic state forms. If you download forms, they may be set up so that you can enter information directly into them and then print them. If this is an option, use it. Your forms will be much easier to read and understand.

If you do not have access to a computer, or your state has nothing online, you can go to family court and obtain the forms there. If you obtain the forms this way, you will likely have to handwrite on them. Do so as neatly as possible and ask the court employees questions if there is anything you don't understand.

Family Court Hearings

When you are scheduled for a family court appearance, be there on time. If you need to cancel, call in advance. Just not showing up may mean a ruling against you in the case. Most courthouses have security and you may need to go through a metal detector or have your belongings searched before you are allowed to enter the courthouse.

Family court is generally lower key than divorce court, often because there aren't as many attorneys. Despite this, you will make a better impression if you wear business-like clothing and are timely and polite.

If you are representing yourself, the court will explain to you how to call witnesses and present evidence and may even assist you in preparing subpoenas. Keep in mind it is a formal hearing and not an informal opportunity to talk to the judge.

Some family court require couples to attend mediation before they can go to court for a custody case. For more information about mediation, see chapter 6.

What Family Court Cannot Do For You

While the relief available in family court is pretty wide ranging, there are some things that the court cannot help you with. Family court cannot grant you a divorce or annulment (unless your family court handles these cases and you file a petition asking for that). Family court cannot divide up marital property or debts. To accomplish these items, you'll need to take the steps discussed in the next chapter.

Chapter 4

***

First Steps in a Divorce

Once you've made the decision that you want to move forward with getting a divorce, the choices and first steps can seem a bit overwhelming and intimidating. While it's true that divorce as a whole can be a huge, life-consuming process, the best thing you can do is take things one day at a time and one step at a time. You will get through the process in one piece.

When you have decided that a divorce is the path you're going to take, there are some immediate things you should do to protect yourself. It may be difficult to think about protecting yourself, your children, or your assets, but now that you are going to be on your own, that is exactly the way you must start to think. Even if you do not believe your spouse would harm you or be extremely unfair on purpose, you're now in a position where the only person looking after you is yourself. It's time to step up and take charge of your life and make your own decisions.

Protect Yourself and Your Children

Protecting yourself and your children, if you have any, from harm should be your primary concern when your marriage is ending. You have nothing if you do not have health and safety. If domestic violence is an issue in your family, your first step is getting to a safe place. Chapter 1 offers information about this.

Often when a marriage falls apart, people change and act in ways they never did before. It is not uncommon for a person you previously felt safe with to become unstable or very angry, to the point where you become afraid. Should this happen, you need to get away from the situation, and find a way to prevent placing yourself in that kind of danger again. If you've moved out, don't go back to the marital home when your spouse is there, or have someone go with you if you must go back. If you've been threatened and you are fearful, you can obtain an order of protection or an order directing the other person to stay away from you. These kinds of court orders can be helpful in calming things down and inserting some distance into the situation.

If you and your spouse clash whenever you see each other, you need to be careful to protect your children from these situations. It is emotionally harmful for them to witness these kinds of fights between their parents. If you have things you need to discuss, do so out of hearing of your children. See chapter 8 for more information about children and parental conflict.

This is the time in your life when you need to shift your thinking so that protecting yourself, your future and your children's future becomes a priority for you. You may not be in physical danger from your spouse, but she may have many ways to sabotage your life and your future. For example, a spouse who spends with abandon can harm your credit rating if joint cards are used. It's time to guard your financial future (more about this later in this chapter). In another example, your spouse may be very skilled at eroding your self-confidence and self-esteem; this is the time in your life when you need to protect yourself and build up your confidence in yourself. It is time to start thinking about what is best for you and your children, independent of your spouse. This can be a difficult change to make in your life, but it is one that you must begin to do now. Some people feel that it is somehow underhanded or sneaky to start protecting themselves and their assets, particularly if the divorce has started in a very amicable way. The fact of the matter is that many amicable divorces turn ugly. You can protect yourself and still remain calm and reasonable.

As you begin the divorce process, you need to focus on building up your reserves of strength. You may also need to rely on other people to get you through this difficult period. This is the time to call in favors and depend on family and friends to help you. You need support as you make difficult decisions and cope with new situations.

Talk to Your Children

One of very first things you will need to do once you and your spouse make the decision to divorce or to physically separate is to talk to your children about the decision you've made. It is usually best for you and your spouse to try to talk to the children together—this sets the tone that you will continue to be parents together and makes sure that they are told in a neutral way. Be honest with your children, but do not share personal details or information they do not need to know. For example, it is important to be clear with your children if you have decided to divorce that you will not be getting back together; however, it is not appropriate to tell them the details of why you have made this decision. General statements about not loving each other any longer or disagreeing all the time are fine, while comments about adultery, emotional cruelty, and so on are not appropriate. The children should not be told it is anyone's fault that you are divorcing.

While it is best to talk to your kids together, if your spouse won't cooperate with you, then you will have to talk to your children yourself. It can be hard to do this alone—you may feel very emotional. Practice what you will say with a close friend or relative. Try not to say anything negative about the other parent. If the other parent talks to the children himself and says negative things, try to rise above it. Your children are not judge and jury and you should not be trying to convince them who is right and who is wrong. Just tell them there are two sides to every story. If your spouse said something that is totally untrue, feel free to simply say that that is not true. Explain that you don't want to say anything negative about the other parent and so you're not going to.

The conversation you have with your children when you first tell them about the divorce is so important because it sets the tone for how all of you will handle the situation. It's important to set expectations now for what kind of parenting schedule you intend to keep. Don't promise your kids that they will see the non-residential parent "all the time" if that isn't the case. Don't tell them that hardly anything will change, because many things surely will. It's ok to try to put a positive, upbeat spin on things, but kids are going to see the downsides no matter what you do, so it's best to just be honest about it all. Give age-appropriate information. Teenagers will want and need a lot more detail than a five year old.

It's important to answer your children's questions as they come up. Kids will likely have some initial questions when you first talk to them, but as the situation evolves, they are likely to have more in-depth questions and concerns (see chapter 8 for more information about helping your children adjust to the divorce). Answer the questions as honestly and sensitively as you can. Try to create an open door policy so your child can come to you with questions at any time. Remember that your child loves the other parent and you should avoid saying negative things about him or her in front of your child.

If you have younger children, it is very important to explain that while moms and dads can stop loving each other, parents always love their kids and that can never change. It is also important that you stress that although you and the other parent will no longer be married that you will continue to be parents together and that you will always be there together for your child. Your child will still have a family—it's just going through some changes.

Kids need details about how the situation is going to affect their lives. Their primary concern is going to be how the divorce will affect them personally. They want to know where they are going to sleep, what their schedule will be, who will take them to school, whether they can still go to dance lessons or soccer, and how things will change for them. Provide as many of these details as you can.

Tips for Telling Your Children about the Divorce

- Keep in mind that this is probably not news to them. They know you've been fighting. They may be surprised about the divorce, but not about the source of the conflict.

- Don't be shocked if your child initially wants to blame someone. In most situations in their lives, kids want to pinpoint who is at fault and it is natural for them to want to do so in this situation also. Explain that it is no one's fault and do not play along if your child tries to set up one of you as the bad guy.

- Talk to your kids only once you have a plan. Sitting down and saying we're getting a divorce but not being able to offer any details about who will live where or when they will see the other parent creates a lot of uncertainty and anxiety.

- Buy some age-appropriate books about divorce for kids and share them. It's likely your kids know other families that have divorced, but some good books can help them work through their own family's situation.

Tell the Important People in Your Life

It's likely that your family and close friends already know you've been having marital troubles. Telling these people the news about what has been decided can be very hard in some cases (if, for example, you know your mother will be crushed or if you know your friend is very anti-divorce), and a relief in others (getting it out in the open and being able to openly move forward can take a burden off your shoulders). Take your time sharing your news and do it at the pace that feels right to you. You're not obligated to issue a press release to every person you know. Tell only those you want to. Often as you move along in the coming months, the information will naturally come out in conversation with co-workers and acquaintances.

Those who don't know what you've been going through may be shocked at the news, especially if you were able to put up a good façade. Sometimes people can be overly nosy, asking for details and information you may not want to share. It is perfectly ok to say you aren't ready to talk about something or that you'd like to keep some things private.

One set of people who should know about the divorce is your children's teachers. Your child is going to be dealing with the situation and may display some evidence of this at school. It is very helpful for teachers to understand what may be causing a change in behavior or demeanor. The school social worker or guidance counselor may be able to offer assistance to your child. Some schools have support groups for children of divorce. At the very least, letting your child's teacher know about the problems at home will allow him or her to have a better understanding of how your child is feeling and reacting. It's actually quite common for kids to go into school and immediately announce that mom and dad are getting a divorce or that dad has moved out. Talking about it helps them process it and school is a place that is solely their world where they feel comfortable just blurting things like this out. Giving the teacher some advance warning can be helpful.

Protect Your Assets

Although divorce is very much about emotions, it also unfortunately is about dollars and property. When you and your spouse decide to divorce, or when you physically separate, you need to begin thinking about how to protect your own assets, as well as the joint assets of the marriage. You cannot and should not assume that your spouse will act fairly. People do a lot of crazy things during divorces, and it is impossible to know just how your spouse may react. Assume the worst and hope for the best is the motto in this situation.

Joint assets will be divided in the divorce—either through a settlement or by a decision by the court—however, it will be months before you get to that point. Until then, you want to ensure that joint assets are preserved. See chapter 9 for more information about asset division in the divorce.

Bank Accounts

If you don't already have a bank account in your individual name, it's time to open one. This is an important step in establishing credit in your own name and taking charge of your own finances. The money in joint accounts is something you need to consider. While the money is in a joint account, you and your spouse both have the right to withdraw the entire amount. If possible, you and your spouse should talk about these accounts and agree to split the money and close the account. If that's not possible, you personally can safely withdraw half. If you are very concerned about your spouse squandering all the money in a joint account, you can remove it all and place it in a separate account and leave it alone. This will show the court your goal was to protect the asset, not to claim it and spend it. It is also possible to go to court (once a divorce case has been begun) and get an order freezing the joint accounts, or dividing them. If the statements are being sent to your spouse's address, access the account information online so you can keep track of what is happening with the account, or go into the bank and have the address changed.

If your children have bank accounts and your spouse is listed as a joint owner, you may be concerned about the safety of the money in those accounts. Withdrawing it and opening a new account for the child may be a protective step to take. If you do not have access to these accounts, be sure to obtain balance statements and account numbers so that you can provide this information to your attorney. Should your spouse withdraw this money, the court will require him or her to restore it.

Cash

It is a good idea to have some cash on hand, in a safe place. If your spouse suddenly decides to freeze joint bank accounts and credit cards, you could be left in a very tenuous position if you do not have a separate account or credit card. Having some emergency cash is a good idea at this point in your life. If you only have joint accounts the money will come from there. It is perfectly acceptable to take some of the joint funds for your own use.

Credit Cards

If you do not have a credit card in your name, without your spouse on the account, this is the time to open one. This will help establish your own individual credit and will give you the freedom to make purchases.

Your joint credit cards are something you should be very concerned about at this point. Since you are both authorized to use them, you are both also responsible for paying them. If your spouse goes out and charges thousands of dollars and doesn't pay, you're considered responsible as far as the credit card company is concerned (purchases made after the date of separation can be addressed in your property settlement or judgment, but the problem is that is probably months away and if you wait, you're likely going to damage your credit rating).

Because of the potential problems with joint accounts, it is a good idea to close them if possible. If there are balances remaining on the cards you may be able to work out an agreement about who will be responsible for what portion, and transfer that balance to individual cards. If you cannot agree, this will be worked out in your divorce, but in the meantime, you can place a hold on the account so that no new charges can be made to it and one of you can make the minimum payments until things are settled. If account statements are being sent to your spouse, you can access them online to keep tabs on what is happening with the account.

Another problem to consider is the possibility of your spouse opening joint accounts without your knowledge. This could have happened while you were together, or after the separation. Because of this, it is a good idea to get your credit report and check. You can obtain a free report from each of the three credit reporting agencies by going to www.annualcreditreport.com. You're not entitled to receive your spouse's report—only your own. If you notice any accounts you did not authorize, contact those companies and tell them and ask them to cancel the accounts. This is also information your attorney will need—fraud is a serious offense.

When you have your credit report, this is a good time to sort through accounts you have open. You likely have some that you no longer use. Closing them may be a good idea because it will free you up for future credit you may be seeking, such as for a mortgage or car purchase. It will also prevent your spouse from using them without your knowledge.

Investment Accounts

If you and your spouse have joint investment accounts, you might want to freeze these (call your broker and direct that the account be frozen) so that no funds can be withdrawn without both of you signing. Another option is to withdraw half and reinvest it in your name only, however this may trigger a capital gains tax, so it is best not to do anything without consulting your attorney.

You may be able to change the beneficiary on your retirement accounts prior to divorce. Check with your plan administrator for information.

Safe Deposit Boxes

If you and your spouse have a joint safe deposit box, you can ask the bank to require both signatures to open it. You can also remove the items from the box and place them somewhere your spouse cannot access them if you are concerned about their safety. If your spouse does this before you can, let your attorney know and he will make sure these items are recovered or accounted for in the divorce.

Bills

There are several considerations when it comes to household bills for the marital home. If you move out, you will want to get your name removed from the account so that you are no longer liable for payment (note however that the court can order you to pay these even if your name is no longer on them). If you remain in the home, you may want to change the accounts to your name alone so that you get the bills and can be sure your spouse won't order that utilities be turned off. The down side of this is that doing so makes you the one who is responsible for paying these bills (unless the court orders your spouse to pay them, which is a definite possibility).

Control Your Spending

Divorce is a financial blow to anyone. Paying legal bills and court costs and managing household expenses with one income (or no income if you are un-employed) is just difficult. This is the time in your life for some serious belt-tightening. It can be tempting to give in to the freedom that living on your own provides and spend freely, knowing you have no one to answer to but yourself. However, this will soon catch up with you.

The best way to get a grip on your situation is to make a budget. Gather together all of your bills and calculate what your average monthly expenses are. For items that are not monthly (such as vacation, holiday spending, car registration renewal, etc., divide the amount by 12 to determine how much you need to allocate each month towards the expense. Because it is easy to forget about some expenses, use this budget form to help you create a complete picture of all of your expenses.

Monthly Budget
Household

Rent/mortgage _____

Home equity loan payments _____

Real estate taxes (if not included in mortgage _____

Homeowner's (if not included in mortgage) or renter's
insurance _____

Homeowner association fees _____

Gas _____

Water _____

Electric _____

Telephone (including local and long distance _____

Cell phone _____

Internet access and email _____

Cable _____

Home repairs and maintenance _____

Appliances and appliance maintenance _____

Food (include take-out by do not include dining out _____

Alcohol _____

Household supplies _____

Baby sitters/child care _____

Children's school and activity expenses _____

Children's allowances _____

Pet food and supplies _____

Vet expenses _____

Household help _____

Charitable donations _____

Furniture purchases or maintenance _____

Lawn and yard expenses _____

Other _____

Personal

Clothing _____

Coin laundry and dry cleaning _____

Haircuts and styling _____

Gym membership _____

Personal care services (nails, salon, facials,
    shoeshine, etc. _____

Other club memberships _____

Life insurance premiums _____

Health insurance premiums _____

Health insurance co-pays _____

Prescription costs _____

Vision care costs _____

Dental costs _____

Medical supplies or equipment _____

Hobbies _____

Tobacco expenses   _____
Other   _____

Financial matters
Contributions to retirement accounts   _____
Taxes (amounts you owe in income tax, property tax,
    etc. which are not included elsewhere)   _____
Bank charges   _____
Finance charges on credit cards   _____
Payments and finance charges on personal loans   _____
Monthly contributions to medical savings accounts   _____
Other monthly deductions from pay not included
    elsewhere   _____

Transportation Expenses
Car loan or lease payment   _____
Auto insurance   _____
Repairs and maintenance   _____
Average for license, inspection and registration   _____
Bus, taxi, train, plane costs   _____
Gas   _____
Car wash   _____
Parking and tolls   _____
Other vehicle expenses (include boat motorcycle,
    RV, other cars)   _____
Other   _____

Entertainment
Dining out   _____
Movies, theater, shows, attractions   _____
Books, newspapers, magazines   _____
Video/DVD rentals   _____
Vacation   _____

Babysitters   _____

Other   _____

Gifts

Holiday gifts (include all holidays you buy gifts for)   _____

Birthday, anniversary, wedding, baby, hostess,
    retirement gifts   _____

Cards, wrapping paper, gift bags, decorations   _____

Other   _____

School

Tuition   _____

School books and supplies   _____

Student loan payments   _____

Activity and sports fees   _____

Uniforms and equipment   _____

Daycare   _____

After-school day care   _____

Other   _____

Other

_____   _____

_____   _____

_____   _____

_____   _____

Once you have created a complete list of all of your expenses, you need to compare it to your gross monthly income. Don't be surprised if your expenses appear higher than your income (this is a common situation when you are recently separated). This is a signal that you need to find a way to cut costs, or find a way to bring in more income. One way to increase your household income is to seek child or spousal support payments from your spouse.

This is not a good time to incur a lot of debt. So many things are up in the air right now, that you probably don't really know what your situation will be like in a year. Racking up a lot of debt is just going to make it harder for you to get on your feet financially. Now, that being said, you have credit cards for a reason and one reason is to bail you out in an emergency. This is definitely a time in your life when you are in an emergency. If your spouse empties the bank account and you have no money for groceries, go ahead and use your credit. You need to have an eye on the long-range implications of your spending, but you also have got to simply survive day to day right now.

The budget you've just created is an important tool, not only for your own organizational purposes, but it's also a document you will be asked to provide to the court in the divorce. You've just done all the hard work of looking up the numbers and putting them together in one place and when you're asked to complete a financial affidavit for the court or your mediator, you'll be prepared to just transfer the numbers over. Note that your attorney might advise you to tweak your numbers to increase your expenses on paper. This is a discussion you should have with your attorney, especially in light of the fact that providing false information on an affidavit is perjury.

The Marital Residence

If one of you has not already moved out, it is a good idea to talk to your attorney before deciding to do so. Moving out can give the other person a strategic advantage in the divorce proceedings, as grounds for proving abandonment. It can also affect who ultimately will receive the house in the property settlement.

If you remain in the home, do not change the locks without checking with your attorney, since the rules about this vary from state to state. If you are living in the home and are unable to change the locks yet, you will want to take some precautionary measures, such as using a sliding chain lock while you are in the home (preventing access even if your spouse has a key to the deadbolt) and removing or hiding valuables so your spouse cannot take them while you are out. Remember, as with all marital assets, you can remove them to protect them, but not for your own gain.

How to Find an Attorney

Now that you've decided you're going ahead with a divorce, you need an attorney. There are many ways to find an attorney. If you've used an attorney in the past and liked her, ask her for a referral to a matrimonial attorney. There are many attorneys with general practices who also handle divorces and many of them are excellent; however, to be assured you are getting someone with the most experience and qualifications, seek out someone who specializes in matrimonial law.

If you have family members or friends who have used matrimonial attorneys that they liked, get the names of those professionals. You can also call your state or local bar association and ask for a referral. Many have special referral programs where they require attorneys to have a certain amount of experience before they can receive referrals in specific subject areas.

You can also contact the American Academy of Matrimonial Lawyers (www.aaml.org or 312-263-6477) and use its referral service. Attorneys referred through this organization must have extensive experience in this area of law.

How to Evaluate an Attorney

As mentioned earlier in the chapter, the first thing you want to consider is how experienced the attorney is in the matrimonial field. Attorneys who primarily handle divorce and family law have handled more cases and presumably have more knowledge than those who handle divorces along with everything else. They also have more connections with judges and other attorneys, and familiarity with the court process and court personnel.

Schedule a free consultation with the attorney you've selected and consider it a job interview for the attorney. Do not be intimidated and instead focus on asking questions and deciding if this is a person you trust and want to work with. Some questions to ask include:

1. *How long have you practiced this type of law?* Ideally you want someone who has been doing this for at least three years.

2. *How many cases of this type have you handled in the last six months?* An attorney who has handled ten divorce cases in six months is someone who definitely specializes in this area; however, if you live in a less populated area, it may be difficult to find an attorney who just does divorces.

3. *What are your fees?* Ask for information about in-court and out-of-court rates. Ask if a retainer fee (an up-front payment, similar to a down payment) is required. Determine if a separate rate is charged for paralegal work or if you will be charged for expenses.

4. *What are the court fees?* Each jurisdiction has its own fees, so ask what they are.

5. *How much do you think a case like mine would cost?* If the attorney is unable to estimate, you should get a second opinion.

6. *Can a payment plan be worked out?* Many attorneys are willing to do this. Be concerned, however, if an attorney suggests a lien against your home in exchange for legal work.

7. *What are the chances of my spouse paying some of my legal fees?* As mentioned, the court may order the moneyed spouse to pay the legal bills of the non-moneyed spouse.

8. *Do you provide a written contract?* Always insist upon this.

9. *Who will handle my case?* If it won't be the attorney you are interviewing, ask to speak to the person who would be in charge of the case.

10. *How likely is it I will get what I want? What am I asking for that is not realistic?* You really want an attorney who can be realistic with you and not promise you the moon.

11. *Is this a case you would try to settle?* Most cases can be settled and a settlement is much less expensive than going to trial.

12. *How quickly do you return phone calls?* Your calls should be returned within twenty-four hours.
13. *What do I do if there is a problem after hours?* Most attorneys do not accept calls after hours, but the fact of the matter is that all divorce crises do not happen between nine and five.
14. *How long would you anticipate this case lasting?*

In addition to weighing the answers to these questions, you need to consider how the attorney and his office makes you feel. There is a lot of personal choice involved in selecting an attorney. Some people prefer a woman or a man, some choose someone they feel is intimidating, while others want someone friendly and accessible. You need to decide what you are comfortable with and what will help you feel you're getting the best service.

Look around the attorney's office while you are there. Friendly staff is a good sign. Piles of disorganized, messy files can be something to be concerned about. Consider how convenient the office is for you to get to, since it is likely you will need to go there several times.

How to Afford an Attorney

Your divorce is likely to be an expensive proposition. You can plan to spend several thousand dollars at the very least, and much, much more depending on how complicated and lengthy your case is. When you're already dealing with the financial strain of living on one income, the thought of paying this amount of money can really get your heart pounding.

There are many ways to come up with the cash to afford your attorney. Probably none of them makes you want to smile, but they are solutions. The thing to remember is that you are paying for your freedom. Try to think of it as the necessary costs for making this important change in your life.

You can tap into investments or retirement funds available to you. You can work out a payment plan where you pay your attorney a set amount each month until the balance is paid off. You may be able to sell an asset, such as a home or vehicle to come up with the money. You can ask that the court order your spouse to pay your legal bills (this is only likely in a situation where your spouse has many more financial resources than you do). You can also ask a family member or friend for a loan to help you pay your legal bills. You can cash advance a credit card. You can take out a personal loan, a loan against a retirement account, or a home equity loan. There are many possibilities available.

In addition to considering how you are going to afford your divorce, you should consider some ways you can reduce the total cost of the divorce itself. You and your spouse can meet and determine a settlement agreement in which you work out custody, child support, spousal support, and division of assets and debts. Before you do this, it is very important that you seek the advice of an attorney so that you understand what your rights are and what a court would award in your situation. You and your spouse can handle all the paperwork of the divorce yourselves (see later in this chapter for information). You can also hire a mediator who can help you reach a settlement together (see chapter 6 for more information). You can instruct your attorneys that you do not want to go to trial and instead want them to settle your case. You can hire collaborative attorneys (see chapter 7 for more information). You can organize all of your bills, paperwork, and documents so that your attorney does not have to spend time doing this. You can refrain from calling your attorney more than is absolutely necessary. Each phone call will cost you, so the fewer calls you make, the less you will end up paying.

How to Handle a Divorce Yourself

It is possible to handle a divorce yourself, without an attorney. The first rule to remember though is that if your spouse gets an attorney, you probably need to as well. Handling paperwork and hammering out agreements together is one thing, but facing down, on your own, an attorney with years of experience in this field is another thing completely. Another option you should consider is hiring a paralegal. Paralegals are much less expensive than attorneys and can assist you in preparing the paperwork for your case.

Should you decide you want to handle the divorce yourself, check to see if your state or county provides you with an online or hard copy packet of forms and instructions. Some states have established self-help centers for family and divorce court cases where you can go for assistance. Check your state court Web site to see if your state offers this, or call the court clerk's office and ask.

There are also books that include specific state forms that you can use. It is important to follow all instructions carefully and meticulously. When dealing with court forms, you must make sure you check the right boxes and select the right options, otherwise you can lose some of your rights. It is also important that you carefully follow the filing instructions. Certain documents must be filed at certain times and failing to follow those requirements can lead to your papers being rejected.

Refer to the mediation checklist in chapter 6 for a list of all of the decisions that must be made in a divorce. While this checklist is designed for use in mediation, it can be used when you are handling a divorce yourself. Sit down with your spouse and talk through all the decisions in this checklist and reach agreements for all of them.

Always make copies of everything. Put all your documents in a file and take it to court every time you go. Staying organized is imperative. If you reach a point where you feel like you are in over your head (something you may encounter if you have to go beyond the basic forms the state gives you and write something they do not provide), you can always hire an attorney for a limited period. You could pay him to draft the papers for you or talk with you about how to do it yourself.

Deciding What Type of Divorce You Want

There are several pathways your divorce can take. You can decide what you think is best for you, but remember that your spouse plays an equal role in this process as well.

Uncontested

Also called a default divorce, in this situation, one person files papers and the other does not respond or appear, or files a form saying he does not wish to contest the divorce. This type of divorce is the quickest and most inexpensive. The person who filed the papers does have to appear in court (in some states you can send in an affidavit in place of a personal appearance). You don't automatically get everything you ask for—the judge decides what he believes is fair in the case. For example, if you are a young, healthy person ending a short marriage and ask for lifetime alimony, the judge is going to deny it. The judge isn't there to rubber stamp what you are asking for—he is there to apply the law to your case.

There are several different types of situations that can result in your divorce being uncontested. If you serve your spouse and she fails to respond or appear, then the case moves forward as uncontested. If you and your spouse agree on the terms of the divorce, one person files the paperwork and the other deliberately does not respond or appear.

The last situation is if you do not know how to find your spouse. This is actually more common than you would think. Lots of people separate and go their own ways and lose touch with each other (deliberately, in some cases). If you don't know where to locate your spouse, you first have to make an effort to find him or her—check the last address, call mutual friends, and contact his family if you know where they are. Check with his or her last known employer. Google the person. The court might require that you check military records and tax assessor records as well. Once you've done all of the above, and carefully documented everything, you let the court know you can't find your spouse, and you will likely be able to give notice by publication. This means the court will require you to publish a notice in a specific newspaper and this will serve as legal notice. If your spouse doesn't appear or respond, you can then go ahead with your case as uncontested.

Simplified
In some states, you can obtain a simplified or expedited divorce, which is a fast-track process. This is usually available to couples married for a short time without children. Usually you agree to waive the right to alimony and have no

significant assets or debts that need to be divided in the divorce. This type of divorce can usually be handled yourselves and has only a small amount of paperwork. It is also usually a much faster process than other divorces. If you have a prenup that requires alimony then you do not qualify.

Contested

The term *contested* makes the divorce sound as if it is argumentative and difficult. Really, this term just means both of you appear in the case. Most divorce cases settle before they go to trial, but after papers and motions have been filed. In fact, it's quite common for a divorce to be settled outside the courtroom doors on the actual day of the trial. Most courts now have procedures in place that require settlement conferences with the judge's law clerk or other court personnel to encourage settlement early in the case. If your case doesn't settle, though, it will go to a trial.

How to Begin the Divorce Process

Whether you are handling the case yourself or are hiring an attorney (or don't know which you're going to do yet), it is helpful to understand the basic steps in a starting a divorce case.

Residency

Before any paperwork can be filed in a divorce, you (or your attorney) have to make sure you qualify to get a divorce in the state in which you are living. Each state has what is called a residency requirement, which requires that you have lived in your state for a certain period of time before you are able to file for a divorce there. This is to ensure that people are not traveling to states where the laws are more favorable to get a divorce (this is called forum shopping). Note that if one of you is in the military, you can file in the state where the military spouse is currently stationed and you don't need to meet that state's residency requirement.

State Residency Requirements

Alabama	6 months or 180 days
Alaska	No requirements
Arizona	90 days
Arkansas	60 days
California	6 months or 180 days
Colorado	90 days
Connecticut	12 months or 1 year
Delaware	6 months or 180 days
District of Columbia	6 months or 180 days
Florida	6 months or 180 days
Georgia	6 months or 180 days
Hawaii	6 months or 180 days
Idaho	6 weeks
Illinois	90 days
Indiana	6 months or 180 days
Iowa	12 months or 1 year
Kansas	60 days
Kentucky	6 months or 180 days
Louisiana	6 months or 180 days
Maine	6 months or 180 days
Maryland	12 months or 1 year
Massachusetts	None if the reason for the divorce happened in the state, 12 months or 1 year otherwise
Michigan	6 months or 180 days
Minnesota	6 months or 180 days
Mississippi	6 months or 180 days
Missouri	90 days
Montana	90 days
Nebraska	12 months or 1 year
Nevada	6 weeks
New Hampshire	12 months or 1 year
New Jersey	12 months or 1 year

New Mexico	6 months or 180 days
New York	12 months or 1 year
North Carolina	6 months or 180 days
North Dakota	6 months or 180 days
Ohio	6 months or 180 days
Oklahoma	6 months or 180 days
Oregon	6 months or 180 days
Pennsylvania	6 months or 180 days
Rhode Island	12 months or 1 year
South Carolina	90 days (1 year if only one spouse is a resident)
South Dakota	No requirement
Tennessee	6 months or 180 days
Texas	6 months or 180 days
Utah	90 days
Vermont	6 months or 180 days
Virginia	6 months or 180 days
Washington	No requirement
West Virginia	None if married in the state, 12 months or 1 year otherwise
Wisconsin	6 months or 180 days
Wyoming	60 days

Paperwork

Once you've determined that you are qualified to divorce in your state, you will need to prepare a petition or complaint—the document that opens the case and gets served to your spouse notifying him or her about the case. This document includes the reasons for divorce, what you are asking for, and details about your date and place of marriage. You will also likely need to complete some other forms for the court, and pay any filing fees. You file these papers in the county in which you live. You may be able to file papers by mail, or you may have to do so in person.

When you complete papers, type or word process them whenever possible. If you must handwrite, do so neatly. Always use full legal names. Be prepared with social security numbers for yourself, your spouse, and your children. Once the papers are filed, the case will be assigned a number. It is important to keep this number. Always get a receipt for any papers you file, and keep a copy of the forms themselves, so that you have proof of what you filed.

In the next chapter we will discuss the divorce process and how the case will proceed.

Chapter 5

———— ✥ ————

The Divorce Court Process

Although divorce is an emotional journey, it is also above all else a legal process. Because a divorce is a legal proceeding, there are rules and procedures that you must follow and work through. The process itself can be a bit frustrating, particularly if you live in an area with courts with heavy schedules. You may have a long wait to get to the finish line.

The good news about divorce procedures is that they are fairly clear cut and if you just follow the steps, you will complete the process. The court is a bureaucracy, but it is one that demands respect and compliance.

Understanding How Courts Work

The first thing you must understand is that divorce courts are very busy. Your case is but one of thousands moving through the courts. The only person who really cares about your case is you. The judge has too many other cases to pay much attention and your attorney, while paid to be your advocate, is not personally affected by the outcome in the same way that you are. You must be in charge of your case and follow up on everything. You can't assume that anyone else will look out for your interests.

Another important fact to understand is that courts are all about paper-work. To get anything done in court, you (or your attorney) have to use the right form. This can be confusing if you are representing yourself, but if you ever are unsure what to do, ask the court clerks. Because of the importance of paperwork, if you are representing yourself, you need to keep copies of every scrap of paper involved in the case. Some states allow electronic filing of forms. Check your state court Web site for information about this option.

Courts are also all about procedures that are set in stone. Everything must be completed in a step-by-step process, fulfilling every requirement. This is how the court makes sure that everyone's rights are protected. It may seem time consuming, but it is this careful process that ensures that every detail is taken care of. You must cross all your Ts and dot all your Is. The only way you ever get anything in court is by formally asking for it. If you don't ask for it, you don't get it. Being meticulous pays off.

Understanding the Roles of All the Players

There will be several people in the courtroom in addition to you and your spouse and it can be helpful to understand who they are. If you have an at-torney, he is there to represent you and tell your side of the story to the judge. When you do have an attorney, your role is to be quiet and let him or her do the job. When you represent yourself, you must speak for yourself. It is fine to ask questions if you don't understand what is happening.

The judge is the person who makes the decisions in your case. At times, you may meet with people other than the judge who are in positions of au-thority. Before the case goes to trial, you may meet with the judge's law clerk or a matrimonial referee or hearing officer. These court personnel may try to encourage settlement, be able to formalize any settlement you reach, or be able to hear portions of the case (such as child support). You should treat these employees as respectfully as you would a judge.

Also in the courtroom is a bailiff or court security officer, who is there to ensure the safety of the participants and may be the person who calls your case to start. The court reporter types every word said while court is in session so that there is an official record of it. These records are called transcripts and are available for purchase from the court reporter. (You may need to purchase one if you are handling the divorce yourself because often you must file the transcript at some point in the proceeding. If so, get the court reporter's card so you can obtain the transcript.)

The people who work behind the counter outside the courtroom are court clerks, and they are the people to approach if you need help with anything. They can help you understand which form to use and how to complete it. They are also the people to talk to about rescheduling court appearances.

How to Approach Your Divorce Case

The most important thing you can do is have patience. You will need patience as you wait for your case to be scheduled, patience as you wait for your case to be called, and patience with the slow and plodding progress of the case through the proper procedure. Getting angry won't help and it won't get you results.

Try to think about your case as a checklist. You have to work your way down the checklist to complete it. Every single item must be marked off and taken care of before you can move on to the next one.

It is important to remember that to everyone but you and your spouse, your case is just one in a string of many. It's just another day at the office and no one there is going to be as emotionally charged and involved as you are. There is nothing you can do that will make the other people care as much as you do. All you can do is make your case, and offer reasoned and rational arguments.

Grounds

The grounds for a divorce are the legal reason for the divorce. Practically speaking, there are probably lots of reasons why people divorce, but each state has very specific laws that dictate what reasons you can use to get a divorce in court. Grounds available often include adultery, abandonment, imprisonment during the marriage, and cruel and inhuman treatment. One person in the marriage must accuse the other person of one of these acts. If both spouses do not agree, the one bringing the case may have to actually prove the grounds (this is called having a grounds trial).

Many people want to use adultery as their grounds, because they are hurt that their spouse had an affair. There's often a desire to want to show the world what a creep the other spouse has been and expose his or her sins. In most states, you must be able to offer proof from a third party about the adultery. Your word alone is not enough, and therefore it can be very expensive to prove (you may need to hire a private investigator). Adultery trials can be quite ugly and many attorneys recommend steering away from this as grounds. The easiest grounds to prove is usually cruel and inhuman treatment (sometimes called extreme cruelty) because fighting and arguing is often enough, and this happens in just about every divorce.

No-Fault States

Most states make no-fault divorce (in which neither party has to blame the other) an option. In these states you can simply tell the court that you have irreconcilable differences or an irremediable breakdown. You don't need to prove anything and you don't need to say bad things about each other. This can often make for a smoother divorce, with fewer bad feelings. Many states only allow you to use a no-fault option if you have lived apart for a certain period of time (months or years). If you and your spouse live in a no-fault state and don't want to wait this long, you can use a fault grounds and get a divorce immediately.

States that Allow No-Fault Divorce

Alabama	2 years separation required
Alaska	
Arizona	
California	

Colorado	
Connecticut	18 months separation required
Delaware	
Florida	
Georgia	
Hawaii	2 years separation required
Idaho	5 years separation required
Illinois	2 years separation required
Iowa	
Kansas	
Kentucky	
Louisiana	180 days separation required
Maine	
Massachusetts	
Michigan	
Minnesota	180 days separation required
Mississippi	
Missouri	
Montana	
Nebraska	
Nevada	
New Hampshire	
New Mexico	
North Dakota	
Ohio	1 year separation required
Oklahoma	
Oregon	
Pennsylvania	2 years separation required
Rhode Island	3 years separation required
South Dakota	
Tennessee	2 years
Texas	3 years separation required
Utah	3 years separation required

Washington
West Virginia   1 year separation required
Wisconsin
Wyoming

Covenant Marriage

Arizona, Arkansas, and Louisiana have covenant marriages available as an option when people get married. The idea behind this was to create a marriage that was somehow more binding and harder to end than a regular marriage. It is still possible to get a divorce if you have entered into a covenant marriage (it's not true that divorce is not allowed), although you have to jump through a few more hoops. Before you can seek a divorce, you have to try marriage counseling. You will have a longer waiting period before you are eligible for a divorce and you are required to use a fault grounds. Consult an attorney who can guide you through the necessary steps in this situation.

Service of Process

If you are going to be handling the service of papers in your case, it is essential that you find out what your state requirements are and follow them to the letter. If you don't, you may have to start over. Many states require that you file your papers first, then serve them, but this is not the case everywhere, so be certain you find out what your state rules are. The simplest way to handle service is to hire a process server (sometimes your local sheriff's office will do it). You cannot do the service yourself, so you will need to find a friend or relative who can help you. If you have an attorney, she will arrange for service and it will not be something you need to deal with.

There are several ways you can serve papers, and again, the requirements vary from state to state, so it is important you find out exactly how it must be done in your state. Personal service generally means the papers are personally handed to your spouse. Usually an affidavit has to be filled out by the person who served them, to verify that it actually happened. You may be able to mail the papers to your spouse (but check your state laws—some states only allow mailing if you also personally drop papers off at the home or workplace as well).

If you don't know where your spouse is, you need to make a reasonable effort to find him or her. What is reasonable may differ in each state, so be sure to research this as well. Once you've done what you can to find him or her and come up empty handed, the court will likely require you to publish your notice in a newspaper (in the legal notice section of the classifieds), to give your spouse an opportunity to see it. If there is no response, then your case will continue as if it were uncontested.

If your spouse is not served, and you have not qualified for or completed service by publication, your case cannot proceed. It is a basic requirement of our legal system that a person receive notice of a case against him. If that notice is not received, the case cannot continue. You likely have a certain period of time in which you must get the papers served or the case is dismissed.

How to Respond

If you have been served with papers by your spouse, you may be unsure what you are supposed to do. The first thing you should do is read the papers. If you can afford an attorney, this is the point at which you need to hire one. She can help you understand exactly what the papers say and mean if you are unsure.

The papers will indicate a date by which you must respond. Usually you respond by sending a written answer or response (there is a specific form to use for this and you will need to locate it for your state) to your spouse and to the court. You may also have the opportunity to just appear in court without sending any papers. If you don't have an attorney and don't understand what to do, call the court clerk's office and ask them how and when to respond. They can provide you with a form to use or talk you through filling in an enclosed form.

It is very important that you do respond within the timeframe required. If you don't, you will default on the divorce and the case will proceed without you and you won't have any say in what happens. It is sometimes tempting to ignore problems that seem insurmountable, but in this case, shoving the papers in a drawer will not make the situation go away. It will simply make things much worse for you. If you don't respond, you lose your chance to present your side of the situation to the court. This could mean the court could order you to pay child support or spousal support. The court can decide custody of your children and handle the division of your marital assets and debts. All of this will be done without your input. The judge will make a decision based on what the law allows and the facts your spouse presents.

Forms and Fees

If you are handling your own divorce, you need to become familiar with your court's forms. The court may require that you only use their forms, or they may allow you to create your own, as long as you follow certain rules about formatting and headers. Check with the court clerk for information about this.

There is a form for everything in court. If you are ever unsure what form to use, or where to get a form, ask the court clerk. If you have a pro se divorce packet or Web page for your state, this should provide most of the forms you need. You can find sample forms in Appendix B.

When completing forms, keep in mind that they are designed to cover every situation. There will likely be questions that do not apply to you. Cross them out or write in "N/A." Answer everything else as completely and fully as possible. It is possible to amend forms you have filed if you make a mistake, but it's easier to just do it right the first time. Pay particular attention when you are asked to have a form notarized. This means you have to take it to a notary (there is likely one in the court clerk's office) and swear that everything in the document is true. If you lie in this kind of document, it is a serious perjury offense.

Just as there is a form for everything, there is likely to be a fee for many things as well. Every time you file a form, find out if there is a fee required. The easiest way to do this is to call the court clerk, or to go there in person. If you do not have the necessary fee, you aren't allowed to file the form (unless you qualify under your state's indigency exception, which applies to people who are below certain income levels), so it is important to be aware of this in advance. Some fees are minimal—a few dollars—while others can be over $100. Court clerks usually accept money orders and cash. Many will accept personal checks, but it is best to be certain of this in advance.

Procedures

An important question about procedure is where you will file your divorce. Once you've made sure you meet your state's residency requirements (see chapter 4), you will want to file for divorce in your county of residency. Go to the county courthouse and file them with the court in your county that handles divorce cases. You can find information on your state court Web site.

The divorce process starts with the filing and service of a petition. Your spouse then has the chance to answer this. In some states, you may then file a document called a complaint, which offers more details about what you are asking for. Your spouse has a chance to respond to that. At any time after the initial petition is filed, you can file motions for temporary relief (sometimes called pendent elite relief)—temporary child support, spousal support, residence of the home, custody, visitation and so on. These orders make some temporary decisions so immediate needs are taken care of and everything can remain somewhat stable throughout the court process. Once the initial papers have been filed, the divorce will either move to an uncontested or rather simple court process, or your attorneys will begin the discovery process.

Discovery is a period of time in the divorce case where each side gathers information. Your attorney will gather information from you and witnesses that are prepared for your side, but she can also request information from your spouse's attorney, and may subpoena records (such as bank records, school records, business records, and so on). If you do not have an attorney, you can do discovery yourself, however it will be difficult to understand what you can access and how to access it. The court can issue subpoenas on your behalf if you want to issue any. A deposition is a type of discovery, and involves the taking of sworn testimony outside of court. Your attorney could depose your spouse. Depositions usually take place in a lawyer's office. A court reporter is present to record what is said. The testimony given at a deposition can then be used at trial as evidence and can help your attorney be prepared for what might be said there.

Attorneys will have settlement meetings and settlement conferences with the court and amongst themselves to try to reach a resolution. If no settlement can be agreed upon, the case is scheduled for trial. If you represent yourself, you will attend these meetings.

How to Streamline the Process

All of the above procedures can take months. This can be very frustrating if you want to just get to the trial and move on. There are several things you can do that will expedite the process. The first is to reach a settlement. If you are motivated to wrap things up, you should be able to come to an agreement. If your attorneys cannot get you to a complete settlement, mediation may be able to do so. An attorney has experience in reaching settlements, but a mediator is specifically trained in this area and may be able to guide you to a conclusion where your attorneys could not.

If a settlement is not forthcoming, you are left with the traditional court process. Shortening the discovery period is one way to move things along. Your attorney may also be able to ask for summary judgment (immediate decision by the court) on several points, which can bring some resolution. You can also keep all settlement hearings brief, by making it clear you will not negotiate and that you want the case scheduled for trial.

How to Behave in Court and at Trial

If you've never been in court before, you may be unsure about how to dress. It is a good idea to dress appropriately, because your appearance does make an impact on the court. To make the best impression, men should wear a coat and tie and women should wear a pant suit, skirt suit, or dress. If you aren't comfortable with this, a dress shirt for men and a business-like outfit for women is fine. Avoid all of the following:

- clothing that is revealing, low cut, or suggestive
- dirty, worn, or ripped clothing
- sneakers
- sweat pants or sweat suits
- flashy jewelry
- T-shirts
- jeans
- sandals or flip flops
- leather clothing
- jewelry or clothing that makes noise when you move
- heavy makeup
- hair styles designed to be provocative
- visible body piercings (other than one set of earrings)

When you arrive at the courthouse, you will be required to go through a metal detector and your bags and belongings may be searched. Never bring a weapon of any kind into a court house—it will be seized. Food and beverages are not permitted. Avoid gum or mints, since it is rude to have something in your mouth if you are asked to speak to the judge. If you bring a cell phone with you, you must turn it off while you are in the building. Never go into court with earphones in your ears, even if your MP3 player is not on.

When you are in the courtroom, sit next to your attorney. If you do not have an attorney, sit where you are directed to (usually the person bringing the case sits on the left and the other person sits on the right, but this can vary by location). If you have an attorney, she will do all the talking. If something comes up during the proceedings and you need to talk to your attorney, write a note indicating that and your attorney can ask for a break.

If the judge asks you a question, respond to it. You can refer to the judge as "Your Honor." While you are in the courtroom, you should not talk with your spouse. If you have attorneys, they will do the talking. If not, you are both there to address the judge, not each other.

If you are called to testify, you will have to swear to tell the truth. If you lie while testifying it is perjury and can be charged as a crime. Answer questions as directly and honestly as you can. If you don't understand something, say so.

Trial Procedures

The person who filed for divorce (the petitioner, plaintiff, or complainant) presents his or her case first. The defendant or respondent has a chance to cross-examine all witnesses presented. The respondent then gets to present his or her case and the petitioner or plaintiff can cross-examine. If there is a Law Guardian or Guardian ad litem, he has the opportunity to present witnesses as well, and these can be cross-examined by both parents.

The court does not allow any evidence that is hearsay—not presented by the direct source. For example, you could not testify that your neighbor told you she heard your husband yelling at your kids. The best way to present that evidence would be to have the neighbor testify about what she directly experienced. Any evidence that is presented to the court must be authenticated. You can't just hand the court what you say is a bank record. You need someone from the bank to testify or complete an affidavit that it is an official record. If you want to enter a photograph into evidence, you must have the person who took the photograph verify it is authentic. Although these rules can seem somewhat restrictive, they are in place to protect everyone who is involved.

After both parties have presented their cases and cross-examined each other's witnesses, there is usually the opportunity to make a closing statement or closing argument. If you are representing yourself, this is your opportunity to sum up what your points are and to tell the court clearly what you are asking for (such as custody, child support, and so on). The judge will not make a decision on the spot, and instead will likely issue a decision within a few weeks. Your divorce is not final until the final judgment or order of the case has been entered.

Name Changes

If either one of your changed your name upon marriage, you have the right to change it back after the divorce. To do so, you need to request the court's permission. A request for a name change is normally included in the complaint or petition and then becomes part of the divorce decree. You are not required to change your name back. However, it's a good idea to include this clause even if you think you don't want to change your name, in case you should change your mind in the future. If you do not get permission to change your name as part of the divorce, you will have to go through a separate legal process later, should you decide that is what you want to do.

Removal of Barriers to Remarriage

In some states, you can request that your spouse make every effort to remove any barriers to a future remarriage. This means that he will participate in whatever annulment process is required by your religion, should you choose to seek an annulment. It does not mean you definitely plan to seek a religious annulment (see chapter 1 for information about legal versus religious annulments); however, it gives you the option to pursue it in the future.

Chapter 6

Divorce Mediation

Divorce mediation is an important alternative to traditional divorce. In a regular divorce, you and your spouse are pitted against each other. If you have attorneys, they each work hard to prove that the other spouse is wrong. Everyone is trying to win. It's a competition to see who can convince the judge he deserves the most money, custody, child support, and spousal support.

Mediation is a completely different process. The idea behind mediation is that it took two people working together to create your marriage, and so it ought to take two people working together to end your marriage. Mediation is a cooperative process in which you and your spouse are encouraged to work together to find solutions to the issues in your divorce that are acceptable to both of you.

In mediation, no one wins or loses. There is no competition. There is no mud-slinging or contests to see who can present (or make up) the most damning evidence in court. Instead, you and your spouse sit down with a trained mediator in an office and work together to decide how you are going to resolve the issues facing you. You can take as long as you want to work through this. You can explore creative and unusual options, and if they happen to work for you, you can implement them. You have the power to shape your divorce settlement, instead of a judge who has never met you or your children.

How Mediation Works

Mediation is designed to be a calm and collaborative process. You and your spouse choose a mediator together. You then meet with the mediator, usually once a week. The mediator is a neutral third party who is not invested in the outcome of the case in any way. The mediator guides you through all of the decisions that must be made in the divorce. She acts as your guide and your assistant, pointing out possible solutions, educating you about the law, and isolating areas of agreement. The mediator does not make any decisions, but instead is there to help you and your spouse make the decisions together. She encourages you, points out issues you may have missed, and helps you think through all the choices and options before you.

The mediator works for both of you, and is very careful to make sure that she is completely impartial. This usually means the mediator will not meet with or speak to the parties separately—unless they both consent.

Everything you say in mediation is confidential—the mediation room is meant to be a safe zone where you and your spouse can come and talk freely. Mediators have strict rules that do not allow voices to be raised or name calling to occur. Most mediators also require that you sign a document stating you agree not to call the mediator as a witness should you end up in court.

You and your spouse talk directly to each other, unlike in a traditional divorce where your attorneys talk for you. You can each propose solutions and talk through the implications of different scenarios with each other. Instead of having a judge, who is a complete stranger to you and your children, make decisions about how all of you will live your lives, you and your spouse make your own decisions that fit your lives. The mediator helps you stay on track and can redirect you back to the issues at hand, should you stray into territory that doesn't need to be covered in the session.

The purpose of mediation is to come to a complete agreement that will settle your divorce. The mediator will prepare a separation agreement, settlement document, or memorandum of understanding which sets out everything you have agreed upon. This document will then be converted to legal format, or filed as is with the court. You will not have a trial and will at most have a brief court appearance acknowledging the settlement agreement.

How to Decide If Mediation Can Work for You

Mediation is an option for almost every divorcing couple. There are a few situations, however, in which mediation is not a good idea. If you have experienced domestic violence in your relationship, mediation is not a good alternative because there is the possibility of coercion. If you and your spouse have such a volatile relationship that you cannot sit in the same room or agree on anything, then mediation may not be a good choice for you. If one of you is completely opposed to a divorce or separation entirely, you won't get very far in mediation. A severe mental illness is also a red flag that mediation will not work—you both must be able to make decisions. If you and your spouse have already worked out all the issues before you and have decided to do an uncontested divorce or a simplified divorce, mediation may be unnecessary for you. In all other instances, mediation is something you should consider and offer as an option to your spouse.

In order to be successful in mediation you need to be able to speak your mind and be clear about what will work for you. You cannot defer to your spouse and you can't sit back and expect the mediator to carry the load for you. You must be prepared to take an active role in making the decisions that are going to impact your life. This means knowing your own mind and being able to think about your future and what you need. There is no one to stand up for you or protect you other than yourself, so you must commit to doing so.

If you mediate, both you and your spouse are required to make complete financial disclosure to each other. This means completing a questionnaire or affidavit about your financial affairs. This document is usually filed with the court along with your agreement. If you do not believe your spouse will provide complete or honest information, then you need to talk to an attorney and pursue a traditional divorce in which information can be subpoenaed.

If you are undecided about whether mediation might work for you, set up a consultation with a mediator and get a feel for the process. You might decide you want to at least try it out. You can end mediation at any time, so if it isn't something you are comfortable with, you can walk away.

Benefits of Mediation

Mediation has a long list of benefits. It simply provides the best way to end a marriage in most cases. People who mediate are more likely to abide by their mediation agreement. Because they had a say in creating it and because it is tailored to their lives, people are more likely to follow the agreement. A divorce decree imposed by a judge feels intrusive and some people feel compelled to rebel against it.

Families who mediate are much less likely to return to court. There are some families that get caught in a revolving courtroom door. They never learn how to solve their own problems, and so they come back to court every time one of them sneezes. If you mediate, you learn how to work together and find solutions to difficult problems. Mediation not only helps you resolve today's problems, but it gives you the tools you need to resolve future problems as well. You are better prepared for future conflicts and problems and already have a technique in place that allows you to find solutions together.

Mediation is much better for children. You and your spouse create a parenting plan that is custom designed for your lives and those of your children. You work together to make arrangements with which everyone can feel comfortable. Because mediation discourages fighting and encourages cooperation, you will better be able to parent together afterwards. There is less emotional damage involved for your children because you are not at each other's throats throughout the process. Instead, you work through your issues in a calm and thoughtful way that allows you to make good decisions and treat each other with respect.

Mediation is less stressful. You aren't placing your fate in the hands of a stranger. While there certainly are tense moments in mediation, and you are still dealing with the strain of ending a marriage, it all happens in a much more controlled and calm fashion. You don't have to worry about testifying, appearing in court, being cross-examined, and putting together the best case possible. Instead, you devote your energies to finding solutions. If something is proposed that does not work for you, all you have to do is say so. You aren't bound by anything until the end of mediation when you sign an agreement.

Mediation moves more quickly than a traditional court divorce. In a traditional divorce, you will have court dates spread over many months. In mediation, you meet on a regular weekly or bi-weekly basis and move step by step through each decision facing you. You are always making progress and moving forward, and you do so on your own timeline, not one imposed on you by a court system.

Because you and your spouse agree to all the terms of the divorce, mediated cases have a very low appeals rate. In traditional divorce, in some states, almost half of all contested cases are appealed. An appeal drags your case on for years and is extremely expensive. In mediation, there is no reason for an appeal because you have personally agreed to everything (although you do still have the right to appeal).

Mediation is private. Court divorce cases are public record. Mediation, however, happens in private. Everything from your sessions is confidential, except for the final settlement agreement that is filed with the court. You don't have to stand up in court and say bad things about your spouse or worry that the details of your life will be of interest to other people.

There is less pressure in mediation. It's actually quite common for people to agree to settlements outside the courtroom door and later regret it, feeling as if their attorney pressured them into it. Just the atmosphere of having to make an important decision while standing in a public hallway, knowing you have five minutes to make up your mind can lead people to make bad choices. In mediation you can take all the time you need to make a decision.

Mediation can help you work out problems and issues that traditional divorce is not equipped to handle. You can talk over any issues and agree to anything. One of the best things about mediation is that it pays careful attention to your parenting plan and allows you to craft a plan that is as detailed as you need it to be. If you go to court, a judge will simply lay out where the child will be on what days. In mediation, you can work out details, such as rules you will both have in your homes, how you will communicate with each other about schedule changes, where you will do drop offs and picks ups, how you will tell the children about the divorce (if you have not already done so), and whether you will buy large holiday gifts for the child together. These are all very important points that can have a great impact on your life and which mediation allows you to work out. Other factors mediation allows you to deal with include when and how you will physically separate, how you will tell family and friends, how you will avoid each other at mutual friends' houses, and so on. You can even talk about things such as how you treat each other and how it makes each of you feel. There is room in mediation for any issue or problem you bring in the door.

Mediation encourages your involvement in the case that is, after all, about your life. In traditional divorce, you are discouraged from talking to your spouse and instead are told to let the lawyers handle it. In mediation you do all the talking and are not disconnected from the case in any way. You're supposed to interact with each other.

Mediation offers a lot of control over the situation. You have absolute control not only over the numbers and terms, but also over the exact wording that is used in your agreement. Often people complain that they agreed to one thing when talking to their attorney and when they get the divorce decree they find that it is worded completely differently. In mediation you have control over every word of your agreement. You also have control over the process. You decide what to discuss each week, and how quickly you want to move forward.

Drawbacks of Mediation

While the benefits of mediation are huge, there are some aspects of it you must be prepared for that are difficult. First of all, mediation requires you to make a complete shift in how you think about your divorce. Some people just want it to be a contested situation and aren't ready to work cooperatively with each other. Some people need the conflict of the divorce process to help them work through their feelings and reactions. If that's what you need, that's fine, but mediation is not going to be the forum to help you with that.

To succeed in mediation, you must be able to sit in a room face to face with your spouse and talk to him or her. Some people simply don't want to do this and if so, mediation may not be the best choice. Other people think they can do it, yet find that it is too overwhelming when they actually are there—particularly if you are still hung up on the concept of the divorce itself and your spouse just wants to move forward through the issues.

In mediation you must take responsibility for yourself, your actions, and your choices. This can be difficult to do. Divorce is certainly an eye-opening time in your life and having to be so brutally honest about yourself can be an added burden. In mediation, there really is no place to hide. You may have to come to grips with the fact that both of you caused the divorce. For example, if you go into mediation thinking your spouse decided to stop being an active partner in the marriage and it's all his fault, you might have to face the fact that you started to drift away from him years ago and you in fact also stopped making an effort.

Mediation requires that you provide respect and real consideration for options and suggestions offered by your spouse. You may be at a point where you are disgusted with him or her, or completely annoyed. Working through this so that you are able to seriously and carefully consider everything your spouse says in mediation can be a challenge.

Mediation is, simply put, hard work. It takes a lot of your time and requires you to focus intently during sessions. You have to think and make decisions and create plans. It is very much an active process. If you've ever gone to a therapist, you know you can sometimes leave a session and be emotionally drained and exhausted. Because mediation is similar to therapy, it can create the same reaction. You're making tough decisions and struggling with a lot of emotions. It can feel very intense.

In mediation, you also must compromise. No one is going to walk out the door with everything they want. There are no winners and there are no losers. You have to be prepared to give some things up in order to gain other things. If you aren't prepared to do that, mediation will be very challenging for you.

Mediation requires you to take a step back from your situation and set your emotional issues to one side so you can deal with legal and financial decisions. This can be difficult to do since in divorce the tangible assets often begin to represent emotional issues. For example, a dispute over who gets the lawn mower can really be rooted in the resentments and problems of your marriage, which you are still likely trying to process and work through. Setting aside all of those feelings so you can look at the bottom line of the financial worth of the lawn mower can be hard.

Another difficulty in mediation is that couples often hit a wall somewhere in the process. They cannot find a solution to a decision they are facing and cannot agree. This is actually quite common and happens in almost every mediation. You must be prepared to keep trying. Sometimes setting that issue aside and coming back to it later when other things have been decided is helpful. Approaching the problem from other directions and with other techniques can also get you through it (your mediator will help you do this). You must be prepared not to just give up when you hit a rough patch.

There are still many attorneys who simply don't believe in mediation. If you've hired an attorney, he may not encourage you to try mediation, or if you bring it up, he may try to dissuade you. Some attorneys view it as taking business away from them. They also are slightly insulted at the implication that their way of doing things may not be what is best for their clients. Some attorneys refuse to believe that a mediator who has a therapist background can ever be knowledgeable enough about divorce law to handle mediation competently. Other attorneys simply are not very familiar with the process and don't understand its benefits. If you hire an attorney who does not support mediation, you will have a difficult time of it.

Costs

When people hear about mediation, one of their common reactions is concern about cost. A mediated divorce is, in fact, much less expensive than a traditional court divorce, even one that settles without a trial. In a traditional divorce, you pay two attorneys to work on the case, which can result in tens of thousands of dollars, depending on how complicated the case is. In media-tion, you each hire an attorney, but only consult with him or her for a few hours. You then both meet with a mediator whom you pay by the hour (often at a lower rate than attorneys charge for trials). Because you are able to reach agreements much more quickly than an attorney is, your case is completed in a much shorter time period. You don't need to pay an attorney to draft mo-tions, collect documents, prepare evidence, interview witnesses, have settle-ment conferences, or appear in court.

Mediator rates vary depending on the mediator's experience and his or her background. In general, attorney mediators tend to charge more, while thera-pist mediators tend to have a lower hourly rate. (We'll discuss the differences between these two types of mediators in the next section.) You can expect to pay a mediator between $75 and $300 an hour, with costs varying across the country (rates are higher in urban areas). Average mediation costs range from $3,000 to $7,000, depending on your mediator's rates, and how involved your case is. Most mediation cases are wrapped up within several months, com-pared to contested divorces, which can take over a year.

Most mediators require a retainer fee to be paid up front, which is used to cover the cost of activities outside of the mediation meetings (such as drafting the agreement, corresponding with your attorneys, and handling your phone calls). You are then usually expected to pay at the end of each mediation ses-sion, although some mediators prefer to bill you.

Mediator Qualifications

There is no formal licensing of mediators, so anyone can hang out a shingle claiming to be a mediator. Because of this, it is important that you inquire about the mediator's training and experience. Many mediators are either at-torneys or therapists. Mediation is a profession that bridges both of these spe-cialties. Mediators need to have legal knowledge and also understand relationships. Both attorney and therapist mediators can be equally good, al-though they often have different styles. Some mediators continue to practice as therapists or attorneys and handle mediation as part of their practice.

Others focus only on mediation. You definitely want to find a mediator who has an advanced degree in law or mental health. There are now some colleges and universities that do offer degrees in conflict resolution, so that is another pathway a mediator could have followed.

Since there is no licensing of mediators, you will want to know what kind of training your mediator has. You should only use a mediator who has had at least a 40 hour training program. You also want to be sure you are working with a mediator who has experience in divorce and family mediation and has handled many mediations. Most mediators are members of a state or national mediation association, such as The Association for Conflict Resolution. It is also important that mediators continue to receive continuing education, so that they can be aware of changes in the law and in the mediation field. Most professional mediators have access to other mediators they can consult with on their cases (confidentially, without revealing identities). This allows the mediator to get another opinion or assistance in a difficult case.

How to Find a Mediator

There are several ways to locate a mediator. If you know someone who has used a mediator, get the name from him. If you have an attorney, ask her for a referral to mediation. If you are seeing a therapist, ask if she can recommend a mediator. Your local or state bar association (you can find a list in the appendix) can likely refer you to an attorney who is a mediator in your area. You can also locate a local or state mediation association and find names of local mediators there. You can contact the Association for Conflict Resolution (www.acrnet.org or 202-464-9700) for names of mediators in your area as well. In some areas, there are large group practices made up of many mediators. They may be advertised in the phone book or online. Some courts maintain lists of area mediators as well. If your local Better Business Bureau runs a community dispute program, it is staffed by people trained in mediation and you can ask them for names of mediators.

Once you have a few names, call and talk to a mediator on the phone. Ask a few preliminary questions to get a feel for the person. If you like what you hear, set up a free consultation. Both you and your spouse should go to the meeting, since it is important that both of you are comfortable with the mediator. When you meet with the mediator, ask a lot of questions, such as:

- What are your fees?
- What total cost would you project for our case?
- What training do you have?
- How many divorce mediation cases have you handled in the last year?
- Do you participate in continuing education?
- How available are you for sessions?
- What final document do you prepare?
- Do you provide a contract to your clients?
- Do you also maintain a practice as an attorney or a therapist?

Why You Need an Attorney as Well

Many people are surprised to learn that even though they are using a mediator for their divorce, they still need an attorney. The mediator is there to work with both of you. He cannot provide you with any legal advice—only legal information. It is important that you retain an attorney who can meet with you and give you an opinion about how your case would be resolved in court, so you know what the alternatives are. The attorney is also there to fully explain to you what your rights are and how the law applies to your case. You can meet with your attorney at any point during mediation to get his or her opinion about the decisions that you are facing. It can be very helpful to go to your attorney with a child support or alimony proposal and have him or her tell you that it is far too low or far too high.

Your attorney does not go to mediation sessions with you. Once you have completed mediation, the mediator will send the written agreement to your attorney for review. Your attorney or your spouse's attorney will take the agreement and file it with the court. If your mediator does not require that you hire a separate attorney, you should be concerned. It is considered standard practice to require clients to retain separate attorneys who can advise them about the law.

Other Professionals and Mediation

As you participate in mediation, your mediator may suggest that you involve some other professionals. One referral may be to a therapist, so that you or your spouse can work out the emotional ramifications of the divorce. If you are using a mediator who is also a therapist, it is not appropriate for him to conduct marriage therapy with you since that is a separate process from mediation. Similarly, it would not be appropriate for an attorney mediator to represent you in the divorce.

Another common professional involved in mediation is an appraiser. If you have a home or business, or other valuable asset, you need to be able to put a dollar figure on what it is worth so that its value can be divided in the divorce. In a contested divorce, it is likely both you and your spouse would have to pay for separate appraisers. In mediation, you can agree to use just one, or you can each hire your own and then compromise on what the true value is.

Financial advisors and accountants may also be brought in. A financial advisor can help you make educated decisions about investments and retirement savings. Accountants or tax experts can be brought in to discuss the tax ramifications of decisions you are facing.

If you have children and have come to mediation after beginning a divorce or custody case in court, it is likely there is a Law Guardian or Guardian ad litem assigned to your case. She will have to sign off on any agreement about custody that you reach in the divorce and may even attend sessions if you find it helpful. Custody evaluators are commonly used in contested divorce cases to offer an opinion about what kind of custody arrangement would be most beneficial for the child. This kind of expert can be brought into a mediation case as well if the parties are unable to reach an agreement about custody.

Court-Ordered Mediation

In some states, mediation is mandatory before you can proceed to court. Because most cases do settle without a trial, these states are trying to divert people from the court system and into mediation in the hope that they will settle sooner rather than later.

There are two types of court-ordered mediation. Non-reporting mediation requires that you and your spouse attend a certain number of mediation sessions before you return to court (should you need to). The mediator simply tracks the number of visits and shares that information with the court. Nothing you discuss in mediation is shared with the court. If you fail to reach a resolution, it doesn't impact your court case in any way.

Reporting mediation is a different animal. In this instance, the mediator reports back to the court on what was discussed and what progress was made, if you do not reach an agreement. The mediator sends a report to the court and can indicate which spouse was cooperative and which was not. The report may also indicate what the major points of disagreement are, what your respective positions are, and what the mediator feels would be a good solution for your situation. In this kind of court-ordered mediation, you may need to be careful about what you say and do, because if you do not reach a settlement, the entire process is open to the court and what you've done or said in mediation can hurt your case, should you go to a contested court proceeding.

Something else to be aware of when going through court-ordered mediation is that this process is a step apart from regular mediation. It focuses less on the needs of the parties, and more on reaching an agreement at whatever cost. Regular mediation has an element of therapy in it in which the couple learns to work with each other, understand each other, and put aside their differences. Court-ordered mediation often has a strict timeline or number of visits, and the mediator is under pressure from the court to bring the parties to a resolution. There is less freedom to discuss a wide range of issues.

Preparing for Mediation

If you and your spouse have agreed to use mediation, you will want to give some thought to the process in advance. One thing you and your spouse definitely should do is discuss how you will pay the mediator's fees. You could split it (evenly, or apportion it according to income) or one spouse could pay the entire cost. If you can decide this in advance, it will save you time in mediation, because this is the first issue the mediator is going to want to resolve, so it's best to do it off the clock if you can.

Another step in preparing for mediation is to complete the budget form earlier in this book. Gather all available information about your joint assets and debts and create a list of these. At some point in the mediation, you will be asked to provide this. If you and your spouse have already divided some property, write down what has been divided. If you agree about how to divide other property, write this down as well. Coming to the mediator with a list of agreements will make her job much easier and save you time and money.

Hire an attorney and consult with him before your first mediation session, so that you will have obtained the necessary legal background information you need to make informed choices as you move through mediation. Your mediator may insist on holding off on the first session until you've had a chance to do this, so getting it out of the way will mean your first session can be scheduled sooner.

Before you start your sessions, take some time to sit down and think about how you want the mediation to go. Imagine yourself and your spouse working cooperatively. Think about how you will deal with feelings that may come up during mediation and how you will work around them or through them. Simply envisioning you and your spouse moving successfully through the mediation process can help things go smoothly.

Do not expect there to be immediate results from your mediation. It can take several sessions for the mediator to gather all the needed information and get to know you.

As you mediate, your mediator will likely use a checklist similar to the one below. You can look over this checklist before mediation so that you are prepared for some of the issues you will be working through:

Mediation Checklist

Parenting Plan

- ☐ Decision making (Sole, joint, divided)
- ☐ Living arrangements (Primary residence)
- ☐ Time-sharing schedule ("Regular schedule")
- ☐ Beginning and end, day and hour
- ☐ Notice
- ☐ Travel arrangements and cost
- ☐ Holidays
- ☐ Long weekends
- ☐ School breaks (February, Spring, Christmas)
- ☐ Summer vacation
- ☐ Birthdays (Children's, parents')
- ☐ Other special occasions (Mother's Day, Father's Day, etc.)
- ☐ Other understandings
  - ☐ Child care when ill
  - ☐ Telephone access
  - ☐ Gifts
  - ☐ Travel (length of time, geographic location)
  - ☐ Laundry
- ☐ Extended family ("grandparent's rights")
- ☐ Relocation
- ☐ Religion
- ☐ Decisions requiring mutual consultation
- ☐ Notification regarding illness, emergency authority
- ☐ Visiting if child is sick in bed 2 days or more

- ☐ Access to records, notification of address and telephone numbers
- ☐ Provisions for review or modification
- ☐ Child(ren)'s voice in decision in remarriage
- ☐ Sexual partners
- ☐ Dispute-resolving mechanism—at least four hours of good faith mediation within thirty days prior to court (if cannot resolve themselves)

Support
- ☐ Child Support
  - ☐ Amount
  - ☐ Time of payment
  - ☐ Emancipation definition
  - ☐ Escalation/reduction/suspension
- ☐ Child care costs
- ☐ Summer camp, lessons, special expenses
- ☐ School tuition
- ☐ College
  - ☐ What is child expected to do?
  - ☐ What will parents do?
  - ☐ What will be set aside now?
- ☐ Weddings, Bar Mitzvahs, Graduations, Confirmations, and so on
- ☐ Spousal maintenance
  - ☐ Amount
  - ☐ Time of payment
  - ☐ Duration
  - ☐ Escalation/reduction/suspension
- ☐ Medical insurance (medical, dental, optical)
  - ☐ Who provides for children, spouse
  - ☐ Duration
  - ☐ Access to records, notification
  - ☐ Arrangements for submission to insurance, reimbursement
- ☐ Unreimbursed medical, dental, optical, orthodontia, and related expenses

- ☐ Life insurance
  - ☐ Type
  - ☐ Amount
  - ☐ Duration
  - ☐ Beneficiary arrangements
  - ☐ Access to records, notification
- ☐ Disability insurance
- ☐ Provisions for disability, unemployment, etc.
- ☐ Need for financial planning for retirement, etc.

Property
- ☐ Bank accounts
- ☐ Notes receivable
- ☐ Investments, stocks, bonds, mutual funds, tax shelters
- ☐ Marital residence
  - ☐ Duration of occupancy
  - ☐ Mortgage/rent obligations
  - ☐ Taxes, insurance payments
  - ☐ Repairs, "major repairs"
  - ☐ Sale
    - ☐ Price
    - ☐ Division of Proceeds
    - ☐ Buy-out rights
    - ☐ Fixing up expenses
- ☐ Other real estate
- ☐ Retirement funds
  - ☐ IRA, TSA, 401(k)
  - ☐ Keogh plans (self-employed)
  - ☐ Pension plans
  - ☐ Social security (if married 10+ years)
- ☐ Business, partnerships interest
- ☐ Licenses and degrees
- ☐ Other assets (tax refunds due, patents, royalties, etc.)

- ☐ Personal property
  - ☐ Cars
  - ☐ Boats, RVs, etc.
  - ☐ Jewelry, antiques, other items of large value
- ☐ Household effects
  - ☐ Division of items
  - ☐ Provision for removal, storage
- ☐ Debts and loans
  - ☐ Mortgage, home equity loans/lines
  - ☐ Car loans
- ☐ Warranties re: existence of other marital property/debt

Other

- ☐ Income tax filings
  - ☐ How to file (joint, separately)
  - ☐ Cooperation in filing, if joint; deductions, if separate
  - ☐ Division of funds, assessments
  - ☐ Prior year's joint returns refunds/assessments
  - ☐ Dependency exemptions
- ☐ Future mediation fees
- ☐ Legal fees
- ☐ Estate rights waiver, need to revise wills
- ☐ Religious annulment (including "Get" law or other religious considerations)
- ☐ How to proceed (immediate divorce, separation agreement)

Moving Mediation Along

To keep your mediation moving along, make sure you are meeting weekly or bi-weekly. Failing to have regular sessions will slow things down. Not only will there be longer waits between sessions, but you will also need to use valuable time at the beginning of each session as your mediator recaps where you are at. You can lose steam if you don't keep plugging away at it.

There may be some things you and your spouse can discuss and work out outside of mediation sessions. You may be able to sit down one evening and work out how you will divide the household belongings or calendar out a parenting plan that will work for your family. Don't be afraid to do these things on your own.

Always do any homework the mediator has assigned. Failing to do it will just hold up the entire process, or take valuable mediation time as your mediator helps you work through the homework during a session.

The End Result of Mediation

When you begin mediation, your goal is to work through the process and walk away with a completed memorandum of understanding or settlement agreement. This document will completely resolve all the issues in your divorce. One of your attorneys will file the document with the court and your divorce will then be legalized.

Mediation has other end results, perhaps the most important of which is that you've found a way to cooperate and make joint decisions, even at a time in your life when you're trying to get away from the other person. Mediation will also have given you the skills to work out any future conflicts, such as those about custody, child support or alimony that may arise.

Mediation should also provide closure to your marriage. One of the problems in traditional divorce is you work for months to move through your case and go to court and are then are left hanging as you wait for the decree to come to you in the mail. You never say goodbye to each other or have any formal sense of wrapping things up. In mediation, you can wrap things up right in the mediator's office. There is no sense of the unknown, because you have just crafted the entire agreement together. Some couples have closure ceremonies as well. A closure ceremony can be whatever you want it to be. Some couples simply shake hands and wish each other well. Others burn a copy of the marriage certificate or have a reverse unity candle ceremony (instead of taking two flames and making them one, they light the separate candles and blow out the unity candle together). The key is that mediation allows you to work through the situation together and come out on the other side of it together. You're less likely to walk away with bad feelings and more likely to be able to respect each other in the future. Having the opportunity to say goodbye and thanks for the good times is a civilized way to bring a real end to the marriage.

What to Do if Mediation Is Not Successful

Sometimes mediation is not successful. One of you may decide that you don't want to have to compromise, you can't seem to agree about anything, you can't stand to sit in a room with the other person another minute, or the mediator is not helping you make decisions.

No matter what the problem is, you should not give up on mediation yet. You've invested time and money in this process and it is normal to feel frustrated at times. Give it another chance. Express your frustrations to the mediator. He may not know you feel this way at all. Get it out in the open and you may be able to find some solutions for it. If this doesn't work, consider finding another mediator. Sometimes a mediator is just not a good fit. Look for someone else with whom you feel comfortable.

Talk to your attorney about how you're feeling. She may be able to offer some helpful suggestions for settlement that you haven't thought of yet. Just getting the perspective of another professional in this field can be very valuable.

If you try all of this and you still feel mediation isn't going to bring you to a complete resolution, don't walk out the door yet. Ask your mediator to write up an agreement laying out all the things to which you and your spouse have already agreed. There may only be one item or there may be a whole list. You want to document that progress and be able to take it with you. Now that you are leaving mediation, you'll be going to court and you want to reduce the amount of time your attorney has to spend on the case. If you've already agreed to a parenting plan, there is no need for your attorney to have to rehash or renegotiate that.

Chapter 7

Other Alternatives to Divorce Trials

While mediation is a very popular and friendly alternative to a contested divorce, there are some other options available to you if you want to avoid a trial. Divorce law is evolving and working to meet people's expectations by offering a variety of non-confrontational dispute resolution methods. If traditional mediation does not work for you, you may wish to consider some of these options.

Arbitration

Many people are more familiar with the term arbitration than they are with mediation. Arbitration has been used for years in labor and business disputes, and so many people have heard the term in that context. Its use in family law is a new advance. Like mediation, arbitration is an out-of-court dispute resolution method. The key difference between arbitration and mediation is that in arbitration a neutral third party actually makes the decisions (or offers a recommendation) instead standing by impartially and assisting the parties in making the decisions themselves, which is how divorce mediation proceeds.

In family law cases, formal binding arbitration is one option. You can go to an arbitrator and have him or her issue a decision that is binding in your case, after hearing all the evidence and testimony (although the rules of evidence are generally much looser in arbitration than they are in court proceedings). These arbitrators are often retired judges. The parties agree that they will be bound by the decision made by the arbitrator (they also agree in advance what rules the arbitrator will follow), and an appeal is only possible if you can prove the arbitrator was biased, exceeded his or her authority, or made a very large mistake of law. This type of arbitration is very much like going to trial with your case, except you are actually paying the judge for his or her services. The benefit to binding arbitration is that if you are in a jurisdiction where the court calendar is full, it could be many months or years before your court case is heard. Arbitration speeds things up considerably and gets you to a resolution much more quickly than if you have to wait for the court. Arbitration proceedings are private and not open to the public.

More and more states are creating non-binding family law arbitration programs as part of their alternative dispute resolution programs. In these programs, an experienced family law or matrimonial attorney or retired judge sits down with attorneys for each side and listens to them present their cases. The parties may or may not be a part of the procedure. Some of these arbitration proceedings involve informal testimony and presentation of evidence, while others are more low-key. Once all the information has been presented, the presiding attorney or retired judge considers it and makes a recommendation about how he thinks a judge would decide the case. This is only a recommendation and no one is bound by it. This recommendation is useful though because it can move along settlement negotiations. The recommendation is usually not revealed to the judge, should the case go to trial. This method is especially helpful in a very complicated case where the parties are resistant to settlement. It may make more sense to pay a non-binding arbitrator to hear the case (and note that in some jurisdictions these are volunteer programs with no fees involved) than it is to pay your two attorneys to continue to go to court and fight it out. Hearing what an impartial third party thinks and getting a good idea of how a judge would rule can be very helpful in encouraging settlement.

Collaborative Law

Collaborative law is a burgeoning field and one that is receiving a lot of attention. This solution appeals to people who don't feel they are able to go to mediation and negotiate for themselves. Collaborative law is based on the idea that the parties and attorneys in a divorce case should work cooperatively together to find solutions that will benefit the entire family. The goal is to remove the confrontational aspect of the proceeding and make it into a joint problem-solving situation.

In collaborative law, each party hires a collaborative law attorney. Many attorneys and practices now specialize in this area. You can find one by calling your local or state bar association or checking the yellow pages of your phone book or the Internet. You can also contact the International Academy of Collaborative Professionals (www.collaborativepractice.com or 415-897-2398). Many states now have collaborative law associations (see appendix A) as well who can refer you to an attorney in your area.

A collaborative law attorney will only work on collaborative cases and will not accept cases that are litigated (handled through the traditional court system). You and your spouse must each hire a collaborative law attorney of your own. The two attorneys work together to find a mutually agreeable solution to the issues in the divorce.

The attorneys may meet alone, or ask that the parties participate in the meetings. The attorneys do the negotiating, but work *with* each other instead of against each other. They are each there to represent their client's point of view, but the overall approach is to find and create areas of agreement. The attorneys do not act in an adversarial manner, but instead treat each other like partners who are working towards a common goal. The objective is to reach a settlement that will be drawn up, signed, and submitted to the court. If you and your spouse are unable to reach a settlement through the collaborative process, you will each need to hire new attorneys who will handle the divorce in a traditional manner. The collaborative attorneys do not continue on in the case if a settlement is not reached.

Some attorneys have formed large collaborative law practices, which include not only attorneys, but also custody evaluators, accountants, financial planners, and therapists. These professionals are all housed under one roof and can be brought in to assist with your case. They all approach the case with the mindset of collaboration and helping the parties reach an agreement.

The benefits of collaborative law include the comfort of knowing an attorney is handling your case every step of the way. The pressure is not on you to make legal decisions without close guidance (this offers an important safety net for many people who are uncomfortable with mediation). You don't need to do the negotiating yourself and you don't even have to talk to your spouse at all if you don't want to. The goal of the case is to find a solution that will work best for the family, and confrontational behavior is not encouraged. The idea is to be fair to everyone.

The drawbacks of collaborative law are that it is more expensive than traditional mediation. You pay two attorneys to do negotiations, while in mediation you just pay the mediator. You and your spouse do not negotiate directly, so things can sometimes be lost in translation. It can take longer to work through the process, since the attorneys must arrange their schedules around each other, meet, and then come back to you to discuss where things are at, and then meet again in order to make any decisions. If you are unable to reach a settlement, you essentially start from scratch with a new attorney, and you end up spending more all together.

Co-Mediation

Co-mediation is a variation on divorce mediation. In co-mediation, two mediators work with the couple. Sometimes these mediators are male and female, or attorney and therapist, in order to give a more balanced feeling to the process. Co-mediators may take turns leading the sessions, or may moderate them together; however, both mediators are always present during any session.

Co-mediation can be more expensive than regular mediation, because there are two professionals present. However, some couples find that having two mediators of different sexes or professions helps them feel more comfortable and helps the process move forward more quickly.

If you are considering co-mediation, be sure you meet both mediators ahead of time and ask them about their qualifications. Find out how many co-mediation cases they have done together and how they arrange the sessions.

Shuttle Mediation

Shuttle mediation is another style of divorce mediation. Shuttle mediation is designed for couples who want to mediate their divorce, but are unable to sit in the same room and talk with each comfortably. In shuttle mediation, the spouses are seated in separate rooms after first having one joint session with the mediator where the ground rules are set up. The mediator meets with each spouse separately, then shuttles to the other room to present the options and solutions offered by the one spouse to the other.

Sometimes two co-mediators do shuttle mediation, with each assigned to one spouse. Shuttle mediation takes longer than regular mediation, because the mediator has to restate each person's position to the other, and carry messages back and forth, but for highly confrontational couples, this may be the only way they can mediate their divorce. This method can be very successful for these types of couples. Instead of sitting in a room steaming about the other person, and responding to the tone of the words said instead of the content, the couple can get some distance from each other and direct their attention to the decisions before them. The mediator provides a buffer zone between them.

There are times in a traditional divorce mediation case when shuttle mediation may need to be used for part of the process, particularly if the couple gets highly agitated or is grappling with very emotional issues. The couple is separated for these difficult concerns and then continues in joint sessions the rest of the time. Sometimes taking a break like this can help the mediation process move along and achieve more progress than if you continue to sit in the same room and butt heads.

Attorney-Assisted Mediation

Attorney-assisted mediation is yet another permutation of traditional mediation. In this type of dispute resolution, the parties work with one mediator who guides them through the process. The difference is that the parties are allowed to bring their attorneys into mediation sessions with them.

This method is used when the case involves very complicated legal issues which would require the parties to constantly have to stop the session and go set up appointments with their attorneys for advice on how to handle them. Attorney-assisted mediation is also sometimes used when one of the parties feels as though he is not being heard, and needs an advocate in the room to encourage him or her to speak up, or who can speak for him or her.

Both parties can bring an attorney, or just one. The session can be arranged so that the attorneys are simply observers who are available to step aside with their clients to offer advice on the legal issues. It can also be arranged so that the attorneys assist with the negotiating.

This type of mediation does include added expense since you must pay your attorneys for the time spent in mediation. The benefit is that it allows couples to mediate who might not otherwise be able to do so.

Long-Distance Mediation

Long-distance mediation is used when the parties are physically separated by long distances. If you have already separated and are living in different states, it is likely going to be very difficult for you to meet on a regular basis in person to do mediation. Long-distance mediation uses video conferencing to virtually bring the parties together in the same room, so that mediation can occur.

One of the problems with this type of mediation is that the party who is appearing via video may feel left out of the process, since the other spouse is sitting in the same room with the mediator. It is very important that ground rules are established which allow the distant spouse to feel confident discussions are not happening behind his or her back.

It is also possible to conduct long-distance mediation via speakerphone, but it is not as effective because body language and facial expressions play a huge part in communication. Video conferencing can also reduce the understanding of tone, expressions, and body language, so it is important that a fairly large screen be used and that all parties take the time to spell out exactly what they mean.

Negotiating on Your Own

Instead of paying a mediator or other specialist, you and your spouse can try negotiating an agreement on your own. It can be hard to change your behavior towards each other and sit down to a productive and cooperative meeting, but doing so can save you thousands of dollars and a lot of emotional angst. Agree on an agenda ahead of time and stick to it. Don't let yourselves be distracted by other issues or problems. Work only on the items on your list and you may be able to make progress.

If you are going to be discussing your parenting plan, take some time to think about what would work best for the children. Consider both of your work schedules and lifestyles and consider when you each have time to parent. If you have teens, ask them what their feelings are about the situation and what they would prefer.

If you are going to discuss property division, it is helpful to first make a few lists before you meet with your spouse. List items you must have, items you are willing to negotiate on, and items the other person can have. (One negotiation tactic may be to put some items you don't really want on the maybe list, so that you have some things to give away in the negotiation.) If you both make these lists, you'll probably find there are quite a few things you agree about. You can then spend your time and energy discussing the things that are still in dispute. There are a few ways to work out these disagreements. You can assign a dollar value to each item and total them and agree each spouse is entitled to roughly half of that value, and then perhaps take turns choosing items from the list. You can also make trades, such as, "I'll let you take the china cabinet if you let me keep the dining room table."

If you are negotiating spousal support or child support, you need to first understand what your state guidelines and requirements are, consider the rest of your property settlement, and take a hard look at your individual budgets.

It is possible to trade off a better deal on the property settlement for less spousal support.

Once you and your spouse have reached an agreement on any of the above, clearly write out what you've agreed to. You can then give this written understanding to your attorney or mediator who can incorporate this into your settlement. Note that even if you don't settle the entire divorce, these agreements can be submitted to the court as stipulations and incorporated by the court in the final decision. If you don't have attorneys, you can go to court and read the agreement to the court. This is called an oral stipulation and if the judge agrees with your settlement, it will be incorporated into your divorce decree.

Chapter 8

Children and Divorce

I f you have children, you are likely very concerned about how the divorce will affect them and how you will work out a parenting arrangement for them. Divorce does have an impact on children, but there are many things you can do to minimize the effects and help them through it. Because your children are an important part of your life, it is natural to be concerned about what the divorce is going to mean in terms of the time you get to spend with them. It is definitely possible to have healthy adjusted kids after a divorce, and it is also possible to have a solid relationship with your children, with lots of time together after you divorce. The most important thing you can do is to think about how your actions and words impact your child, and work with your spouse to parent together in a way that supports and nurtures your children and their relationships with both parents.

Helping Your Children through the Initial Separation

It is common for children to have a wide range of reactions when they adjust to the initial separation. Some children may seem outwardly to not be affected at all by the news (but give them time and they will come to you with their questions and concerns). Others may be sad, angry, scared, nervous, worried, or anxious. As time goes on and the child has time to experience what the separation really means, you can expect more reactions, such as frustration, exclamations about the situation not being fair, and blame. You can also expect your child to act out over situations and problems that seem to be unrelated to the divorce, but because they are so out of character you can be sure they really do stem from the family problems.

This is all normal, although it is hard for everyone involved. You need to have patience and give your child room to react and adjust. Make yourself available to talk to—kids often have questions suddenly and out of blue when you least expect it, such as while standing in the grocery checkout lane, driving to soccer, or as they are drifting off to sleep. Be prepared for the unexpected. Remember to try to focus in on what the child is really asking and is really concerned about, instead of superimposing your own ideas about the situation.

Types of Custody

Before you can even begin to form a parenting plan together, it is important to understand what the custody options are when your marriage or relationship ends. There a variety of arrangements possible. The biggest distinction is between legal custody and physical custody.

Legal Custody

Legal custody refers to parental authority and decision-making power. Parents can have joint or sole legal custody. Parents who share joint legal custody are supposed to make important decisions about the child together. These include education, health, religion, and other major decisions. In theory, joint legal custody requires the parents to truly cooperate. In reality, often parents agree to or are awarded joint legal custody simply because it is a way of making the parent who does not have primary physical custody feel better about the situation. Using that wording can make the agreement more palatable—parents like to be able to say, "I have joint custody of my children." Often this designation is in words only—parents who couldn't work together before are not magically transformed into cooperative parents by a court decree. Often the residential parent ends up being the one who makes many decisions about the child without the other's input. However, if you have joint custody, trying to make it work is very important. Any cooperation you can achieve will benefit your child.

On the other hand, just because one parent is given sole legal custody does not mean that the other parent is completely shut out of participating in decisions about the child's life. Your custody arrangement is what you make of it. However, the parent with legal custody has the final say in making important decisions.

Physical Custody

Physical custody has to do with how the child's time is shared by the parents. There are an infinite number of ways time can be shared—any possible schedule permutation can you think of. However, there are a few ways these arrangements can be characterized. First, let's consider the child's primary residence. In most custody arrangements, the child has one home base—the parent's home at which she spends the most time. This parent is sometimes referred to as the residential or primary parent.

If one parent is given sole physical custody, it means that the child spends all of his or her time with that parent and does not see the other parent at all. This is rare, except in cases of abuse or neglect. Parents can also have joint or shared physical custody, which means they share the child's time in a relatively equal way, such as alternating weeks or months, or splitting the weeks in half. As great as this sounds, it doesn't work for many families. Most commonly one parent is given primary custody or residential custody and the other is given visitation.

How Custody is Determined

When a court decides custody, the judge uses what is called the best interests rule. Decisions about parenting time are made based on what is in the best interest of that particular child in that particular situation. There are no absolutes—such as fathers shouldn't have custody, being gay means you're a bad parent, or working means you shouldn't have custody. The court looks at the specifics of your family's situation and makes a decision based on what is going to benefit your child the most.

The court considers each person's parenting skills and abilities, past history, history of wrongdoing (crime, child abuse, or substance abuse), mental health, stability, and ability to create a warm and loving home. The court is also interested in the parents' schedules and work commitments. It makes no sense to give one parent time with the child on a Saturday if that parent works every Saturday. The past history of parenting is also key. If one parent has been the primary caretaker of the child, the court will likely want that situation to continue unless there is a problem with it.

The court is very interested in how willing a parent is to assist the other parent in maintaining contact with the child. Purposely keeping the other parent away from your child is custodial interference and can be grounds for a complete reversal in custody. It is an absolute rule that children benefit from spending time with both parents, unless a parent is harmful or potentially abusive to the child (physically, mentally, or emotionally). It is a rare situation in which a court will order that there be no contact between a parent and child. Another important rule is that courts prefer to keep siblings together, so it is a rare situation in which one parent will get custody of one child and the other parent custody of the other.

Siblings

Sometimes parents think about splitting siblings up—have one live with mom and one live with dad—as a way to make things more fair. This is usually a bad idea. Siblings need to live together under one roof in most circumstances. Splitting them up is not wise because it can damage their relationship and cause feelings of resentment towards the parents.

Supervised Visitation

Supervised visitation is contact between a parent and child that is monitored by another responsible adult. This is often ordered by the court if there is a history of abuse, substance abuse, or creating a harmful or unsafe environment for the child. There are several kinds of supervised visitation. Often a family member or friend (many times it is a grandparent) is asked to provide supervision. All visitation happens at this person's home and the responsible adult is supposed to be present the entire time (actually "supervising"). The problem with this type of supervision is often the person supervising becomes too lax and leaves the parent and child alone for periods of time, or fails to supervise at all.

Another type of supervised visitation occurs at an agency that has a formal supervised visitation program. A trained professional remains in the room, monitoring contact between parent and child. These programs are hard to find and are often overbooked and under-funded. There is also a concern about the atmosphere—these programs tend to be very institutional.

Supervised visitation should be used only in very rare cases, and the goal is often to get to the point where supervision is no longer necessary. A parent who is ordered to have supervised visitation often also has to attend parenting classes.

Parenting Classes

Most jurisdictions now require that all couples going through a divorce attend co-parenting or divorce parenting classes. These classes go over the basics of the information covered in this chapter and stress that parents must learn to set aside their differences and parent together for the benefit of their child. In some locations, completing the class is required; in others, it is simply recommended.

There is another type of parenting class that comes up in divorces. In some instances, the court determines that a parent does not have adequate parenting skills, and orders him or her to attend a parenting skills class, where the basics of discipline, listening, child care, healthy lifestyles, and emergency medical care are taught. Unfortunately, these classes have become somewhat of a weapon, with each party trying to tell the court that the other needs to go, despite both parents possessing adequate parenting skills.

Co-Parenting

Generally speaking, co-parenting refers to two parents continuing to function as a parental unit after a divorce. Instead of going their separate ways and never speaking or cooperating, co-parents continue to see themselves as a parenting team who must work together and rely on each other to raise their children together. Joining together in this way is the best thing possible for the child, who needs to know he still has two parents who care enough about him to work together. Co-parenting is possible in most cases, except when there is domestic violence or control issues which make it impossible or unsafe for the parents to have direct contact with each other.

No matter what kind of custody and visitation schedule is in place, almost anyone can be co-parents. Co-parenting is not about equally sharing time or even making big decisions together; it is instead a state of mind. Your divorce has not ended your parenting relationship. In fact, you will be parents together for the rest of your lives, even after your children are adults. Co-parenting is a cooperative approach to the years ahead of you and a way of including both parents in the child's life.

Co-parenting does not mean second-guessing each other or having no individual freedom. Since you are each essentially parenting alone, you have to have the ability to make decisions on your own. What it does mean is trying to face the big picture of parenting together—working together to solve problems in your child's life, presenting a united front on things such as curfews and household rules, and sometimes joining together in a happy way to celebrate your child's accomplishments or milestones. Viewing each other as partners in your child's life is at the root of co-parenting.

Deciding Where Your Children Will Live

The first step in making arrangements for your children is deciding where and with whom they should live. In some families, this is obvious—there may be one parent who stays at home or works from home, or there may be a parent who works irregular or long hours, making that home less hospitable. If the decision is less obvious in your case, think first about what your respective schedules are. If one person has a schedule more fitted to school hours, this is an important factor. Another consideration is where you will both be living. If one person will remain in the marital home and the other is moving to a small apartment, that may help you decide. If you're both moving, but one person is remaining in your current school district, that's another important factor.

If possible, you want to keep things as normal as possible for your children, so remaining in the same home or school district will go a long way towards adding a sense of normalcy to their lives.

If residency is decided by a judge, he will be very interested in the past—who was the primary caretaker for the children, who took them to doctor appointments, who helped with homework, who went to games, and so on. The past is an important indicator; however, the needs of the children are the most important concern.

How to Create a Parenting Plan

Once you have decided where (or if) your child will have a primary residence, you need to next consider a schedule. If you and your spouse are unable to work out a parenting schedule, the court will do it for you. The most common schedule set up by the court is every other weekend and one night per week. This means your child would primarily live with Parent A. Parent B would then have a schedule which would allow him to see the child every Wednesday evening (this is often from about 4 to 8 p.m.) and then every other weekend from Friday afternoon to Sunday afternoon. If you are not comfortable with this kind of schedule, you should work very hard to create one together without judicial interference. Note that even if you do agree on a parenting plan together, it is subject to approval by the court (it is a very rare situation in which a court would reject a custody settlement).

The idea behind this basic schedule is that it allows both parents to have an equal amount of weekend time with the child (which is when most working parents of school-age children get to spend quality time with their children) and the non-residential parent will have contact every week, in order to stay connected and be involved.

You and your spouse are free to create any parenting plan on which you can both agree. Your goal is to construct a plan that allows the child optimal time with both parents, yet still creates a sense of having one home and being grounded in some way. While plans that alternate entire weeks or months may work in some situations, in general they are confusing and hard for children to adjust to. You want to create a plan with which your child will feel comfortable and with which you both can comply. Something that looks great on paper but is simply not practical given your individual schedules is not a good idea.

When creating a parenting plan, you need to take into consideration what your lives are like on a normal day-to-day basis, but then also consider those out of the ordinary times—summer, holidays, vacations, business trips, and so on. You need to talk about these aspects of your lives and how best to schedule your child's life during these events as well. You also must consider what your child's schedule is like. It is very important that your child be able to continue the things he loves—sports, music, dance, art, and so on. You can certainly schedule visitation on the same day a child has an extracurricular activity, but the parent whose time it is that day should plan to take the child to and from the activity. Don't penalize your child by making him or her miss an important activity for visitation. Teens should have a big say in the visitation schedule because not only do they have extracurricular activities, but they also have a social life that is very important to their development and they may have jobs as well.

When considering a holiday plan, you may want to consider some of these holidays or special days:

- New Year's Day
- Valentine's Day
- Passover
- Easter
- Mother's Day
- Memorial Day
- Father's Day
- July 4th
- Labor Day
- Rosh Hashanah
- Yom Kippur
- Halloween
- Thanksgiving
- Hanukah
- Christmas Eve
- Christmas Day
- New Year's Eve

Many parents create a list of holidays that are important to them and either alternate through the list (this year you get Easter, I get Memorial Day, you get July 4th, I get Labor Day, etc), choose set holidays each will always have (Mom always gets Mother's Day and Thanksgiving, Dad always gets Father's Day and Christmas Eve), or select certain holidays that they will alternate by year (this year I get Thanksgiving Day, and Christmas Day. You get the day after Thanksgiving and Christmas Eve. Next year we switch). When considering how to divide holidays, think about what days are truly important to you and what your family traditions are. Some families always have their celebrations on Christmas Eve. If that is the case for you, then it makes sense for your child to always spend Christmas Eve with you and your family and Christmas Day with your spouse and his or her family.

An important note here is that many divorced families have found ways to share important holidays together. This can be especially helpful in the first few years after the divorce. Inviting the non-residential parent over for Easter or Passover can be a wonderful gesture that not only heals some of the rift, but also lets your child know that he is part of one intact family. Some families who celebrate Christmas plan to spend Christmas morning together. It means that the non-residential parent doesn't miss out on those magic moments, and the kids get to have both parents together for a special day. This is just an option, though—if you can't do it without being unpleasant to each other, then it is best to see the kids at different times.

Parents should also keep in mind that holidays are when we make them. If you will not be with your child on an important holiday, make phone contact that day, and then plan to celebrate the holiday the next time you and your child are together. You can have just as much fun on a day that is not the official holiday (sometimes more so because the expectations are different).

It is common for parents to work out a time-sharing arrangement in terms of the child's summer vacation. Some families agree each parent gets a month, parents alternate weeks, or agree that each parent can schedule a week's vacation with the child at some point during the summer. Whatever works for your family is fine. Some residential parents get upset at the idea of the non-residential parent taking the child away on a vacation. In some situations this is a bad idea—such as if parental kidnapping has been a concern, or if the non-residential parent lacks important parenting skills. In most other situations though, a trip together can be fun for the child, and a residential parent who stands in the way of it may be thinking emotionally.

Parents should also consider the child's birthday as a day to share or at least discuss sharing. If you are able to enjoy this day together as a family, that can be a good plan. You could split the day in half between the parents; however, this may be hard to do if it is a school day. If you plan a party for a weekend, then everyone can be involved. At the very least, the nonresidential parent should have phone contact on the child's birthday.

UCCJEA

The Uniform Child Custody Jurisdiction and Enforcement Act (UCCJEA) is a law adopted by every state except Massachusetts, Missouri, New Hampshire, and Vermont. The law is used to determine which state should hear a custody case when there is a conflict over where the case should be heard. This might happen if the parties lived in Nebraska during the marriage and then the mother moves to Kansas, taking the child with her, and files a custody (or divorce) case there. The basic rule is that if the child has lived in the state for six months before the case was filed, that is his home state. If the child has not lived anywhere for six months, then the state with significant connections to the child can hear the case. The law also sets out how custody orders should be registered and enforced across state lines. Note that emergency orders can be made in any state.

You can read this law online at www.law.upenn.edu/bll/archives/ulc/fnact99/1990s/uccjea97.htm

Grandparent Rights

If you have a very acrimonious divorce, with one parent not getting a lot of time with the children, the grandparents on that side of the family may be concerned that they are going to be cut out of the child's life. This can happen with any grandparents, however—you may be feuding with your own parents and keeping the kids away from them out of spite or because you believe they are a bad influence.

It is a good idea to try to maintain reasonable relations with all grandparents, because these people are important to your children. If you don't think you can do so, you may find yourself in a situation where the grandparents go to court to seek court-ordered visitation. These court cases are messy and usually difficult for the children. Laws about grandparent rights vary from state to state, and generally it is rather difficult for a grandparent to be granted permission by the court to ask for custody or visitation of a grandchild. However, a grandparent who can show an ongoing relationship with the grandchild may have a shot at getting the court to continue that relationship. The rule of thumb here again is the best interests of the child in most states.

These kinds of cases can be avoided if you put your personal feelings aside and schedule one day a month for the grandparent to spend time with the child. However, if you have serious concerns about the child's safety or well-being while with the grandparent, you will want to avoid any time spent alone with the child.

Relocation

Relocation is an issue in many divorces. It is not uncommon for a parent to want to move away and start a new life somewhere else after a divorce. When you have a child, though, picking up and moving is not simple. If you are not the residential parent, you have the freedom to move anywhere you want. Doing so, however, will require an adjustment to your parenting plan. If you move five hundred miles away, it is not reasonable for you to continue to attempt to see your child every weekend or once a week. When the non-residential parent moves, longer, less frequent visitation is usually put in place. It is also important that the parent has the right to frequent telephone and online contact with the child.

Legally, it is much more difficult for the residential parent to move away. The test for relocation is usually what is in the best interest of the child. If moving means a better life—with a higher standard of living due to the parent getting a better job, a bigger support system due to family being closer, or a parent's remarriage into a better situation, it is likely the court will allow the move. A move that is done out of spite, in order to punish the non-residential parent with no real benefit for the child, will be denied.

Relocation is a difficult decision for the court to make. On the one hand, it is essential that a child have regular contact with both parents, but on the other hand, the court wants the family to be able to thrive economically and socially. Relocation hearings are often very emotional and difficult for everyone involved. If the relocation is granted, a visitation plan will be set up, usually involving long stretches over the summer and school vacations. Phone and Internet contact is usually part of the plan as well.

How to Deal with the Other Parent

The key to making your parenting arrangement successful is respect. You must respect the other parent. You likely have a lot of bad feelings towards the other parent, but you need to find a way to separate your parenting from those feelings. Your goal is to create a good life for your child and you can do that by parenting together in a respectful and cooperative manner.

You must make a shift in how you think about each other. When you are parenting, you need to think of your former spouse as your child's other parent, and not as your ex. The problems you had in your relationship need to be separate from your work together as parents. This is a very difficult mental shift to make, but it is essential to successful parenting after the divorce. Your child loves the other parent and needs him in her life. Your child will be healthiest and happiest if both her parents have important non-conflicting roles in her life. Supporting the love between your child and the other parent, and ensuring the other parent has an important role in your child's life is your responsibility as a parent.

Flexibility is the other key to success. You have a schedule, but you need to be flexible with each other. Today the other parent may ask for a change, but tomorrow it will likely be you who is running late, suddenly has a business trip scheduled for your weekend, or wants to take your child to a special event on a day you aren't scheduled for. Cut each other some slack. Also, try to approach your time sharing on a monthly basis. Don't be uptight if you have three hours less with your daughter this week than you are supposed to. Things tend to even out over the course of a month, so try to look at the schedule in a long-term way rather than an in a to-the-minute manner.

If you and the other parent can't seem to talk reasonably or work together and seem to always get into fights or arguments when you are talking about parenting or exchanging your child, you may need to change the way you think about and approach the situation. Obviously, what you are doing now is not working. You need to find a way to distance yourself emotionally from the situation. The solution to this is the business transaction model. View each encounter or conversation with the other parent as a business transaction. You have an objective to complete—such as exchanging your child, making a schedule, talking over a decision about summer camp—and so on. Act as if this is a business negotiation. When you go to the grocery store, you need to buy the groceries, so you put them on the belt, wait for them to be rung up, and pay the cashier. You don't harangue the cashier about how she's looking at you, or what she meant by her last statement and you don't obsess about who she's dating or how she treated you the last time you were there. You simply assume the best and work through the situation in an impersonal, detached, and mildly pleasant way. Of course you will still have feelings about how the other parent is treating you or what she is saying, but you keep them to yourself and do what is necessary to get through the transaction. If you have trouble holding your tongue, remind yourself that you're doing this because it benefits your child. That is your motivation for getting through the situation.

In most parenting situations, biting your tongue is the best policy. You aren't going to get anywhere if you allow yourself to say everything you're thinking. It's fine to have a meeting with the other parent in which you hash out big problems from time to time, but you have to realize that you can't change the way the other parent behaves and you have no control over his or her life.

You have to learn to step back and let your ex parent in his or her own way. It may not be the way you would do it, but if it doesn't cause harm to your child, you're best to just stay out of the way. Each parent has to forge his or her own way after the divorce, even if one parent has more experience and the other is pretty clueless. Your child's relationship with his other parent will be stronger and healthier if they are left to develop it on their own.

Uncooperative Parents

If your spouse refuses to cooperate with you when it comes to parenting, you will be in a difficult situation. You'll probably feel anger at his insensitivity and you will probably worry about how this will impact your children. While it's always best if you can talk to each other and cooperate, it's not the end of the world if you can't. That's why courts create parenting plans—so the rules are laid out for both of you.

If you have a co-parent who follows the letter of the law, but not the spirit (for example shows up on time for visitation but does everything to make your life difficult, like forgetting to bring back the kids' clothes or telling the children untrue things about you), you have to try to work through it as best as possible. You have some legal avenues that could help you. For example, in a very volatile divorce it is not uncommon for the custody order to include a provision that the parents may not say derogatory things about each other in front of the children.

If you can't seem to get your co-parent to act like an adult, you just have to accept that, and move on with your life. It can be really hard to continue to act like a reasonable human being when your ex does not. You have to keep reminding yourself that defusing the situation is best for the kids. Yes, there are going to annoying things that happen, but if you minimize the contact between the two of you and make sure your children are well cared for when with him, you have done all that you can.

Helping Your Children Cope with Parental Conflict

Your children are aware that you and your spouse don't get along. Just because it's something they are aware of does not mean it is something they should have rubbed in their faces. Your goal is to protect them from the conflict and disagreements as much as possible. Although your spouse is not your favorite person in the world right now, there are a lot of things you can do to shelter your child from the conflict between you.

The most important thing you can do is resolve not to fight in front of your child. This means no snide comments, no dirty looks, no slammed doors, and no angry words. This can be difficult to achieve if your situation is very volatile, but making the effort will benefit your child.

Keep your children out of your conflicts. Don't talk to them about problems you are having with the other parent. Don't ask them to carry messages. Saying, "Tell your father if he doesn't pay the child support by Friday, we're going back to court," is distressing to your child because it forces him to deliver a message that is not going to be well received and the child will feel he is to blame for causing the other parent's anger. Even asking a child to carry a written message is not a good idea. It is also important to display respect for the other parent in front of your child. Your child loves the other parent and you need to show respect for that, even if you feel none for the other parent as a person. It is important to display respect for the other parent in front of your child. Your child loves the other parent and you need to show respect for that, even if you feel none for the other parent.

Never put your child in a position where you ask him or her to tattle on the other parent. It is perfectly fine to ask questions about what the child did with the other parent—you're interested in your child's life. It is not ok to pry for details about whom the other parent is dating, what the other parent said, how much money the other parent spent and so on. Your role is to be interested in your child's life, but not be a snoop.

Do not ask your child to take your side or choose one parent over the other. Even if you truly believe your child would rather live with you or spend more time with you, you must understand that children want to please their parents and it is likely your child will tell you exactly what you want to hear, then turn around and tell the other parent the same thing.

Never use your child as a shoulder to cry on or a dumping ground. The emotional troubles of your marriage and divorce are hard for *you* to deal with—they are overwhelming and terrifying to your child. Of course some days you will be sad or angry, but your child does not need to know the details about why and should not be used to comfort yourself.

Although you may take these steps to shield your child from the conflict, it is likely she will still be aware of it. Answer your child's questions about the problems between you and your spouse in as neutral a way as possible. One way to handle these questions is to say something like, "Mom and Dad disagree about some things, but we're working through it and trying to find a solution." Reassure your child that she has nothing to do with the tension between you.

What to Do When You Can't Agree About the Parenting Plan

As you and your ex parent together after the separation and divorce, there will definitely be times when you don't agree. Clearly there are things you don't see eye to eye on, or you wouldn't be getting divorced. When you butt heads, take a moment and try to think rationally about the situation. Ask yourself what you are objecting to. It may be that you don't really care that much about the issue at hand, but you do want to be right, show your ex what's what, or be in control. None of those things benefit your child, so you ought to rethink the situation.

If you and your spouse have a genuine disagreement about the best way to handle something or a path to take, consider having a meeting. Sit down in a neutral place (neither one of your homes is neutral—try a park or coffee shop). Consider alternatives together and see if you can come up with a compromise. Be sure that your discussion focuses on what is best for your child. If you get nowhere, take a break and try again another time. For example, you might want your child to go to Catholic school, Your spouse might be totally against this. You need to talk about why you both feel the way that you do. In discussing it, you might find that your spouse is opposed to it because of the cost. If you work out a compromise where you both share the cost, you may be able to make the arrangement work.

If you still can't reach an agreement, it may be time to seek some professional help. A mediator can help you work out these kinds of disputes rather quickly. If that doesn't work, or you don't want to use a mediator, you can go to court and ask the judge to make a decision for you.

In cases in which a couple cannot agree about custody, it is common for the court or attorneys to request a formal custody evaluation. A therapist or mental health professional meets with the child and parents and prepares a report recommending who should have custody and pointing out the problems in the family or in the way the parties parent. These reports can be helpful in some cases, but often each side gets their own expert and you end up with competing opinions. Experts can be used before a trial (to attempt to provoke a settlement) or for the purpose of testifying at the trial. The parents are responsible for paying the experts' fees.

If your divorce papers have just been filed, or have not yet been filed, and you are unable to work out a temporary plan for custody to get you through the trial, you need to go to the court and ask for a temporary order (sometimes called a pendente lite order) which will be put in place until the final decision is made. If you have not filed divorce papers yet, and do not wish to, see chapter 3 about family court alternatives to divorce court.

How to Prepare for a Custody Trial

First, it must be understood that a trial must be your last alternative. Custody trials are incredibly painful and difficult for parents and children. A trial requires you to rip each other apart and say the worst things possible about each other. After a custody trial, it is extremely difficult to move past the ugliness and parent together cooperatively. The trial is also terrible for your child. He loves you both, and knowing you are hurting each other because of him is very damaging. As much as you try to shield your child from the trial, he is going to know about it and he is going to see the effect it is having on you.

Your child likely will feel he is placed in a situation where he is supposed to somehow choose between you, and know that it is a situation in which he cannot win. Never ever try to bribe your child or convince him about what he should say to the Law Guardian (see later in this chapter for information about Law Guardians) or the judge. It's quite common for kids put in that position to walk into the judge's chambers and proudly report how Daddy is buying them a puppy if the judge lets the child live with him.

If you have been unable to reach an agreement and have no choice but to have a custody trial, there are some things you can do to prepare for it and help your attorney (if you have one) present a good case.

You must learn to document everything. Keep a journal and write down each incident that occurs with the other parent in terms of your child, such as missed visitations or times when the child is returned to you dirty. Write down everything you do with your child. This will help you present evidence of what happens on a daily basis. You should also use a calendar to record when your child is in each household, so that you can quickly reference this information, and be able to show a clear pattern of how your child splits his or her time between parents.

Ask your attorney if it is legal to tape record your spouse without his or her permission in your state. If so, you can make audio recordings of your conversations with him or her that back up your position. This could be useful if your spouse says things to you such as "I don't care what our daughter thinks, She's a dirty little tramp." Getting something like that on tape would be very useful in court.

You should also accumulate and take photographs. Photographs can be used to show the condition of your spouse's home or vehicle, or the condition the child is in when brought to you by the other parent. Photos can also showcase the terrific times you have had with your child and the child's room or facilities at your home for the child. Videotapes can be used in the same way as photographs to provide visual evidence.

Spend as much time as possible with your attorney going over all your evidence and everything you can testify about. Provide a list of witnesses your attorney can call who will support your case. During the trial, let your attorney handle things, but if someone has said something that isn't true or if you've just thought of something very important your attorney needs to ask a witness, write a note, or ask the attorney if you can have a brief recess.

Working with the Law Guardian or Guardian ad litem

In most cases, when you are litigating your custody arrangement, the court appoints an attorney who will represent your child's interests in the case. This attorney is often paid by the state (although parents who can afford to pay the fees may have to) and functions as an independent party in the case. The Law Guardian or Guardian ad litem (different states use different names) is appointed to determine what is in the best interest of your child and to share that information with the court.

The role of the Law Guardian varies. In some states, she is considered an arm of the court, and makes a report to the court about the case, offering an opinion. In other instances, she functions like the other attorneys—calling witnesses, presenting evidence, and taking a position. The attorney might choose what that position is herself, or she might have to take whatever position the children want her to—this differs by state, and even in jurisdictions within states.

However the Law Guardian functions, he is the key to your custody case. The judge takes this attorney's opinion very seriously. He has a lot of influence over the case's outcome. Because of this, you should work very hard to be friendly and accommodating to the Law Guardian. He may wish to come visit your home, speak to your child in private, speak with your child's teachers and doctors, and interview you. Be cooperative. Make yourself available. Be open and honest. Encourage your child to be open and honest with the Law Guardian.

Some people worry that the Law Guardian expects to see a spotless house and perfect parenting. That is untrue. The Law Guardian is there to evaluate your relationship with your child. If she sees a deep bond, real love, and a reasonable amount of care and concern, you have nothing to worry about.

Children do not usually testify in a custody case, unless they are older teens and have something important to testify about, such as abuse they witnessed (being called to testify against one of your own parents is a terrible situation for any child, no matter what the circumstances). Instead, children may talk with the judge in private. The Law Guardian will accompany your child on this visit. These visits are nothing for your child to be nervous about. The judge tries to make the child comfortable and asks a few questions about the situation.

Helping Kids Cope after a Divorce

Telling your kids about the initial separation and helping them adjust to the first few weeks and months is difficult and challenging. However, as the situation settles down and everyone gets used to the routine of the parenting plan, children will continue to need your help adjusting.

While it is difficult to get used to seeing parents on a schedule, once that schedule becomes routine, children may begin to resist it or struggle with it. At first the schedule will be a novelty—new and exciting for your children. But as time wears on, some kids start to feel constrained by it. This is a normal reaction. They need to find out what the limits are and how far they can go. Your role as parents is to be understanding and kind, yet make sure that you are in control of the decisions and schedules. The parenting plan must become part of your child's life, in the same way that a school schedule is. Your child may not always appreciate it or enjoy it, but it is an important part of his or her development to follow it.

It is also common for kids to experience schedule fatigue. It can get very tiring to always be packing up and moving between houses. If this is hard on your kids, you may need to reevaluate the plan. One solution may be to provide more downtime at both homes. Instead of scheduling every minute, let them just hang out. Another option is to make some changes to the schedule so there is less movement between homes, but perhaps longer periods of visitation.

Cooperating and Coordinating with the Other Parent

As you and your spouse move forward with your new parenting agreement, there will surely be bumps in the road. Whenever possible, take the time to negotiate and compromise. Listening to what the other person says is also very important and will help reduce conflict. In addition to this, there are many ways you and the other parent can help each other, support each other, and make a better life for your child.

One thing you might consider is using each other as babysitter of first refusal. If you need to go somewhere during your scheduled time with your child, ask if the other parent would like to baby-sit. This allows you to maximize parental time with your child, and hopefully return the favor to each other. Another suggestion is to work together with the other parent for holiday and birthday gifts for your child. You could compare lists so you don't duplicate items, chip in on large gifts together, or establish a dollar amount above which neither of you will spend (this then eliminates comparisons between the two houses when there is gross overspending by one parent). You can attend parent-teacher conferences together and go to sporting events and recitals together (or at least sit together).

You and the other parent should also attempt to coordinate your home lives so that your child does not have to try to adjust to widely different environments. For example, it makes sense to establish the same bedtime and curfew at both homes. Policies such as no TV until homework is done, no cell phone use after a certain hour, and so on can also help establish common ground rules. That being said, clearly you and the other parent are two individuals and you should have the right to do things your own way in your own home. It's likely you can find some areas on which to agree with the other parent. Everything need not be exactly the same, but similarities will help your child adjust to having two homes.

Functioning as a Single Parent

Learning to be a single parent will be an adjustment for you (as well as for your child). Most of the time, you will be parenting on your own and this means you must learn to stand on your own two feet as a parent. There is no one to back you up, to step in when things get hairy, or to offer you support. You must develop confidence in yourself and in your parenting skills. You have to learn how to find downtime for yourself. You must learn how to find support in your community or through your family and friends. You will make mistakes and that is ok.

It is tempting to think that you must be both mother and father to your child, even if your child spends significant time with the other parent. You need to learn to just be yourself as a parent and to give the best of yourself to your child. It also important to stop trying to fill your child's every moment with you. You are not an entertainer. Your child doesn't need a dog and pony show. Your child just needs a parent who can be there. Whatever the living arrangements are, your child needs time at both houses to just be. He needs to do normal things like watch TV, wash the dishes, play with the dog, and read. Spending those everyday moments with your child is the best way to connect.

Embryos

If you and your spouse underwent fertility treatments, you may have frozen embryos that are being stored. Deciding what to do with this genetic material can be very difficult. Usually when you have the embryos frozen, you will sign an agreement with the lab or doctor specifying how long they will keep them and who has the right to take them out. Typically, these agreements state that unused embryos will be donated for research, for use by other infertile couples, or destroyed.

When you divorce, you want to be certain that there is a clear disposition by the court about these embryos. Some people want to be able to take the embryos and use them themselves after a divorce, and very often the other spouse is opposed to this. Most courts will not allow one spouse to become impregnated with a leftover embryo against the other spouse's wishes, but if it is something you want, you need to find an attorney who is experienced in this area of law who can help you.

Divorced Parenting Rules
- Always be willing to compromise with the other parent.
- Do not use your child as a go-between or a message carrier.

- Do not discuss your feelings about the other parent with your child.
- Always remember that your child needs time with both of you to grow up healthy and happy.
- Never argue in front of your child if possible.
- Do not treat your child like a friend and talk about how sad or confused you are.
- Be flexible whenever possible.
- Think of parenting time as benefiting your child, not the other parent.
- Envision yourself and the other parent as a team.
- Reassure your child that both of you love him and always will.
- Do not try to buy your child's love.
- If you are the residential parent, include the other parent as much as possible.
- If you are the non-residential parent, exercise your visitation.
- Never blame your child for the divorce.
- Be available to answer your child's questions about divorce and be honest, but not too revealing about personal information.

Chapter 9

※

Dividing Your Assets
and Debts

After custody, division of property and debts is the hardest part of the divorce for many people. This is where the fighting gets petty, sneaky, greedy, and ugly. It is very easy to get bogged down with these decisions and spend months fighting over them. How your assets and debts are divided is an important decision, though, because it affects your financial stability and standard of living for years to come.

How to Think about Property Division

Before we talk about how marital property and debts are divided, it is first essential to discuss how to think about these things. For too many people, assets somehow start to become symbolic of their emotions. Working hard to take every last dime can help you feel as if you have vindicated yourself or proven the other spouse wrong. Small battles over things such as whom gets which CDs can sometimes start to become symbolic of the entire divorce. A credit card debt that resulted from your spouse purchasing a large screen TV to which you were opposed at the time can become a proving ground to demonstrate that you were right about that argument and many others in your marriage. You can easily lose your perspective when you are negotiating or fighting over assets and debts. Whether you are negotiating a property settlement together or with a mediator, or hashing it out in court, there are some important mental shifts you should make before you move ahead in the process.

First of all, it may be hard to hear this, but stuff is just stuff. You can buy another can opener, couch, porch swing, or serving platter. Material possessions do not define you, make you a better person, or guarantee any happiness. Getting or being awarded certain items does not mean you've won or taught your spouse a lesson. While it is important that you get a fair share of the marital property, you need to think about the trade-offs. How long and hard do you want to fight over a couple thousand dollars? Is it worth three months of lawyer bills to take a bit more assets? Do you really want to pay your lawyer $1,000 so that your spouse has to pay the $500 debt you are upset about? The property settlement ought to be something that makes sense for you when you look at the bottom-line end result. You need to total up not only the actual dollars, but the emotional toll the process will take on you.

It is very important that you take the time to see your situation clearly. The fact that your ex wants the kitchen table or the computer probably makes you angry. You don't want to be taken advantage of. However, you also need to perceive things for what they are. You can replace many of the smaller household items, so it may not be worth fighting over them. You need to be careful that you do not allow your frustration and anger over your relationship to seep into your thoughts about property. The property settlement part of your divorce is essentially a business arrangement and there is no room for emotions in business. Certainly there are items that have emotional meaning to you—photo albums, trip souvenirs, baby mementos, jewelry, and so on, but most things that you own really are just things that don't change your life.

Now, all of that being said, it is important that you stand up for yourself to ensure that you receive a fair share in the property settlement. Some people become completely disgusted with the whole process and want to just wash their hands of it. It's ok to feel this way, but you also need to think about your future financial well-being. You may be tempted to walk away and say "let her take it all, I don't care." However, while you may be proving that your spouse isn't going to win this emotional war no matter how much property she gets, you may be doing yourself a huge disservice. If you don't want to argue over personal property, at least make sure you get a fair offset for it out of liquid assets, such as bank accounts and investments. Or work toward an arrangement where you take less debt. Your attorney or mediator can help you work through these alternatives.

Marital versus Separate Assets

Your divorce can only divide *marital* assets and debts. Marital assets are those things that you accumulated during the marriage. It doesn't matter which of you accumulated them or in whose name they are technically owned—they came into the marriage and became part of the property of the marriage. The same rule applies to marital debt. It doesn't matter whose name is on the bill, if it was incurred during marriage, it is a debt of the marriage. The reasoning behind this is that if something is acquired or owed during the marriage, it is a product of the marriage—created by the marriage. Therefore it is the responsibility of both parties.

Note that gifts you give each other during marriage are considered marital property, not separate property. An engagement ring is separate property since it was acquired before the marriage. Wedding rings are marital property. If you have separate property, it is very important that you gather records that easily trace the property to when you acquired it before marriage. Bank records, deeds, bills of sale, and so on are proof of this. If you had separate property and sold it during the marriage, the proceeds from the sale remains separate, unless you commingle it (see below).

There are a few exceptions to these rules. Inheritances received during marriage are considered separate property. Gifts given to one spouse by other people are separate property. Personal injury awards or settlements received during marriage are also separate property. However, these types of asset can be converted to a marital asset if they are commingled with marital assets (placed in an account with marital assets and not kept separate) or used as a marital asset, such as to support or provide for the family.

Separate property (or a portion of it) can also become a marital asset if the owner's spouse in some way contributes to its upkeep or increase in value. This often applies to real property. If the husband owned a rental property prior to marriage, and the wife helped with maintenance, improvements, and making mortgage payments on the property during marriage, the increase in the value of the property during the marriage is subject to division in the divorce. The idea is that that spouse helped cause the increase in value and so is entitled to a portion of that increase.

Note that marital assets can't be converted to separate property. You can't withdraw money from a joint account, put it in your solo account and magically have it become your separate property (and if your spouse takes marital assets and tries to do this they will be accounted for in the property division and added in as marital assets). All assets that are part of the marriage have to be accounted for and divided. Just slapping your name on it does not make it yours or make it separate property. Your spouse cannot just take marital property and designate it as his. Anything acquired during marriage that is not separate property is marital property and will be divided by the court in the divorce.

Your State Laws about Dividing Property

Each state has its own individual laws about property and debt division, as with everything else in a divorce. However, there are two major ways in which states approach property division. Most states employ the equitable distribution rule of property division. This means that the marital property is divided in a way that is fair (equitable), but not necessarily equal. The court considers each party's situation and contributions to the marriage and then makes a decision based on what is fair under the circumstances. This can mean that a judge could award more marital property to a spouse who stayed home with the children and did not work, as a kind of compensation for this contribution.

The other property division approach is community property. A community property state assumes that all property acquired by the parties during the marriage belongs to each of them equally because marriage is a joint partnership. In some of these states, property is simply split 50/50, but in others, the parties can show reasons why they should get more than 50 percent. It's a good idea to have an attorney to help you prove this.

Nine states are community property states. These include:

- Arizona
- California
- Idaho
- Louisiana
- Nevada
- New Mexico
- Texas
- Washington
- Wisconsin

In Alaska, you are subject to community property rules only if you signed an agreement (such as a prenup) in which you agreed all property would be community property.

State laws require judges to consider many factors when dividing marital property. These can include:

- The length of the marriage
- The earnings of each party and their earning capacities
- Your ages and respective health
- Your separate assets and debts
- Bad behavior by either spouse to the other during the marriage, including hiding or fudging assets and factors that led to the divorce, or domestic violence
- Children of the marriage, and their ages and needs
- Where the children will live

- Assistance one spouse provided the other in obtaining a degree, establishing a practice, or getting a professional license

Prenuptial Agreements

A prenuptial agreement is a contract signed before marriage that dictates how you will settle property and arrange spousal support (see chapter 11) should you divorce. These agreements are binding, as long as they are entered into freely and honestly. If you signed a prenup, it likely sets out how your marital assets are going to be divided. Your property division is ruled by this agreement and not by your state laws. If you have a prenup and want to challenge the property division laid out in it, your attorney will have to focus on getting the entire prenup thrown out as invalid. The assets and debts then become subject to your state property division laws.

Some couples have post-nuptial agreements (or postnups). This is like a prenup but it is entered into after the marriage has begun. It is treated the same way as a prenup.

Finding Property

Before you or a court can divide your marital property, you have to figure out what exactly there is. This may be simple if you have few assets, or if you believe your spouse has been completely honest with you. It may not be so simple if you were not the person who managed the money or if you have a spouse who has been hiding or using up assets. You may know for certain your spouse is trying to pull a fast one, or you may just have a feeling. If your account balances have gone down, you may have a problem. If your spouse suddenly is earning less, that's another clue. If things of value are just disappearing from around the house, be wary. If your spouse owns a business and suddenly business is bad, or she decides to sell, you could have a potential problem.

To determine what property there is, or should be, dig out all the financial statements you can find, including those from past years (hopefully stored with your tax returns). Make copies of everything, because your spouse could easily take these documents tomorrow. Back up any computer financial records onto disk and store it in a safe place. If statements are missing and your name is on the account, call the financial institution and get copies.

If things are very complicated, or very ugly, you will need your attorney's help. She can subpoena records, obtain information from your spouse during discovery (see chapter 5), or hire an investigator who can find assets and records. If your spouse owns a business, you may need an accountant to scrutinize the business's records and transactions.

It is important that you are able to identify all assets. The more assets there are, the more there is to divide and the more you will receive.

Valuing Property

Before property can be divided, it has to be assigned a value, so that it can be added into the totals of what each spouse is getting. You and your spouse can agree as to the value of an item, or you can get experts to provide valuations. The problem with value, of course, is that it is often subjective. Even if you hire two separate qualified experts, they will probably come up with different numbers. Regardless of the black-and-white value of an item, you and your spouse might have different levels of attachment to it. One common example is the marital home. One spouse might have no problem selling to the highest bidder, while the other spouse may be emotionally attached to the home and have difficulty selling at almost any number. Because of this, the home may truly be more valuable to one spouse than to the other.

If you are attempting to do valuation yourselves, you can rely on valuation guides such as the *Kelly Blue Book* for cars, which show average values. A common mistake people make when valuing objects is to assume that a used object has the same value as a new object of the same type. No matter what it is, unless it is a collectible that increases in value as you own it or real property, its value decreases with age. Don't make the mistake of agreeing with your spouse that you will get a certain amount of household objects valued as though they were new, while your spouse takes an equal value in something such as cash or stock. In terms of strategy, whatever items you want, you should seek to have them undervalued and have items your spouse wants overvalued. If you are negotiating values yourselves, lowball or high-ball these items in your negotiations to try to get the values closer to what you want.

Another important point is that usually in a divorce, items are divided using their value as of the date of separation. If you're in court in December and you actually moved out of the house back in March, everything will be divided based on what it was worth in March. It's important to be savvy about this, because some things have likely increased in value since that time, while others may have decreased or remained the same. If you agree to let your spouse keep the house valued at $250,000 as of the date of separation, he may really be walking away with a home that is now worth $275,000; however, if real property values in your neighborhood have sunk, the home's value may have actually gone down.

Special Considerations

Note that when you or the court is dividing up property, the marital property is looked at as a whole. You don't go and divide every single asset between you. Instead, each party ends up with roughly half of the total value of all the assets. So if you have a house with equity of $20,000, you don't necessarily have to sell the house and give each person half. One person could keep the house and the other could take an investment account worth $8,000 and $2,000 worth of personal property, for a grand total of $10,000, or half the equity.

If you and your spouse lived in a community property state and then moved to an equitable distribution state, property you bought or obtained in the community property state will likely be treated as community property in your divorce. Say, for example, you lived in California, bought a house there, and then later moved to New York but kept the California home. If you file for divorce in New York, the California home would be divided under California community property laws.

How to Divide Household and Personal Goods

If you and your spouse are trying to divide up household items yourselves, it can be hard to decide how to do it. (Even if you don't intend to take on this task, it's likely the judge will not get into the nitty gritty of dividing up each book, CD, and towel and instead will tell you to split it in half or assign a dollar value to which each party is entitled.) There are some rules of thumb you can use to help you make these decisions.

First of all, consider need or interest. If you are moving out and are buying a home or apartment that comes with a refrigerator and stove, you do not need to take the marital fridge and stove. If your spouse is moving out, he probably does not need all the coffee cups. Half will suffice. If you don't ski, don't ask for the skis. It can be tempting to add things to the list of what you want just because you know your spouse will want the same thing—it may seem like a great way to stick it to him or her, but in the end it just means your settlement will take longer to work out and it will increase the bad feelings between you.

Consider the children's needs. The children need to be comfortable at both homes; however, they probably need to have the most amenities and provisions at the home where they spend the majority of their time. There's nothing wrong with a child sleeping on a pull-out couch every other weekend, but to leave a child with nothing to sleep on the rest of the time makes no sense. It's perfectly fine to move some toys, clothes, and other items to the non-residential parent's home; however, if the children are old enough they should have some say in what they want to keep where.

Keep sets together. Things that come as a set, such china, silverware, matched furniture, collections, and so on are worth more all together than they are if they are split up. While it may be no big deal to split up your daily silverware, doing so with your good silver is not wise since it then has no resale value. If you can't agree about a set, it might make sense to agree to sell it and split the proceeds, and then you can each go buy what you want.

If you try to catalog and value every single item in your home, you're going to be spending months with a calculator. At some point you have to realize that you simply can't total things to the very last penny and must simply start to divide assets in a way that seems fair. It's likely that you can adequately do so without haggling over whether the alarm clock is worth $2 or $4.

Real Estate

The most common misperception about property division is that the home must always be sold. This is not true at all. It is definitely possible for one person to keep the home after a divorce. When dealing with real property, there are a number of considerations. First of all, if the property was purchased during the marriage using marital funds, it is a marital asset, no matter whose name is on the title or the mortgage. Too many people think that because the home is in their spouse's name that they have no right to it. The total value of the home must be added into the pot of money that must be divided in the divorce. The marital home is often a hot point in a divorce. It symbolizes a lot of things and is much more than just a piece of property.

There are several ways to deal with the marital home.

- You can sell the home and split the profits, after paying off the mortgage, home equity, capital gains taxes, and the realtor. This is a good option if the home has a very high monthly mortgage payment that would be a burden for one or both of you to pay towards each month after the divorce. Also, it is not uncommon for both parties to want to start fresh after the divorce, in a new place, with no ties to the marriage. You can each then take your portion of the proceeds and walk away and do whatever you want with it—buy a house or condo, invest it, pay off other debts, or buy a boat to sail around the world in. One of the main stumbling blocks to this plan of action is that you will both need to agree on the listing price and the offers you accept. If you have difficulty agreeing with each other, this may not be easy. The best way to solve this problem would be to agree to follow the recommendations of your realtor. When you divide the proceeds, you need to consider who has been making the mortgage payments since the separation and compensate that person for those costs.

- One person will remain in the home. The other spouse will quitclaim (sign a legal document transferring ownership) the deed to him or her. The spouse remaining in the home will refinance the mortgage so that it is in that person's name only, and be solely responsible for paying the mortgage. The value of the equity in the home is credited to the spouse remaining there. She may have to pay the non-residing spouse a portion of that equity, or trade off other assets in exchange for keeping the home. The main stumbling block with this method is that you must agree on what the value of the home is so you can determine what the equity really is.
- One or both spouses will continue to own the home and rent it. If it is jointly owned, it will need to be treated as a business venture by the two people—splitting expenses and profits.
- One person remains in the home and the deed is quitclaimed; however, the mortgage remains in both names, and the non-residing spouse must contribute to (or perhaps even pay all of) the monthly payments. This type of arrangement can be done in lieu of spousal support.
- One spouse remains in the home and gradually buys out the other spouse's interest. This option may work if there aren't a lot of other assets to offset against the value of the equity. The downside is that you continue as joint owners, which can lead to tension.

It is important to understand the difference between the deed and the mortgage. This is something many people do not understand when transferring real property after a divorce. The deed is a legal document that lists the owners of the property. The property cannot be sold without all deedholders agreeing. If a property is sold, the profits belong to both deedholders. If your spouse quitclaims the deed to you as part of the property settlement, you become the sole owner of the property and are the only one who can make decisions about it or profit from it. Note, however, that even if only one spouse is listed on a deed, if the property was bought during the marriage, it is marital property.

The mortgage is an entirely different story. A mortgage is a legal agreement between the borrowers and the bank. If you sign the mortgage, you agree to be responsible for the entire debt. If both of you are on the mortgage, the bank has the right to come after both of you if the mortgage is not paid. It doesn't matter if the judge ordered just one of you to make the payments, or if you have an agreement that one of you will pay it. As far as the bank is concerned, you are both liable.

If a judge orders one of you to be solely responsible for the mortgage, this does not change the terms of your agreement with the bank. The bank is not a party in the divorce and the judge has no authority over it. The only way to change your obligation to the bank is to have the person who is remaining in the house refinance the mortgage in his or her own name. You can ask if the bank will allow you to execute a document (called a release) releasing the non-owner spouse from the mortgage, essentially taking his or her name off the mortgage and placing all responsibility on the owner spouse. The benefit to this is that you can keep the same interest rate and terms. However, the bank has no incentive to do this for you (it would rather have two people on the hook than just one) and it may be difficult if not impossible to get your lender to agree to this.

If the court orders your former spouse to refinance the mortgage or to be solely responsible for it and she fails to do, simply leaving the existing mortgage in place, you can go back to court to complain. The judge will enforce the order and possibly hold your ex in contempt if she blatantly disregards the order. If the person who is supposed to pay the mortgage does not make payments, the bank will come after the other person listed on the mortgage. The only recourse is to go back to court and ask to have your ex reimburse you for any costs for which you're being held responsible.

If you are dividing other real property, such as a vacation home or rental property, you have basically the same options as those listed above for the marital home. The process may be easier though since other real property is not usually as much of an emotional hot button. It is usually much easier to agree to sell this type of property.

Businesses

If you or your spouse owns a business, the business is a marital asset. If the business was owned before marriage, the increase in value to the business that occurred during marriage is likely a marital asset as well. Small businesses are tricky to work with in a divorce because they are very difficult to value. Placing a value on the business is the most important part of the process. It is much more complicated than considering what the business has in the bank and how much the real property and equipment owned by the business is worth. Businesses have receivables, accounts payable, contracts, and the goodwill of their customers. It is also important to compare the business to other comparable businesses to get an estimation of value. Since all of these things must be considered, you will need to consult an expert when placing a dollar value on the business. There are business valuation specialists who will do so for a fee. Unless you're in agreement, you'll likely want two experts and it's likely they will give different numbers. You may need a forensic accountant who can carefully examine all transactions relating to the business and uncover hidden assets, or improper transactions. In small business in particular, cash sales may play a large role in the business; these can be very difficult to trace if they are not documented properly.

If the business is jointly owned, it is certainly possible to continue on as joint owners after the divorce, but you need to consider how well this would work and if you are really able to work together for the best interest of the company. You may need to create an agreement about what your individual responsibilities would be and how you will resolve any disagreements.

One spouse can buy the other out—exchange other assets in order to be able to become the sole owner of the business. The business could also be sold, but a sale must be conducted in a way so that both parties believe it is done fairly and so that an equitable price is received.

Social Security and Pensions

If you've been married more than ten years, your and your spouse's Social Security benefits are marital property that can be divided. These benefits aren't paid until retirement age, but they can be divided in anticipation of the payout. If you remarry, you won't be entitled to receive benefits through your ex-spouse.

Military benefits are another type of retirement benefit to consider. Payments to retired military are called retired pay. Up to 50 percent of this pay can be awarded in a divorce (and up to 65 percent including child support). The court can actually award more, but this will have to be paid personally by the retired service member, not by the military. A military pension is technically considered property, not a pension plan.

The portion of pensions and retirement accounts, such as 401(k)s and IRAs, which accrued during the marriage are considered marital assets as well. These accounts are a different animal than other assets, because, in general, you don't want to cash these in until retirement (you pay a hefty penalty if you do, and with a pension plan you actually have no access to the money before retirement age no matter what), so you're negotiating about money you will get in the future. The problem with this is that nothing in the future is certain. You could die in six months, and never see a dime of this money. Or you could live to be a hundred and need every penny of retirement money available to you. You can take loans against retirement accounts; this way you avoid penalties. However these loans must be repaid within a five-year period in most cases.

Dividing pensions and retirement accounts is a complicated and highly specialized business. There are attorneys who do only this and your attorney may need to hire one to handle this aspect of your case. You should never agree to a distribution of these types of assets without having a specialist look at the numbers and use specific formulas to calculate value. These assets are not easily divided and require specialized documents called QDROs (qualified domestic relations orders). If you have an attorney for nothing else, you need one for this.

Investments

Investments are one of the easiest assets to divide because they rarely have any kind of emotional meaning or symbolism. Because the value of investments fluctuate with the market, you will get half the value as of the day you separate an investment into separate accounts. For settlement purposes, use the value of the investment as of the date of separation as your negotiating point.

Investments have a cost basis. This is the amount you paid when you first bought the stock or mutual fund. It is the dollar amount you put into it. The good news is that when you divide up assets in a divorce, you don't owe any taxes on them. The bad news is you take the original cost basis with you. If you bought a stock for $1 and it is now worth $5, should you decide to sell it, you'll have to pay tax on the $4 profit. If you have a choice, opt to take the property that has shown the least amount of growth, so that if you need to sell it, you will owe less tax than if you took the investment with the lower cost basis.

Pets

Pets are considered assets, even though to many people they are like children. Some people get into "custody" cases over pets. While custody laws do not apply to pets because they are technically property, some judges will listen to testimony and evidence about who could provide better care for the animal. In some cases, a court could issue a time-sharing (visitation) arrangement for the pet, but most of the time, ownership of the pet is just given to one person. (If there are children, it's a good bet the pet will stay where the children are.) Although you might not think of your pet as a thing of value, it does have value, particularly if you own a purebred animal and most definitely if the pet is used for breeding or showing.

Debt

Often when people think about property settlements and divisions, they only think about the assets, but the debts have to be divided as well. Debts are usually divided using their value as of the date of separation. Often one spouse will continue to use one credit card and the other spouse another one after the divorce, racking up their own individual charges on them. Dividing as of the date of separation ensures you're only talking about debt that was incurred by both of you. Debts are handled the same way as assets under the law. Community property or equitable distribution is used to divide them. If you can show that your spouse incurred the debt during marriage, without your knowledge and with the intent of you being responsible for it after the divorce, it is likely the court will assign that entire debt to your spouse. Other debts incurred for items only your spouse would use and which you did not know about may also be assigned to the spending spouse. Student loans taken out during marriage are marital debt.

Joint Debt
There are several ways to divide joint debts:

- Pay them off entirely. Using assets from the marriage, pay off all debt so that you both start off fresh. You may want to do this for just some of the marital debt.
- Divide them. Agree (or have the court order) who will be responsible for which. Close the joint account and transfer the balance to an individual account.
- Agree to pay them off together. Doing so is a dangerous proposition though. If you leave a joint credit card debt and agree to each pay half every month, if your ex doesn't pay, you're on the hook and your credit rating and credit score will be harmed. Your only recourse is to take your ex back to court for failing to pay and have the court order him or her to pay you. In this type of situation, it is important that your original divorce decree specifies you will indemnify each other and hold each other harmless for your individual portions of the debt being assigned to you. That way, if your spouse fails to pay, you have a clear avenue to sue him or her to recover the amount you're being charged with.

Bottom line: You really should close all joint accounts no matter how you plan to pay them. Get those balances transferred into separate accounts so that you are no longer responsible for each other's failure to pay.

Non-Concrete Assets

In addition to all the things you can see, count, and touch, there are other non-tangible assets that need to be divided. These include stock options, licenses and degrees, frequent flyer miles, and more. All of these items have value and it is important to make sure they are included in your total property division.

Stock options are often a benefit of employment. An employee is given the right to buy a certain number of stocks at a certain price—usually well below the market value. These options may have dates at which they become viable some time in the future. Stock options acquired during marriage are a marital asset and must be divided. The spouse who receives the options from his or her company must pay tax on them before transferring them to the other spouse. The spouse who receives the options gets them with a cost basis equal to the amount on which the employee paid tax.

Frequent flyer miles are given by airlines and also earned through special credit cards. These miles can be used to get free tickets or upgrades on future flights, and they can be very valuable. All frequent flyer miles accumulated by either of you during marriage are marital assets (even if you earned them while on business travel—if the miles are in your name, they're a marital asset). These miles can be transferred to anyone, so moving them around is not a problem.

Licenses and degrees are a specialized area of matrimonial law. The idea is that if you get your license to practice medicine, or earn a degree in engineering during the marriage, this is an asset that is owned by both of you. Even though you may have been the one who went to school or took the bar exam, or even underwent training to get your hairdresser's license, the value of that degree is part of the marital assets and must be divided. When we say divided, remember we do not mean taking the actual item and splitting it up. Obviously, if you cut a medical degree in half and gave one piece to each spouse that would not have any real value. What we are talking about is determining the value of that degree or license and adding that value into the marital pot.

Often this license or degree is valued by considering the worth of the business or practice it has allowed you to have. A medical degree has allowed you to open your cardiology practice, for example, and that practice can be valued. However, even if you haven't opened a practice based on your license or degree (maybe you just graduated, or you've stayed home with the kids for a while), it still has a value in and of itself because it gives you the potential to earn income. Each state has specific court precedents about how these assets are handled. Talk with an attorney to find out how these types of property are handled in your state.

Patents, trademarks, and copyrights are other non-concrete assets. If either of you wrote a book or received a patent during marriage, that intellectual property has a dollar value and it goes into the pot of money to be divided. Other assets you might not think about include gym or club memberships, tickets/season's tickets to sporting events or performances, and subscriptions to magazines, newspapers, and services (such as Netflix or Napster).

Tax Consequences

Taxes are an important (and possibly expensive) consideration when dividing property, so it is essential to clarify what your tax liability will be and talk with your attorney about ways to minimize it.

If you sell the marital home, it is subject to capital gains tax. However, the first $250,000 of gain (the increase over what you paid for the property) for each of you is excluded, meaning it is not taxed. (The total excluded is $500,000 if you sell the home together and lived there for two years before you sold it.) There is no exclusion for the sale of a second or vacation home.

If you transfer retirement accounts between spouses, it is not a taxable event, unless you don't roll the funds over into a similar account. If you cash in the account, you'll pay tax, but if you put it in your own IRA, it is not taxable.

Dividing Your Property Yourselves

You and your spouse can absolutely decide that you want to divide your property yourselves. For many small items, this method works best. When it comes to larger assets, it is a good idea to create a list of all the items that need to be divided and what their approximate value is. Do this for assets and debts. Then sit down together and talk through the list. Some things may seem obvious—you will each probably keep your own cars and car loans, for example. Other things may be harder, such as the house (read the section earlier in this chapter about your options).

The best way to handle this is slowly and carefully. You will likely need to sit down and talk about the division of your property a few times, and spend some time on your own thinking it through in between your meetings. If you have difficulty, consider seeing a mediator. It is very important that you talk with your attorney before agreeing to anything final. There are tax implications that you may not be aware of and there may be options you have not considered, so be sure to get some legal advice before shaking your spouse's hand about any agreement.

Once you have reached an agreement, you'll want your attorney or mediator to draw it up as a formal stipulation or settlement which can be submitted to the court. Even if you don't agree on the other areas of your divorce, you can submit this settlement to the court to close this issue.

The Sneaky Spouse

If your spouse is working overtime to hide, move, or steal assets, you need to be on your toes. If your spouse removes items from the home, make a list of everything that is missing, with an approximate value. This list can then be presented to the judge and deducted from the property your spouse would be awarded.

If your spouse takes money from accounts or investments, hold on to the statements showing the previous values and try to pinpoint the date the asset was removed. Again, this can be deducted from his or her final take.

If you are concerned about your spouse taking things, it isn't a bad idea to go through your house and carefully videotape every room. Open closet and cupboard doors, so that you can get an accurate picture of what is there.

Preparing for a Trial about Property

If you and your spouse are not able to reach an agreement about property (and this is not uncommon because a divorce is primarily about money), you will need to get professional help. You might want to start with a mediator first to see if a settlement is possible. If not, you'll be working with your attorney who will also likely try to reach a settlement by talking with your spouse's attorney.

If no one can agree, then you're heading for a trial. A trial is not the worst thing in the world—it will bring you a solution at least. There are some things you can do to help your attorney prepare for the property part of your trial. Gather all the current information you can about your property and debts. This includes:

- current real property assessment on your home
- all current statements from investments and retirement accounts
- current bills from all debts
- information about all pension plans
- a list of the non-concrete property involved in the divorce
- a list of personal property that needs to be divided
- property your spouse has already removed
- a list of property that is your separate, non-marital property

Spend some time talking with your attorney and preparing to testify (if necessary). Understand that even though you will go to court that day with the intention to have a trial, your attorney will likely spend a lot of time trying to reach a last-minute settlement.

Chapter 10

Child Support

C hild support was designed to protect the children of divorce and ensure that they maintain a lifestyle comparable to that they had before the divorce. It is not intended to be a punishment for the parent paying it, or a reward for the parent receiving it. All parents are required to support their children, whether they are divorced or not. Child support laws are established by the individual states.

Child support can be confusing to some parents. It seems complicated, with all the forms and calculations. Once you understand the way it is determined, the process begins to make a little more sense. The federal Child Support Enforcement Act requires states to set up guidelines for calculating child support. If the parents live in different states, the Uniform Interstate Family Support Act (UIFSA) governs which state will have jurisdiction.

How Child Support Is Calculated

In most states, child support is not calculated just by looking at the non-custodial parent's income. Instead, most states start with the idea that both parents must support their child. Their incomes are compared and child support is calculated based on the state's particular formula. The residential parent is assumed already to be financially supporting the child, so it is the non-residential parent who ends up paying support. The more children you have, the higher the percent of income that is required in child support. If you have a shared custody arrangement where you equally divide time with your child, in most cases, the parent who earns more will pay child support to the other parent, although it is possible to opt out of child support in some cases.

The easiest way to calculate child support is to use an online calculator or worksheet. You can find your state's below.

State Child Support Calculators, Guidelines, and Worksheets

Alabama
http://alabamalawyers.com/Rent-a-MBA_files/alacsc.htm

Alaska
https://webapp.state.ak.us/cssd/guidelinecalc.jsp

Arizona
http://www.supreme.state.az.us/childsup/

Arkansas
http://courts.state.ar.us/aoc/acs_guidelines.cfm

California
http://www.childsup.cahwnet.gov/calculator/

Colorado
http://www.courts.state.co.us/chs/court/forms/domestic/childsupport
guidelines.htm

Connecticut
http://www.jud.ct.gov/external/news/childsupport.htm

Delaware
http://courts.delaware.gov/Support%20Calculator/

District of Columbia
http://csgc.oag.dc.gov/application/main/intro.aspx

Florida
http://dor.myflorida.com/dor/childsupport/pdf/poz8.pdf

Georgia
https://services.georgia.gov/dhr/cspp/do/public/SupportCalc

Hawaii
http://www.courts.state.hi.us/page_server/SelfHelp/Forms/Oahu
/7D004AF15FE5ADBDEEA9E49E98.html

Idaho
http://www.healthandwelfare.idaho.gov/Portals/_Rainbow/Manuals
/cS/css.htm

Illinois
http://www.ilchildsupport.com/

Indiana
http://www.in.gov/judiciary/childsupport/

Iowa
https://dhssecure.dhs.state.ia.us/changechildsupport/AspScript
/Estimator.asp

Kansas
http://www.kscourts.org/ctruls/csintro.htm

Kentucky
http://ag.ky.gov/childsupport/support.htm

Louisiana
http://www.dss.state.la.us/departments/ofs/index.html

Maine
http://www.maine.gov/dhhs/OIAS/dser/manual/chapter-6.html

Maryland
http://www.dhr.state.md.us/csea/worksheet.htm

Massachusetts
http://www.dor.state.ma.us/apps/worksheets/cse/guidelines-short.asp

Michigan
http://courts.michigan.gov/scao/services/focb/mcsf.htm

Minnesota
http://childsupportcalculator.dhs.state.mn.us/

Mississippi
http://www.mdhs.state.ms.us/csemdhs.html#receive

Missouri
http://www.courts.mo.gov/__862565ec0057e8f0.nsf/0/d538248b77951
e45862568e300513e47?OpenDocument

Montana
http://www.dphhs.mt.gov/csed/packet/guidelines.shtml

Nebraska
http://www.supremecourt.ne.gov/forms/supreme-court-child-support
-forms.shtml

Nevada
http://www.leg.state.nv.us/NRS/NRS-125B.html

New Hampshire
http://www.dhhs.state.nh.us/DHHS/DCSS/Child+Support+Calculator
/default.htm

New Jersey
http://www.judiciary.state.nj.us/csguide/index.htm

New Mexico
http://www.nmcourts.com/cgi/prose_lib/csw.htm#introduction

New York
http://www.nyc.gov/html/hra/html/revenue_investigation/OCSE
_child_support_calculator.shtml

North Carolina
https://nddhacts01.dhhs.state.nc.us/home.jsp?TargetScreen=WorkSheet
.jsp

North Dakota
http://www.ndcourts.com/chldspt/

Ohio
http://jfs.ohio.gov/Ocs/services.stm

Oklahoma
http://204.87.68.21/childsupport/guidelines/calc.htm

Oregon
http://dcs.state.or.us/calculator/

Pennsylvania
http://www.pacode.com/secure/data/231/chapter1910/s1910.16-1.html

Rhode Island
http://www.cse.ri.gov/services/establishment_childsup.php

South Carolina
http://www.state.sc.us/dss/csed/calculator.htm

South Dakota
http://dss.sd.gov/childsupport/services/obligationcalculator.asp

Tennessee
http://www.state.tn.us/humanserv/is/incomeshares.htm

Texas
http://www.co.travis.tx.us/records_communication/law_library/pdfs/calculator.pdf

Utah
http://www.utcourts.gov/childsupport/calculator

Vermont
http://www.ocs.state.vt.us/OCS_Guidelines/OCS_External_Guidelines.htm

Virginia
http://www.dss.virginia.gov/family/dcse_calc.cgi

Washington
http://www.courts.wa.gov/ssgen/

West Virginia
http://www.legis.state.wv.us/WVCODE/48/masterfrm2Frm.htm

Wisconsin
http://dwd.wisconsin.gov/dwd/publications/dws/child_support/dwsc
_824_p.htm

Wyoming
http://courts.state.wy.us/Pro%20Se%20Divorce%20Forms/CSMod
/CSMod06.pdf

If your state does not post a calculator or worksheet, and only has the guidelines for determining support, you can use the calculator at http://www.alllaw.com/calculators/ChildSupport/.

When a court calculates child support, the judge starts by using the state guidelines. However, there are other factors that can be considered in most states. The judge can take into account child support or alimony received by or paid by the parent (from another marriage), costs of health insurance and child care, the children's ages and special needs, the parents' incomes, and whether each parent is living with a new partner who contributes to household income. The judge may also consider whether one parent is purposefully trying to reduce his or her income (by working fewer hours, or by working at a job far below his or her qualifications) to avoid or reduce child support. Most states have a required minimum child support payment that every parent must meet no matter what. Even if the parent is unemployed and homeless, this monthly minimum amount will apply.

Child support, when determined by a court, is set at a specified weekly or monthly amount. This does not fluctuate or change in any way, even with the parenting schedule. If the non-custodial parent has the children for one month in the summer, for example, child support is still owed for that time period, even though the non-custodial parent is the one caring for the children. If there is a temporary change in the parenting plan, such as the non-custodial parent having the kids for an extra weekend one month, there is no change to the child support that is owed. The only way child support is changed is by going back to court for a modification (see section later in this chapter).

Duration of Support

Child support generally ends at age eighteen, but this does vary by state. Some states require child support to continue as long as the child is in school or college (often to age twenty-one). Child support can end earlier in certain circumstances. If your child becomes emancipated (is legally declared by a court to be living on his or her own as an adult), gets married, or joins the military, child support ends. Child support does not end if either parent remarries. It does end if the paying parent should pass away.

Other Expenses that Can Be Court Ordered

In addition to child support payments, the court can order, or the parents can agree upon, other benefits for the children. The most common is health insurance. Either parent can be ordered to maintain health insurance for the children. It is a good idea to have a Qualified Medical Child Support Order (QMSCO) put into place, which will formalize the requirement. The insurance company's summary plan will specify what must be included in this order and you can ask for the company's help in preparing it if you don't have an attorney (they won't write it for you, but will tell how to fix one you have written to make it acceptable to them). Medical expenses not covered by insurance (such as co-pays, deductibles, prescriptions, and other costs) can also be assigned to one parent, or split between the parents. Mental health care, dental, and orthodontia care can also be included in a child support order.

It is common for a child support order to include a requirement that the paying parent obtain a life insurance policy naming the children as beneficiaries. This offers financial protection for the children, should that parent pass away before child support ends.

Educational and school expenses are another category that is often included in a support order. Tuition, school supplies, school fees, and more can become the responsibility of the paying parent, or shared by both parents.

Medical and educational expenses are areas where many parents end up having conflict. You need to make things very clear from the beginning. If the non-residential parent is solely responsible for all additional medical expenses not covered by insurance, you should set up your accounts this way with doctor's offices, so that that parent is billed directly. It is sometimes difficult to do so—particularly if your child needs a prescription immediately (drugstores expect payment at pick up—they usually will not bill the other parent). In such instances, you don't have time to get the other parent involved and instead have to seek to be reimbursed later. If you are the residential parent, keep good records and conduct all requests for payment in writing, while keeping a copy for yourself. The same applies to educational expenses. To reduce conflict, tuition should be billed directly to the responsible parent. Keep thorough records for reimbursement of other expenses.

How Child Support Is Paid

There are several ways child support can be paid and each method has advantages and disadvantages. One parent can directly pay the other by cash, check, or money order. This person-to-person method is simple and does not require waiting for any processing time by the state. The receiving parent must keep records and track the payments. Enforcement is more difficult and is not as automatic. If you agree to this type of payment, it is wise to include a provision that if payment is missed for a certain number of months, wage garnishment (see below) will be automatically set up.

Wage garnishment is another method of payment. Child support is deducted from the paying spouse's paycheck and sent either to the receiving spouse or to the state child support enforcement agency. Garnishment requires an extra step of formally notifying the paying parent's employer and setting a court date for the garnishment order. The parent receiving the support must handle all of the paperwork. The employer is legally obligated to withhold the support from the paycheck. The advantage of this method is that payment is made automatically. There are several disadvantages. First of all, the paying parent is likely to find it embarrassing, which might escalate hostilities between you. Second, there are limits to how much can be garnished from wages, so you may not be able to get the entire support amount this way. If your spouse is self-employed, you cannot garnish the wages. You also cannot prevent the paying spouse from quitting his job, which then puts you in the position of having to do more legwork to find the new employer and garnish again.

Wage garnishment is controlled by the Consumer Credit Protection Act, a federal law which limits the percent of wages that can be garnished. The garnishment law allows up to 50 percent of a worker's disposable earnings to be garnished for child support if the worker is supporting another spouse or child, or up to 60 percent if the worker is not. An additional 5 percent may be garnished for support payments more than twelve weeks in arrears.

The third option is to have your state child enforcement agency collect all child support. You can agree to send payment through this organization from the beginning, or at any point while child support is being paid. This is also the agency that will assist you in collecting unpaid child support. The advantage of this method is that the receiving parent doesn't have to do any legwork or keep any records and the parents don't need to have any contact with each other about child support (which can be helpful if you're prone to disagreements about this). Payments are automatically increased with the cost of living. The disadvantages are that the agency may take a small percentage of the payment as an administrative fee. The paying spouse may not appreciate this method as there is no absolutely no slack given for late or missed payments. Another disadvantage is that you're dealing with a government agency, so there is likely to be red tape and backlogs.

State Child Support Enforcement Agencies

Alabama
http://www.dhr.state.al.us/page.asp?pageid=288

Alaska
http://www.csed.state.ak.us/

Arizona
http://www.de.state.az.us/dcse/

Arkansas
http://www.arkansas.gov/dfa/child_support/ocse_index.html

California
http://www.childsup.cahwnet.gov/

Colorado
http://www.childsupport.state.co.us/do/home/index

Connecticut
http://www.ct.gov/dss/cwp/view.asp?a=2353-&Q=305184

State Child Support Enforcement Agencies

Alabama
http://www.dhr.state.al.us/page.asp?pageid=288

Alaska
http://www.csed.state.ak.us/

Arizona
http://www.de.state.az.us/dcse/

Arkansas
http://www.arkansas.gov/dfa/child_support/ocse_index.html

California
http://www.childsup.cahwnet.gov/

Colorado
http://www.childsupport.state.co.us/do/home/index

Connecticut
http://www.ct.gov/dss/cwp/view.asp?a=2353-&Q=305184

Delaware
http://www.dhss.delaware.gov/dcse/index.html

District of Columbia
http://csed.dc.gov/csed/site/default.asp

Florida
http://dor.myflorida.com/dor/childsupport/

Georgia
http://ocse.dhr.georgia.gov/portal/site

Hawaii
http://hawaii.gov/ag/csea

Idaho
http://www.healthandwelfare.idaho.gov/site/3337/default.aspx

Illinois
http://www.ilchildsupport.com/

Indiana
http://www.in.gov/dcs/support/

Iowa
https://childsupport.dhs.state.ia.us/welcome.asp

Kansas
http://www.srskansas.org/cse/cse.htm

Kentucky
http://chfs.ky.gov/dcbs/dcs/

Louisiana
http://www.dss.state.la.us/departments/ofs/Support_Enforcement
_Services.html

Maine
http://www.maine.gov/dhhs/OIAS/dser/

Maryland
http://www.dhr.state.md.us/csea/index.htm

Massachusetts
http://www.mass.gov/?pageID=doragencylanding&L=4&L0=Home&
L1=Individuals+and+Families&L2=Help+%26+Resources&L3=Child
+Support+Enforcement&sid=Ador

Michigan
http://www.michigan.gov/dhs/0,1607,7-124-5453_5528---,00.html

Minnesota
http://www.dhs.state.mn.us/main/idcplg?IdcService=GET_DYNAMIC
_CONVER-SION&RevisionSelectionMethod=LatestReleased&dDoc
Name=id_000160

Missouri
http://www.dss.mo.gov/cse/

Montana
http://www.dphhs.mt.gov/csed/index.shtml

Nebraska
http://www.hhs.state.ne.us/cse/cseindex.htm

Nevada
http://www.welfare.state.nv.us/child.htm

New Hampshire
http://www.dhhs.state.nh.us/DHHS/DCSS/default.htm

New Jersey
http://www.njchildsupport.org/

New Mexico
http://www.hsd.state.nm.us/csed/

New York
https://newyorkchildsupport.com/

North Carolina
http://www.dhhs.state.nc.us/dss/cse/index.htm

North Dakota
http://www.nd.gov/dhs/services/childsupport/

Ohio
http://jfs.ohio.gov/ocs/

Oklahoma
http://www.okdhs.org/divisionsoffices/visd/csed/

Oregon
http://www.dcs.state.or.us/

Pennsylvania
https://www.humanservices.state.pa.us/CSWS/index.aspx

Rhode Island
http://www.cse.ri.gov/

South Carolina
http://www.state.sc.us/dss/csed/

South Dakota
http://dss.sd.gov/childsupport/

Tennessee
http://www.state.tn.us/humanserv/cs/cs_main.htm

Texas
http://www.oag.state.tx.us/cs/index.shtml

Utah
http://www.ors.utah.gov/

Vermont
http://www.ocs.state.vt.us/

Virginia
http://www.dss.state.va.us/family/dcse.html

Washington
http://www.dshs.wa.gov/dcs/

West Virginia
http://www.wvdhhr.org/bcse/

Wisconsin
http://www.dwd.state.wi.us/bcs/

Wyoming
http://dfsweb.state.wy.us/cse_enforce.html

The Purpose of Child Support

Many people mistakenly think that child support must be used directly for child-related expenses. There are no requirements about how a parent must use the money she receives; however, it will certainly look bad to the court if the parent is buying expensive personal items for him or herself while the children are wearing rags.

Using child support for anything that benefits the family is fine. You can use it to pay the mortgage, buy food, install new carpeting, pay a landscaper, go on a family vacation, and so on. The parent paying child support has no right to dictate or even inquire about how the funds are used.

If you are the paying spouse, it can be hard to feel good about child support. Not only do you have less time with your children, but you also have to give money to the other parent. It can seem like a bad deal all around. It's important to remember that the money you are paying is used to help your children maintain a decent lifestyle. Focus on the fact that the money benefits your children, even if you do have to pay it to the other parent. Even if you can't stand your ex, make the payments out of respect for your children.

Negotiating Child Support

You and your spouse can negotiate your own child support payment plan; however, anything you agree to will need to be approved by the court. If you deviate significantly from your state guidelines, you will need to explain why and convince the court to agree with you.

When working out child support, you should always start by calculating what the obligation would be under the state guidelines. If this amount seems fair to both of you, you don't need to go any further. If you continue to negotiate, you will want to look at child support in conjunction with the rest of your financial settlement. If there will be no alimony, paying a little more in child support might make sense. Reducing child support in exchange for a larger share of assets is another option.

When calculating an amount for child support, be sure to create a list of the children's yearly expenses, including:

- Clothing
- Health and hygiene items
- food
- tuition
- school supplies
- school fees and expenses (such as field trips and teacher gifts)
- sports or activity expenses (equipment, uniforms, and fees)
- camp
- lessons (including instruments or other equipment)
- child care
- transportation expenses (including possibly a car, gas, and insurance for a teen)
- entertainment expenses
- toys, electronics, and personal belongings

- parties and celebrations
- allowances
- tutoring and testing (for extra help, SAT preparation costs and test fees, etc.).

The total of these items can help you both to understand how many expenses are purely child related.

If you choose to opt out of the guidelines, some of the reasoning you might use when presenting your arrangement to the court could include

- a child's special needs
- one parent earning much more than the other
- a parent's disability
- the non-custodial parent's dire financial situation
- a shared custody agreement

The key to opting out is to show the court that the child's needs will continue to be met and that both parents are committed to making certain of that.

Tax and Bankruptcy Implications

Child support is an important legal obligation and has an impact on taxes, as well as on filing for bankruptcy. Child support is not an obligation that can be discharged through bankruptcy. Even if you pay child support and go through a bankruptcy, you will come out the other side still owing child support. There are no exceptions. Child support is given top priority among creditors in a bankruptcy case, so it will be paid first. If the parent receiving child support files for bankruptcy, child support is included as part of his or her income.

Child support is not taxable income for the person receiving it and it is not tax deductible for the parent paying it.

Another important tax issue has to do with who will claim the children as dependent exemptions on their tax returns. This means that children who are under nineteen and living at home (or under twenty-four and a full-time student) can be listed on your tax return as dependents and you are allowed to exempt a certain amount of money from your taxable income because of this. The amount changes yearly—in 2007 it was $3,400.

Who will take the dependent exemption is something that can be negotiated in your divorce, or decided by the court. According to IRS rules, the parent with whom the child spent more than half the year gets to claim the child as an exemption. If a child was supported 50 percent by each parent, then the residential parent is the one who gets the exemption, unless there is an agreement to the contrary. If the non-residential parent takes the exemption, he should attach IRS form 8332 to his return every year the exemption is claimed. If you both claim the children as exemptions, the IRS will notice (they cross-reference the social security numbers of dependents and it will be caught).

You and the other parent can make your own agreement about the exemption. You can agree that the non-custodial parent will take the exemption, even though she did not spend more than half the time with the child. If you have more than one child, you can split up the exemptions (if you have three kids, mom could take two and dad could take one, for example). When considering who should get the exemption, explore who will benefit more from it. If one of you is in a higher tax bracket, it may make more sense for that person to use the exemption. Talk with your tax preparer about how the exemption will affect your taxes.

Note that if you have residential custody, you can file your taxes as "head of household," which will give you a higher standard deduction then just filing as single. This is an option available if you have lived without your spouse for at least six months of the tax year, your divorce is final (and you remain single), you pay half or more of your household expenses, and you have a child living with you for at least half the year.

Preparing for a Child Support Hearing

If you and the other parent are unable to reach an agreement about child support, you will have to have a hearing. Whether the hearing is part of your divorce, or held separately (such as if you seek child support prior to filing for divorce, or if you seek a temporary order while the divorce is pending), you need to prepare in the same way. Child support hearings are primarily about accounting. This is not a forum in which you can show what a bad parent or spouse the other person is. Instead, it is a numbers-based process in which the judge or hearing examiner (court employees who often hear these kinds of cases) wants a complete accounting of incomes and expenses. There is room to discuss special circumstances, such as those described earlier in this chapter that would allow an opt-out of the guidelines—situations in which the court could order child support higher or lower than the guidelines dictate. However, barring special circumstances, this hearing is going to be strictly about the numbers—unless there is evidence of one party hiding or concealing income. In this kind of situation, you might have the other parent's boss come in and testify about the tips she makes or the cash bonuses he receives. Or, you might testify about your personal knowledge of the other parent receiving under-the-table income.

If you have an attorney, he will prepare you to testify (if necessary). If you will be handling the case yourself, make sure you are familiar with the child support guidelines and how they calculate out in your situation. If you are going to argue for deviation from the guidelines, bring witnesses who can support your position.

Modifying Child Support

Once you have a child support order, it is not set in stone for all time. Either of you can seek to have it changed in the future. The best plan is to first try to talk to the other parent about what the situation is to see if you can work it out yourselves. If not, mediation is a great alternative to going back to court.

If you return to court, you must show a "change in circumstances" justifying the increase or decrease in child support. If you are the paying parent and you lose your job (quitting doesn't count), this would be a good reason to ask for a decrease. If the custodial parent remarries or moves in with someone, this is also a reason to ask for a decrease, since her household income has increased. If you are the receiving parent, reasons for an increase could include a change in the child's needs (such as diagnosis of a serious illness or disability, need for orthodontia, or private school tuition), or your own loss of income. If you learn the paying parent has gotten a raise, this is justification for an increase.

Some states automatically review each child support case every few years and adjust the terms when the circumstances warrant and to accommodate for cost of living increases. Child support can also be altered if there is a change in the custody arrangement.

The High Costs of Not Paying Child Support

Parents who don't pay child support when they are ordered to face a wide range of penalties. Failing to follow the order could result in prison time, fines, denial of your passport, seizure of your bank accounts, forced sale of your property, garnishment of your tax refunds, seizure of property, and suspension of your driver's license or professional and recreational licenses. It also impacts your credit report, which is now accessed not only by potential creditors, but also by potential landlords and employers (and can affect your ability to get a job or be accepted as a tenant). Child support is a serious obligation, which carries even more penalties for non-payment than most debts.

Because the ramifications are so severe, you must pay the ordered support, even if there is an error in the order or if the child support enforcement agency has made a mistake. Pay first, and get it straightened out later so that there can be no question about being in arrears.

Some parents are so opposed to paying child support that they are willing to have their parental rights terminated to avoid it. If you agree to terminate your rights just to get out of child support, it's possible that the judge will refuse to accept the termination, because it is always in the child's best interest to have two parents when possible. Think of how damaging it would be to a child to find out later in life that his father ended the relationship to get out of making some payments. If, however, you agree to terminate to allow an adoption by a stepparent, or because there has been severe abuse involved, child support would end.

Chapter 11

———— ✠ ————

Spousal Support

Spousal support, also called alimony or maintenance, can often be a sore point in many divorces. Many people ordered to pay alimony feel it is unfair, while those receiving it sometimes feel they don't get enough (and those who don't receive any at all feel the same way). Alimony is designed to help a spouse get back on his or her feet after a divorce. Often there is one spouse who put a career on hold, didn't pursue job opportunities or advancements, or took care of the home, which benefited the spouse paying alimony.

In many marriages there is one spouse who earns more than the other. Both spouses are accustomed to living at that financial level. A divorce can change everything. The non-moneyed spouse may have little job prospects or contacts, may need additional education to get a job, or may be unable to work at all. Leaving him or her completely in the lurch is considered to be unfair. Alimony is designed to even things out and give that non-moneyed spouse a chance to get things together after the divorce. Alimony helps her get on her feet and offers a chance to move forward with some financial support. Alimony is normally considered to be temporary—only to help the non-moneyed spouse make a transition to a self-supporting lifestyle.

Most people assume alimony is only for women, but it is available for either spouse. It is true that most often women are the recipients, which reflects the fact that women often stay home, delay their careers or education during a marriage, or earn less as a rule compared to men (according to the Bureau of Labor Statistics, women earn 80 cents on the dollar compared to what men make). Alimony for men may be on the rise though. According to the American Academy of Matrimonial Lawyers, 44 percent of all attorneys included in a recent survey said they've seen an increase in men wanting alimony

How Alimony Is Calculated

There is no set formula that is used to calculate spousal support, as there is with child support. No one is guaranteed alimony in the same way she is guaranteed child support. Alimony is something that the parties can agree to on their own, or which is decided by the judge by considering a variety of factors. The factors vary by state, but usually include:

- the age of the parties
- the parties' special needs, health, or disabilities
- who has custody of the children
- how the property is being divided
- the income and assets of the parties
- the non-moneyed spouse's employment status, abilities, skills, and need for education or training to return to the workforce
- the standard of living the parties were accustomed to in the marriage
- the role the non-moneyed spouse played in the marriage, such as staying home with children
- whether the non-moneyed spouse has been out of the workforce during the marriage
- whether child care will be necessary for the non-moneyed spouse to get a job

- the non-moneyed spouse's employment history before marriage
- the ways in which the parties supported each other or made it possible for each other to obtain education, training, degrees, promotions, and licenses
- each person's earning capacity, and whether she has purposely taken work that pays less than she could have earned elsewhere

In some states, the judge will consider the parties' behavior towards each other when deciding about alimony. A spouse who committed adultery or was abusive during the marriage can be ordered to pay more. And likewise, if the person receiving alimony did these things, his or her alimony award could be reduced. This is called punitive alimony and is controversial in some instances, because in many marriages, both people have treated each other poorly. In other cases, this type of alimony is meant to compensate a spouse for things the other person put him through in the marriage.

If you're working out alimony payments on your own, you need to consider how both of you will financially survive after the divorce. Alimony is not intended to impoverish one person, while making the other wealthy. If you are seeking alimony, look at your household budget and determine how much more you need to handle all your bills. If you will be going back to school, find out how much the tuition will be and consider what kind of income you can earn while in school. Put all of these numbers together and find out how much money you need on a monthly or weekly basis to keep your head above water after the divorce. It is unfortunate but true that many women find that divorce puts them in a difficult financial position. Alimony is your chance to get help with that.

There are some women who refuse to seek alimony out of a sense of pride—"I don't want anything from him," is a common attitude. The fact to remember is that you aren't asking for a favor; you are seeking something to which you are legally entitled. You aren't being money-grubbing or greedy to request financial compensation for choices made during the marriage. It is unfair for a divorce to leave a woman bankrupt and a man living the high life. There is nothing wrong with requesting alimony. Ultimately the judge will decide what is fair in your situation. If what you are asking is not fair, you won't get it.

If you have a prenuptial agreement, this will decide the amount of spousal support available.

Duration of Support

Many states have a rule of thumb that alimony is awarded for one third the length of the marriage. So, if you've been married 15 years, alimony would be paid for five. Each case is considered separately though and alimony payments can certainly last longer in situations where there is need. If the non-moneyed spouse is elderly or disabled, lifetime maintenance can be ordered, since someone in this situation has no possibility of returning to the workforce and assumed he would be cared for by his or her spouse.

Alimony ends when either party dies. If the person receiving alimony remarries, the payments also end. In some states, cohabitating with another person may end the payments (since presumably the household income is higher).

How Spousal Support Is Paid

Spousal support is usually paid directly from one spouse to the other on a weekly, bi-weekly, or monthly schedule. Wage garnishment (see chapter 10) is a possibility, but is most often used only in cases in which the paying spouse has violated the order and failed to make voluntary payments.

It is also possible to pay alimony in one lump sum. This can reduce conflict between the parties (since there is no ongoing contact about payments) and can provide a sense of closure that isn't possible when alimony payments continue for years. This kind of payment is common when the receiving spouse needs a lot of cash up front to buy a business, buy a home, or pay off debt. A lump sum payment can also be invested and kept as a nest egg or emergency fund.

Alimony can also be paid directly to creditors: The paying spouse could pay tuition, household bills, mortgage payments, medical bills, taxes, insurance and so on. This kind of arrangement can simplify things—the non-moneyed spouse does not have to cash an alimony check and wait for it to clear before paying the bills. It can also be incredibly complicated if the spouse who is supposed to pay fails to do so. The non-moneyed spouse won't be aware of this nonpayment until an overdue bill arrives, and damage is already done to the credit report. Sometimes agreeing to direct payment to creditors can make the paying spouse feel better about the situation. If he knows the money he is paying is going to directly to the mortgage to keep a roof over his children's heads, he may have greater incentive to make the payments.

Because alimony is usually handled between the two spouses, it is important to keep good records and receipts, so that if there is ever a question about what is due, you will have proof. Just as with child support, you can use the money you receive as alimony in any way you would like. You are not required to provide or keep any sort of proof that the money was used to maintain your household or pay bills.

Modifying Alimony

It is possible to modify alimony after it has been awarded, if there has been a change in circumstances. If the paying spouse loses his job, becomes disabled, takes on additional support (by having another child), or if the receiving spouse comes into a sizable inheritance or a higher paying job, has increased need for support and so on, a modification would be possible. State law will decide whether a modification is appropriate based on the circumstances. Your divorce decree can supercede state law about modification if it contains language that specifies when alimony can be modified. It could also include a provision stating that alimony cannot be modified at all. Note that a modification can only be made retroactively to the date you filed the papers requesting the change. So the sooner you file, the better. It is also possible to extend the length of alimony if there has been a change in circumstances (such as the receiving spouse not becoming self-supporting as soon as was anticipated).

You can include a clause in the divorce decree or settlement that alimony is to increase with the cost of living (this clause is called COLA—cost of living adjustment). This increase would be based on a clear standard, such as the Consumer Price Index. Alimony agreements or orders can also include an escalator clause, which automatically adjusts the amount due upward to coincide with the paying spouse's increase in income. For example, consider a doctor who completed medical school and training during marriage and was supported by her spouse. If this doctor is just opening a practice at the time of divorce, her income is going to be quite low compared to the points it will reach in the coming years. An escalator clause allows the alimony to increase proportionately with the income that is actually earned.

Life Insurance

It is common for the paying spouse to be required to take out a life insurance policy naming the receiving spouse as beneficiary. This ensures that even if the paying spouse passes away, the receiving spouse will still be supported financially. Disability insurance is another less frequently used option. The paying spouse can take out a disability policy and, if she becomes disabled (and unable to pay alimony), the other spouse would receive the benefits.

Health Insurance

Health insurance benefits are of huge concern to you when you are going through a divorce, particularly if you currently receive your health insurance through your spouse. There is a federal law that allows you to continue receiving these health insurance benefits after your divorce. COBRA (the Consolidated Omnibus Budget Reconciliation Act) applies to any public sector employer with at least twenty employees. The law allows you to continue your health care coverage for up to three years after the divorce (always check with the contact person at the insurance company who is administrating this though, because in some cases the three years may run from the date of separation). You are responsible for paying the insurance company directly for the full cost of the insurance. (If your spouse has his benefits paid for by his employer and receives them at no cost, this will be a big change for you. However, you will still be getting your insurance at the discounted group rate that the employer has negotiated.) The insurance company can also charge a 2 percent administrative fee for handling the transaction for you. The employer must be notified within sixty days of the divorce for the COBRA benefits to kick in.

Once the three-year COBRA period expires, you will have the option of converting the policy to an individual plan; however, the cost will go up since you will no longer receive a group rate. You can opt out of the COBRA insurance at any time, and if you get a job that offers benefits, it is likely a smart choice to do so. If you go the three-year period under COBRA and aren't sure where to get insurance after that, there are a variety of options. If you are a student, there is likely a program offered through your college or university. If you run any kind of business, you can apply for health insurance through your local chamber of commerce. If you belong to any professional organizations, contact them and ask if they offer any health insurance programs at group rates. You may also qualify for low cost income-based insurance through your state.

If your spouse's employer is not covered by COBRA, contact the human resources office to ask if there are other options for extending your coverage after a divorce. Your state may have a similar law that provides coverage.

If your spouse is in the military, you are only entitled to continue your medical benefits if you have been married over ten years, and if ten or more years of your marriage occurred during your spouse's military service. Spouses who have been married for over twenty years—twenty years of which were during service—are entitled to extended benefits. If you don't qualify, you can pay for the Continued Health Care Benefit Program (CHCBP), which offers health insurance as a bridge between military coverage and regular health insurance.

Tax and Bankruptcy Implications

Like child support, alimony is not tax deductible for the person paying and is not taxable income for the person receiving it.

Your attorney may neglect to mention the deductibility of some attorney's fees. Attorney's fees that relate to tax advice, or which have to do with the production or collection of taxable income are deductible. So, money you spend for time your attorney spends talking with you about tax matters is deductible. Money you spend for the time your attorney spends getting you alimony is also deductible. Ask your attorney to break these fees out separately so that you can easily deduct them.

Spousal support is not dischargeable in bankruptcy (meaning if you go through bankruptcy, your obligation to pay support is not erased by the bankruptcy—the obligation is not affected by bankruptcy). Spousal support you receive if you go into bankruptcy does count as income.

Chapter 12

─── ✦ ───

Emotional and Practical Implications of Divorce

While the actual legal process of divorce is enough to leave anyone drained, divorce has wide-ranging impact throughout your whole life. It is truly one of the largest life changes there is, and it touches just about every aspect of your life. There are a variety of emotions and reactions you will experience as you cope with your divorce and all of them are valid, real and "ok." You may feel at times as if you are emotionally completely out of control, but honestly, that is normal too. Having a good therapist who can help you is important, but so is simply understanding what you're going through and believing you will get through it and survive.

Dealing with Friends

When you get divorced, you may find that your friends get divided in the divorce. It is very difficult for a person to remain friends with both parties in the divorce. Not only is it uncomfortable for your friends to hear both sides of the story, but they often feel they have to choose sides.

Many people in your social circle can probably be traced back to being the wife's or husband's friends to start with. If you went to college with Dave, he and his wife may likely be "your" friends after the divorce. If your spouse met Susan at work, she and her partner may be your spouse's friends after the divorce. This isn't always the case. Your husband may have been the one to meet Susan and introduce you to her and her partner Lidia, but you may be the one who has solidly bonded with Susan or with Lidia.

In most cases, you don't sit down and actively decide which friends are yours and which will be your spouse's. It will happen naturally. You may not feel like returning calls from Jamila, since you feel slightly uncomfortable with her since the divorce. Because of this you just sort of drift apart. You might find that Shawn doesn't return your calls or acts distant when you run into him at the gym and eventually you just don't see each other. This is part of the natural evolution process.

It's likely that you will begin to form new friendships during or after the divorce. Suddenly you're a single person and you might find you enjoy hanging out with other singles. Going to a dinner party with a group of married friends may feel completely uncomfortable now. It can be hard to be the only person in the room who is there alone. If you don't enjoy it, stop going. If you have a good relationship with one or two people in the group, focus on seeing those people alone. If you don't mind going to group activities where you're the only single person, let your friends know. They might assume you will be uncomfortable and not invite you to save your feelings.

You might develop new interests and cultivate friends that share those interests. It's ok to "try out" new friends. Some may be keepers and others not. You'll have fun along the way. This is all part of the growth process that divorce forces you to go through. It may not always be easy or comfortable, but it does move you forward and help you create a new life for yourself.

Dealing with Family

Dealing with family events after a divorce can be particularly difficult because you probably always attended family events with your spouse and now suddenly you're going alone. It takes some adjustment, but you will adjust to it. Here are some tips for coping with your own family:

- If you feel like the odd man out because you're suddenly single, find ways to insulate yourself. Be the one who sits with Grandma and helps her with her walker. Or get involved with the children in the family—nieces and nephews or cousins. Play a game with them or invite them to help you set the table.
- Don't be afraid to ask for directions. If your spouse is the one who always drove to family parties, you may never have actually driven to Aunt Sally's house yourself. You're pretty sure where it is, but actually driving there yourself alone is another thing. Ask for detailed directions if you need to. Or ask your sister to come pick you up.
- Control the conversation. If you don't want cousin Tanya fawning all over you about how she's so sorry and how it must be so hard to be all alone, change the conversation to her eczema treatment or go talk to someone else. It's a family party, not a pity party.
- Understand their feelings. Your family may have liked your ex and may still have friendly feelings toward her. You can't expect your family to suddenly change the way they feel, but you can expect some loyalty.

Your ex's family is another entirely different aspect you will need to deal with. If you don't have children, you have no requirement to ever see or speak to them again, which may be great if you never liked them. However, you may have developed a close relationship with a member of your ex's family and it's ok to continue that relationship. The relative is likely to feel a little uncomfortable about it, so be clear that you totally understand that his or her first loyalty is to your ex who is still family. Tell them that you hope you can continue your friendship and that you don't see the divorce as changing the way you feel about each other.

If you have children, it is important for your kids to have a good relationship with their extended family on your ex's side. Your ex will probably be the one who arranges time with the relatives, but if she does not, you can certainly do so. You will want to establish with your children's grandparents that you want them to have a relationship with your kids and that you support them.

Make it clear that your relationship will be focused around the children—you're not stopping over to visit, you're just dropping the kids off—but that you intend to have friendly relations with them in order to make the kids feel comfortable. It's important not to say bad things about your former in-laws in front of your children. This is their family and you need to respect that. It takes a while to develop a comfortable relationship with the people who used to be your in-laws, but it can be done for the sake of your children.

Asking for What You Need

Friends and family may be clueless about how they can help you. They know you're going through a really rough time, but a lot of people are afraid to say the wrong thing or simply don't know what they can do that would help you. Speak up and tell them how they can help you. You may have a lot of conversations that end with "If there's anything I can do... . ." or "I wish I could help you somehow. . ." Jump in and tell them exactly how they can help you.

You might not know how people can help you. It's time to start thinking about yourself and what you need. Here are some ways people could provide assistance:

- Give friends a list of household items you want to buy used and ask them to check out a few yard sales in their neighborhood. You may also find that a lot of people have items around their house they are happy to donate to you.
- Ask for babysitting help if you have children.
- Enlist people to help you move.
- Invite people over to help you paint your new place.
- Put out the word that you are looking for a new (and higher-paying) job. Ask people to put their networking skills to use for you.
- Let people know when you need some fun. Sometimes you've just got to get away from it all, so suggest a night out or a fun activity.
- If you are not in the market for a date, let people know. There are lots of people who assume you're ready to immediately hook up with

someone new, when in fact you might need some time just to learn to be you. Make it clear that you're not ready so people don't engineer meetings with friends of theirs.

- Let people know what you are ready to talk about. Sometimes people assume that everything about your marriage and divorce is suddenly off-limits and they tiptoe around things and avoid even mentioning your ex. This kind of soft-shoe dance can make some recent divorcees nuts. Your marriage and divorce happened and pretending they didn't doesn't help you at all. Be clear about this.

- Work out holiday plans. The holidays can be a hard time of year, particularly the first year you are divorced or separated. Make it clear if you would like to be invited to parties and get togethers. If you have no plans, drop hints and let people know you're looking to fill up your calendar. If you would rather have some time alone, thank people for their invitations, but let them know you'll be just fine on your own.

Living Alone

If you have been married for many years, learning to live alone can be a challenge. If you married at a young age without much time on your own, it can be equally difficult to adjust to a solo household.

The first thing to do is to arrange your home to suit your own needs. Whether you are remaining in the marital residence, or moving someplace else, your home is yours alone now (unless you are a parent) and it's time to take ownership of the space. If you've always secretly hated the wallpaper in the bathroom, replace it. If you've always slept on the edge of the bed, move into the center.

This is your chance to create your dream home. Give yourself free rein to decorate and arrange it just as you would like it to be, without regard to what anyone else might think about it. If you'd rather have a library or exercise room than a dining room, go ahead and convert it. Whatever makes you happy is the way to go. If you want to make a whole room into a closet, go for it. You need to put your personal imprint on your space. Doing so will make the space very clearly yours and will help you forget someone else used to live with you. A big home project will also keep you busy and take your mind off your problems.

Household Jobs

Living alone may mean learning some skills your spouse had that you are lacking. If your wife did all the cooking, it's time to get some cookbooks and learn how to feed yourself decent meals. If your husband handled home repairs, get a toolbox and look up how to fix that leaky sink on the Internet and go to town. Living alone means learning to be independent and taking the necessary steps to care for yourself and your home.

If you don't have the necessary skills to handle some of the things you or your house needs and you've tried on your own but failed, don't give up. You might have a friend who could do a home maintenance task for you, or help you learn how to do it. You can hire someone to handle things you aren't able to or don't want to do, as long as it fits into your budget. There are people available for just about anything you can think of. You can hire a personal chef to make and freeze meals for you. You can pay someone an hourly rate to put in your storm windows.

The key to handling unfamiliar tasks is not to get overwhelmed or frustrated. Letting things go is not the answer either. You need to find a way to work these responsibilities or jobs into your new life. It takes time to adapt to getting things done on your own.

Loneliness

Another common difficulty with living alone is loneliness. You were used to having your spouse around, and even if you had a lot of disharmony, at least there was another body in the apartment, or someone to watch *Seinfeld* reruns with. The first thing to do is to learn to enjoy your own company. When you are alone you need not be lonely. There are lots of activities or things you can do when you are alone that will keep you busy and help you feel fulfilled.

Music and TV are two things that easily help fill a void in your home. Other voices make you feel less alone.

Creating a home that engages you and gives you things to do will also help you feel less alone. If you buy a bunch of plants, you will have to spend time taking care of them. If you start a collection of baseball cards, you will need to spend time organizing and categorizing them. Photographs of loved ones can also help you feel less alone.

Routines

Developing a routine will make it easier to be alone. One of the hardest things about living alone is that feeling of not knowing what to do. If you develop a daily schedule, you will always have something planned and you won't feel at a loss.

How to Think About Yourself

Another important thing you can do is to stop thinking of yourself as "alone" and instead think of it as "by myself." You are with your own self. You're a creative, bright, and interesting person—you're lucky to have your own company! Start enjoying yourself instead of wishing someone else was there to entertain you.

Bed

Some divorced people miss the physical comfort of another body in the bed. Certainly there are ways to sexually satisfy yourself, but just being alone in a bed can sometimes feel lonely. One solution is to remake your bed. Buy linens you adore, big soft pillows, and warm, fuzzy blankets. A big body pillow can help the bed feel full. If you've always wanted a canopy or a leather headboard, this is the time to add it. Make your bed a sanctuary where you feel pampered, cared for, and comfortable and it won't feel quite so empty.

Safety

Personal safety is often a concern for women who are living alone after a divorce. The first thing you can do is change the locks. Whether you are living in the marital home, or have moved to a new apartment or home, other people have keys to that home. Get the locks changed so that only you and people you specifically choose have keys. Install a security chain or deadlock so that you feel certain no one can get in.

Assess your home with a security conscious eye. Do the windows lock? Do you have outside lights? A security system may be worth the investment for some people. Trim back shrubs near your doors if they make you uncomfortable. Get to know your neighbors if you have moved someplace new—knowing the people nearby can help you feel safer. You may wish to consider having your telephone number be unlisted or list only your first initial, so that it is not obvious you are a woman living alone.

Some women take a self-defense class to learn basic techniques to protect themselves. You and a friend could try this. Learn to be observant above all else. If something doesn't feel right, get out of the location and to someplace safe immediately. Learning to have confidence in yourself is also important. You must learn to feel comfortable in your home alone, and out and about alone.

Managing on One Income

Divorce certainly has financial implications for everyone involved. If you are used to living on two incomes but are now suddenly getting by on one (even if you're receiving child or spousal support), it can be quite a change.

Budgeting

The first thing you must do is create a budget. Now, you probably had to create a budget as part of your financial affidavit for the court in your divorce. It's likely that budget was not completely accurate. Not only do some people pad these budgets to attempt to show greater need in order to get more support (or to have to pay less), but it is also simply hard to know what a realistic budget is for living alone until you've actually done it. Take a month and document every cent you spend, whether it is in cash, by check or credit card. Then write up a new budget for yourself that reflects these actual costs.

Cutting Expenses

If you find that you're living above your means, take action now to reduce your spending. Your life has changed—there are likely some expenses you can reduce to fit in with your new approach, but you have to think critically about your life and situation to notice them. You might be used to subscribing to your local newspaper because your spouse read it. Picking up that paper every morning is just part of your habit, even though you don't even read it. Unless you question what you're doing and why you are doing it, you might continue to have that paper delivered to your house each day and throw away money on the subscription. For every check you write and everything you pay for, ask yourself if you really need or want whatever it is you are paying for. If the answer is no, cut it from your budget.

You may also find that you are in a position where you have to make some tough choices. You may have new expenses to add to your budget (such as a security system, a new puppy, or a home gym) that are parts of your new life. However, in order to afford them, you'll have to cut some other costs.

Planning for the Future

You may be formulating a lot of big plans for yourself. Maybe you want to buy a house, take a trip, backpack across Europe, or start your own business. All of these ventures cost money. The best way to reach those goals is to start saving money today towards them. Your dreams will never come true if you do not create a workable plan for how to achieve them.

If you've received a chunk of money or investments as part of the divorce settlement, it can be tempting to use that money to indulge yourself. In reality, that money is your nest egg. You need to protect it and help it grow. It's definitely fine to take some of the money and do something nice for yourself with it. After all, you just endured a horrible ordeal and you deserve some pleasure. However, most of that money should be put away to help you reach your goals and also to provide you with an emergency fund. It is a good idea to talk to a financial advisor so that you can create a sound plan for how you will manage this money.

Retirement Planning

One thing you absolutely must not cut from your budget is saving for your future. It's essential, now more than ever, that you plan for your retirement. There is no one else who is going to support you. You are the one who has to plan for your own old age. A 401(k) or IRA is a good way to make sure you will have the money you need when you are older. Even if you are entitled to a portion of your ex's retirement plan, you may not be able to count on that if she is not yet vested in the plan and dies before becoming vested. It's a good idea to meet with a financial planner who can help you determine how much you need to save and the best way to do so. Something else to consider might be long-term care insurance (insurance that pays for nursing home or assisted living care). It gets more expensive as you age, so the sooner you buy it, the better.

Disability Insurance

If you don't have disability insurance, you should talk with an insurance agent who can explain what your options are. Right now, you are the only one taking care of you. If you become injured or disabled and can't work, how will you survive? Disability insurance provides a regular income for people who are unable to work due to an injury or illness and this may be the back-up plan you need to feel confident and ready to move forward with your life alone.

Increasing Your Income

If you find your current budget to be tight without a lot of wiggle room, this might be the time to think about how you can increase your income, if decreasing your expenses isn't getting you anywhere. This is a good time in your life to focus on your career and moving forward at work. You could obtain new certifications, attend seminars, learn new skills, and gain experience in new areas. Some people feel very motivated after a divorce to become successful and "show" their ex that the divorce didn't hold them back or get in their way.

This might also be the time to think about adding a part-time job or turning a hobby into a business. This could be the time in your life to take risks and try out new things. As you rearrange your home, you may find things you can get rid of—and maybe sell on eBay or at a yard sale.

Waiting through the Long Divorce Process

The divorce process is ridiculously long. From the time you make the decision that you really do want a divorce to the time you hold the decree in your hands it is most likely more than a year (and often significantly longer). That's even longer than it takes to make a baby! Getting through this long waiting period can be challenging. Once you've made the decision to divorce you're probably ready to get it over with, and yet you have to go through months of decisions, paperwork, and much baloney to finally end your marriage.

It is important to stay busy while you're waiting. Your life has to be about more than court appearances and negotiations. Find the time to do things you enjoy and that lift your spirit. You need to step away from the divorce at times and focus on other things.

It can also be helpful to have a clear picture of how the divorce is supposed to proceed. If you understand that you're waiting for discovery to be complete and a trial to be scheduled or for mediation to be scheduled and a settlement to be signed, you can see the timeline in your mind of what has to happen in order for the marriage to finally be over. If you don't understand where things are at and what has to happen next, talk with your attorney so that you can work the process out in your mind.

It can be very hard to have patience, but this is one situation in which you have no choice. You can decide that you will face one day at a time and remind yourself that soon it will all be over and you will be able to move on with your life.

Self-Esteem

No matter who initiated the divorce, it often has the effect of decreasing self-esteem. The thought that someone important to you no longer loves you or wants to be married to you can be a big blow and one that can make you question your self-worth.

This is the time in your life when you need to remind yourself of all your achievements and abilities. Hang your diplomas, awards, or certificates on your walls. Fill your home with reminders of successes you've had and things you have accomplished. Who you are is not about what your ex thinks about you. It is about the things you have done in your own life.

Although you are probably trying new things and taking risks right now, it is also important to continue to do the things you are skilled at. You need to see yourself succeeding and remind yourself that you are an amazing person.

Depression

A divorce can be very tough to cope with and there are sure to be times when you just feel down. This major life change is very stressful and you may find yourself reacting by feeling depressed. However if you find that you're having a hard time functioning (getting to work, getting out of bed, eating, etc) or have thoughts about harming yourself, it's time to seek professional help. A therapist can help you through this very dark time in your life. Almost everyone going through a divorce sees a therapist—it is simply part of the process and nothing to be ashamed about. It's also important to remember that depression is a medical condition that is caused by a chemical imbalance in the brain. Medication can be very helpful.

If you find that you're managing fine but from time to time feel down, make a list of things you can do when you're feeling that way that generally cheer you up. Simple things, such as buying fresh flowers, getting a massage, buying a nice steak to cook, or hanging out with friends can really cheer you up when you're down in the dumps. Divorce is an up and down process. Some days you feel energized and ready to move on, but others you just want to pull the covers over your head. Get through the bad days so you can experience the good days.

Anger

Divorce stinks, so being angry is a pretty reasonable reaction sometimes. Your ex likely behaves poorly at times, the court system is very slow, your lawyer is expensive, your kids may be having a hard time, and your financial situation may appear less than rosy. Yes, there is a lot to be angry about. And it is ok to express your anger, as long as you learn to channel it in the appropriate way. Getting into a way with your ex is probably not going to help your situation, and blowing up at your lawyer is unlikely to make things move more quickly. Screaming at your kids can make things worse.

Channeling your anger into something productive can be the way to go. Once you've screamed or cried into your pillow, try using your anger to help you rip out those old cabinets in the kitchen or to go for a run. Physical activity can help you work through anger and calm yourself down.

Once you've worked through the burst of anger, take a look at what is making you so angry and think about what you can do to improve the situation. There may be things you can do now or ways to plan to change your circumstances. Much anger is the result of a feeling of powerlessness. If you find a way to change your situation and regain control, you may not feel so angry.

Grief

The end of a marriage is like a death in many ways. Although you likely have very mixed feelings about your ex, it is still sad to see something as important as a marriage end. Grief professionals will tell you that there are five stages of grief: denial, anger, bargaining, depression, and acceptance. These can come in any order and repeat themselves. As you cope with the end of your marriage, it is likely you will go through many of these stages as you work to accept the divorce.

It is perfectly fine to mourn the end of your marriage even if you really don't love your spouse anymore. No matter how it turned out, you invested a lot into the marriage and most likely entered into it with hope and optimism. To see those dreams die is painful.

There is no easy way to work through grief, other than to know it is a process and it will get easier as you move through it. A part of you may always mourn the loss of your marriage, no matter how well you recover from it, simply because it was a part of you for so long. Grief requires patience and the willingness to allow yourself to feel the emotions that come with it.

Being Responsible for Yourself and Your Children

Suddenly you are the one in charge of your own life and possibly the lives of your children. While this can be freeing, it can also be a little frightening to be all alone against the world. It takes some courage to stand up and take responsibility for your own life and that of your children, but it is an essential part of healing from the divorce. You can no longer blame your ex for everything that goes wrong or for many problems. If there is going to be change, it is up to you to create it.

Working after Divorce

At some point in the divorce process, you will let your co-workers in on what is happening. You will also likely need to let your boss or supervisor know since it's likely you will need to take time off for court appearances. Some people prefer not to let co-workers know about the divorce for as long as possible so that work can truly be an oasis from your personal life. Once your co-workers know, it will be harder to keep it out of conversation and more difficult to keep your mind on your work.

Some people you work with will treat you differently once they learn of your divorce. Some single people who were previously friendly might now view you as competition for the opposite sex. Married people with whom you were close might feel they don't have as much in common with you anymore and drift apart.

If your divorce becomes very long and drawn out, you may find you don't have enough personal or vacation time to cover your court appearances. If you get to this point, you need to talk to your boss and explain. You can offer to make up the hours you will miss by coming in early, staying late or working weekends. If this is not an option, a last ditch alternative might be to ask your doctor to document that you have an illness (mental illness counts) that qualifies you to take time off under the Family and Medical Leave Act. According to this law, you can take time off from work, unpaid, and still be guaranteed your position or an equivalent position when you return.

Chapter 13

———— ✖ ————

After the Divorce

Once you've gotten through the settlement or trial process, you probably felt some relief that this very taxing divorce process had finally come to an end. There's good news and bad news at this point. The good news is your marriage is over and you're free to move on. The bad news is that moving on is not as simple as it may sound. There are still many things you need to take care of in order to completely free yourself and there are still problems that may pop up.

Finalization of the Divorce

Although you and your spouse may have reached an agreement, or the judge has made a decision, your divorce is not final until you get the formal decree. This could take a few weeks or a month, depending on how quickly paperwork is processed by your court. You are not legally divorced until you have this paper and you are not free to remarry until this point. If you are unsure when to expect it, ask your attorney or the court clerk.

Actually receiving the divorce papers in the mail may be harder than you anticipate. A lot of people feel they really have experienced all the emotions there are to feel throughout the process, but are surprised at how hard it is to get the notification that the marriage truly is over. Be patient with yourself when you get the news and don't be afraid to ask family and friends for support.

Your Right to Appeal

You always have the right to appeal a decision by the court (including temporary orders). There is usually a brief time after the decision in which you must file your intention to appeal the order, so be certain to find out how long you have if it is something you are considering. An appeal must be handled by an attorney who will prepare a brief for the appellate court in which the judge's decisions are compared with existing law. The appeal only considers whether the judge followed the law. It is not another trial or an opportunity to present more evidence. The appellate court looks only at the record of the trial or proceeding and the briefs that are submitted to the court. No one gets up and testifies. An appeal can take a long time to move through the system, so don't expect anything immediate. If you are considering an appeal, consult an attorney.

How to Deal with Your Emotions

The final end of your marriage likely brings up a lot of conflicting emotions. You may feel relieved and glad to have it over with it, but also sad or nostalgic for the good times. It can also feel quite strange to suddenly realize you are single again (if you've been married a long time, this can be quite a change). Some people have a party when their divorce is final and their friends come to offer support through this big change. Other people find they need to take time to contemplate the change and set goals for themselves in this new era of their lives.

One thing that is not advisable (though it may be tempting) is destroying your marriage certificate. You may need this as proof at some point (it can be used for a name change and could be necessary for other purposes). Stash it in a safe place where you never have to look at it again, but do keep it. Along the same lines, some people feel like they want to destroy their wedding photos or toss their wedding rings. If you have children, keep them. They will enjoy these memories even if you can't (after all, it is part of their history).

The important point to remember is that nothing you feel at this time is wrong. Everything you experience is a valid emotion or reaction to the very big change you are going through. You may find that in the years after the divorce you rediscover or reinvent yourself. It takes time to make these changes, and you probably will find you have a lot to learn and understand about yourself.

Helping Your Children Adjust

Children often have a hard time adjusting to the news that their parents are separating and planning to divorce. By the time the divorce is final, you may think they have come to terms with the situation. However, the finalization of the divorce is likely to be hard for your children, just as it is for you. Many children harbor hopes that their parents will get back together. The finalization of the divorce can dash those hopes, or at least help the child realize how unlikely they are. What might have seemed like a kind of weird and new experience to them has now become a way of life. It may be hard to accept that what was temporary is now permanent and will be for the coming years.

You can help your children through this time of dawning acceptance by being willing to listen and answer their questions. It can be hard to focus on parenting when you yourself are going through a time of upheaval, but you will find a way to be there for them.

If you move on and choose to date, this can also be difficult for your children to handle. Dating someone else again makes it clear that the parents are not going to reunite. It's common for kids to feel resentment or anger towards the dates. You are an adult and are allowed to make decisions for your own life; however, you are also a parent and must think about how your choices impact your children. You might consider dating, but not bringing your new interests around to meet your kids unless they are fairly serious. If you are introducing your child to a date, don't expect an automatic bond. You can insist on respect and politeness, but not love. The best thing to do is to allow your child and your new love interest to gradually get to know each other in relaxed and non-forced ways.

Putting Yourself Back Together Financially

Divorce often has devastating financial repercussions. Even though your divorce is final, you are likely still dealing with the financial impact of the divorce. You may have unpaid attorney fees to deal with. You are learning to live on a new budget. You are also coping with the financial responsibilities the divorce has placed on you such as child support, responsibility for debts, property settlement payments, and alimony. Here are some important financial actions to take after your divorce:

- Sit down once the dust has cleared and create a new household budget for yourself which will take into account alimony and child support (whether you are paying or receiving it), your current income, your current expenses, and the responsibilities the court has placed on you. It's essential to have an honest idea of what your expenses truly are right now. If your lifestyle has changed and suddenly you're going out with friends a lot or playing golf more frequently, for example, your budget needs to reflect that. If your budget is just not workable in your current circumstances, then you will need to consider options such as moving to someplace less expensive, getting a better job or a second job, or cutting back on expenses.
- As discussed in chapter 12, develop a savings plan for yourself. You should also begin thinking about retirement planning. If is it just going to be you (and you do not remarry or repartner), you need to start thinking about how to provide for yourself in the future.
- Obtain copies of your credit reports from all three credit-reporting agencies (www.annualcreditreport.com). You will want to check that the information on there is correct, and request changes for

information that is not (it make take a few months for the transfers and changes relating to the divorce to show up).

Completing Paperwork to Comply with Court Orders

There is a lot of paperwork you will likely need to work through to implement what the court has ordered. Here is a quick summary:

- If there is an order of custody, you will probably need to make some changes to your child's school record, to reflect the new situation. This includes indicating who has custody and who has permission to pick the child up. You may also want to ask the school to send out duplicate report cards and notices to both parents.
- If child support has been ordered, it needs to begin immediately. If payment is being made through the state child enforcement agency, you both will need to make contact with this agency and complete necessary paperwork to ensure payment.
- If life insurance is a requirement of either child support or alimony, the policy needs to be purchased and the beneficiary verified by the other party. If one parent will be handling the health insurance for the children, this needs to be implemented. If one parent is now the person responsible for paying for unpaid medical bills, this information needs to be shared with the health care providers involved, so that billing can be set up.
- You will need to make changes to your financial situation based on how the court has distributed property and debt. This may mean transferring funds, refinancing debt, paying off debt, and transferring deeds and titles.

Paperwork Changes to Protect Yourself

In addition to court-ordered paperwork, there are a lot of steps you should take to protect yourself once your divorce is final, if you have not already done so.

- Make sure your spouse's name is removed from everything that has anything to do with you. Close or freeze all joint accounts and credit cards if you have not already done so. Take your spouse's name off the auto insurance on the vehicle that is yours. Change your life insurance beneficiary if you are not required to list your spouse. Change your medical records so that your spouse no longer has access to them. You likely signed a form saying he could access them without permission.
- If you and your spouse shared a lease for anything (such as an apartment or even a storage space) and you are the person who will retain possession, you need to have the lease changed to reflect the change. Leaving your spouse's name on a lease will give her the right to enter the property without your permission. If you are the person moving out, make sure your name is removed from the lease so that you no longer have any financial responsibility for the lease.
- Change your W-4 (tax withholding) for your pay at work. Before, you might have taken more exemptions because your household was bigger. Reevaluate what kind of exemptions fit your new situation. If your paycheck is automatically deposited, be sure it is going to an account that is yours and yours alone now.
- If you will be receiving health insurance through COBRA (see chapter 11 for more information about this), you need to get in touch with your spouse's human resources department to determine what paperwork you need to complete. You will need to be sure your spouse submits the necessary information to them as well.

Gathering Documents

Now that you and your spouse are going through the final separation of items and sorting things out, there are some documents that you should be sure you obtain and keep. These include:

- your birth certificate or baptismal certificate
- your passport

- your car registration
- insurance papers for your home, life, or car
- your health insurance card
- your social security card
- your medical records
- financial records for any accounts that have become yours
- copies of all joint tax returns for the last seven years (in case there is an audit or if you need to provide proof of income in order to qualify for a loan).

Once you receive your judgment of divorce, you should keep a copy of it in a safe place.

If you are the residential parent, you will want to be sure you have the following documents for your child:

- birth certificate
- immunization records
- Social Security card
- passport
- medical records
- bank statements from the child's account

Name Change, Revisited

If you have chosen to revert to your pre-marital name (see chapter 5 for information about this), you will need to notify everyone who needs to know you are doing so. You may be required to provide a copy of your divorce decree for some institutions. Make sure you notify or change:

- All banks and credit unions
- All credit card companies (including store credit cards)
- Store discount and membership programs
- Investment and retirement fund companies

- Auto insurance
- Titles to vehicles
- Deeds
- Mortgages
- Vehicle registrations
- Driver's license
- Children's schools
- Club or gym memberships
- Health insurance (make sure you get a new card)
- Dental insurance (make sure you get a new card)
- Disability insurance
- Health care providers (yours and your child's)
- Library card
- Passport
- Newspaper and magazine subscriptions
- Utility companies
- Union
- Veterinarian
- Dry cleaner
- Employer
- Frequent flyer programs
- Voter registration
- Student loans
- Personal loans
- Internet service provider
- Property tax registration
- Flexible spending accounts

In addition to the above list, you also must notify the Social Security Administration (SSA) about your name change. Failure to do so can delay your tax refund. To change your name, you need to show the SSA your divorce decree and one other form of identification that has your married name and your photo (your driver's license will work). For more information, visit the Social

Security Administration web site at http://www.ssa.gov/pubs/10120.html. You can make the change by mail or in person (if you do it by mail, you have to mail your ID and hope it is returned to you).

You also need to change your passport. How you go about this depends on how old your passport is. If it is less than a year old, there is no fee and you will need to show your divorce decree. If the passport is older than a year, then you will be charged a fee and will need to show your decree and other identification. For more information, visit the State Department Web site at http://travel.state.gov/passport/get/correcting/correcting_2654.html

If you have moved as a result of the divorce, you will want to include address changes along with name changes. You change your address with the US Postal Service online at https://moversguide.usps.com/ or at your local post office.

Taxes

It is a good idea to talk with your tax planner about your newly divorced status. Now that you are divorced, you will be filing your own taxes. If your spouse has always been in charge of this responsibility for your household, you will need to learn what kinds of information you need to save and how to organize it. It is also a very good idea to talk with your tax preparer about how head of household filing status (see chapter 10 for more information about this) will affect your tax responsibilities. You may want to consider taking some steps, such as contributing to an IRA, which may decrease your tax burden.

Rewriting Important Documents

Now that you are divorced, you likely will want to change your will so that you can remove your spouse as an heir. You can simply destroy your existing will and have a new one written to reflect your current wishes. You are welcome to leave your will intact with your spouse listed, but most people want to make this change. If you have children, you will want to name a guardian, should your spouse not be alive to care for them.

If you have a health care directive (also sometimes called a living will or health care power of attorney), you will need to change this document as well if you had listed your spouse as the person who could make medical decisions for you. You can simply destroy all existing copies to make this change. You are welcome to keep the current document listing your spouse if you wish to keep it in place. If you do not have a health care directive, this is a good time to get one.

You may have executed a power of attorney in the past, giving your spouse the right to make financial and business decisions on your behalf. Destroy all existing copies (this may mean getting them back from banks or other financial institutions). You may wish to have a new one completed naming someone else.

Obtaining a Religious Annulment

If you would like to obtain a religious annulment from your church, you don't have to wait for your divorce to be final. Start by talking with your local clergy about how the process works and what steps you will need to take.

Enforcing Child Support

If you are the parent who is receiving child support, there may come a time when you find that support is not being paid on time and you need to take action to get what is legally yours. Here are some steps you can take:

- If payment is being made through your state child support enforcement agency, they will handle enforcement procedures.
- If payment is being made through wage garnishment, you can return to court to enforce penalties for failure to make the payments. If payment is not being made through garnishment and is supposed to be paid directly to you, wage garnishment is a simple way to get it enforced. You will need to return to court and get an order permitting the garnishment. You can get a garnishment put in place for the

current amount of child support as well as the arrearages that are owed. Wage garnishment can be enforced in any state, so moving away will not affect the ability to collect.

- If you are trying to collect child support from a parent who does not have a regular job or is paid in cash, it can be more difficult to get your money; however, your state child support enforcement agency can be very strident in its demands, which include telephone calls, revocation of state licenses, withholding of tax returns (up to $500 for arrears), liens against property, and so on. If the delinquent parent receives payments from the government (such as payments to private vendors and federal retirement payments), these payments can also be garnished to pay for overdue support. (Note that Social Security, railroad retirement, federal student loans, and other programs are not subject to garnishment.) The case is eligible for what is called an Administrative Offset when the non-custodial parent owes at least $25 in past due support and is at least thirty days delinquent in his or her child support payments.

- If your spouse is withholding child support, you cannot withhold visitation in retaliation. Refusing to comply with a visitation order can be considered custodial interference and is grounds for a change in custody. It may not seem fair that your spouse can skip payments, yet still have the privilege of visitation, but it is important to keep in mind that visitation is set up to benefit the child. Your child should not be punished because your ex does not make payments.

- Go to court and obtain a judgment against your ex for the unpaid funds. Then seek to have his wages garnished to pay the judgment.

Enforcing Alimony and Property Division

Enforcing alimony and property division is more difficult than child support. While we have created a nationwide network of agencies that cooperate with each and share information when it comes to child support, those who are trying to enforce alimony or property division orders are mostly on their own. There is a federal law in place, called the Revised Uniform Reciprocal Enforcement Support Act (RURESA), which allows an ex-spouse to use the court in his or her own state to enforce an alimony order against an ex living in another state. In practical terms however, these cases are not given a high priority.

If your spouse is behind on alimony or is refusing to follow the court's orders about how property must be divided, your only recourse is to go back to court and seek to have the court order enforced. Often it takes several court appearances before the judge's order has any bite to it. You need to obtain a judgment for the unpaid amount and then can seek to have wages garnished to pay off the judgment. You may get some help from the district attorney's office in trying to collect unpaid alimony, but for the most part you have to rely on yourself.

Enforcing Other Orders

There may be other court orders that your ex is not complying with—such as an order to take out life insurance, to sign over a deed, to hand over property, to follow an order of protection and so on. If an order is not being filed, you have to go back to court to have the court enforce it.

Making Changes to the Parenting Plan

Your parenting plan is something that should change over the years. As your children grow older, their interests and schedules will change. While it might make sense for a four year old to have visitation three nights a week, this kind of schedule most likely will not work for a school-age child. Be prepared to make changes to the plan over the coming years.

If possible, have a conference with the other parent once or twice a year to review how things are working. If you can work together to make the changes, everyone will be happier. Creating the schedule yourselves will mean you can create one that is personalized for your family and directly meets your child's needs. If you go back to court to have the plan modified, you likely will not get one with as much attention to detail.

You may experience a situation where you and your ex have different opinions about the parenting plan and simply cannot agree. Situations change. Your ex might have lived farther away and now has moved close and wants more time. You could encounter a situation where you ex has developed an alcohol or substance abuse problem and you are concerned about your child's safety and well-being with him. Living arrangements change also—your ex might have remarried and a volatile relationship could have developed between your child and the new spouse. There are many different permutations of things that can go wrong and require you to go back to court.

If you do return to court, you'll be facing another custody trial. The standard for a return to court is usually a "change in circumstances." Almost every family faces a change in circumstances every few years, so this test is usually easy to meet. Both of you will present evidence and witnesses, as well as your point of view to the court. A Law Guardian or Guardian ad litem will be appointed to represent your child. The judge will make a decision based on what is in the best interest of the children.

There are some families that treat the courthouse as if it were a revolving door. They come in and out and can be regularly seen there every couple of years. Avoiding this kind of behavior is best for your children. Every time you return to court, your child faces uncertainty about his or her living arrangements. This can be disturbing and disruptive. Working out your problems on your own is the best choice whenever possible.

Some people constantly return to court because they're just never happy with their current situation. The fact of the matter is that you are divorced and must share your child's time. The situation can never be what is your ideal. Instead, you need to learn to live with the schedule you have and celebrate the time that you do have available.

Moving Past Your Divorce

Up to this point, you have probably found that a lot of your attention has been focused on the divorce. Divorce is an all-consuming process, as well as one that is emotionally draining. You were right to focus a lot of your energy on the divorce. You had very important decisions and problems that needed to be dealt with. Now that your divorce is over, it is hard to completely let go of that. You may be so used to being in conflict with your ex that it is simply second nature.

It's time to let go of the conflict. The divorce is over and you need to move on with your life. You cannot and should not spend any more of your energy on your ex. You can't change what has happened, but you can control what lies ahead. It's ok to find that you are still working through some of the things that happened, or adjusting to the changes the divorce has brought. However, it can no longer be the focus of your life. You've got to find other ways to fill your time and thoughts.

Planning for Your Future

The divorce has created a very visible shift in your life. You will likely often see your life as split in two parts—life before the divorce and life after. The divorce has given you a chance to create a new future for yourself. There are so many things that are possible for you now. You could go back to school, get a new job, move, take up a new hobby, start exercising, begin saving money for a big trip, meet someone new, find new friends, and basically reinvent yourself.

Try to see the divorce as an opportunity to discover new things and try new adventures. You have a lot of options in front of you, and only you can decide what will work best for you in the coming years and decades. Take some time now to write a list of all the things you want to do before you die. You may not ever get to everything on the list, but at least it gives you a place to start and incentive to dream. If you set goals, you can create plans for how you will achieve them.

Appendix A

Resources

More Books by Brette Sember

15 Ways to Improve Your Co-Parenting

The Divorce Organizer and Planner

How to Get Custody of Your Dog

How to WIN Your Custody Case

The No-Fight Divorce Book

Parenting Together Apart for the Residential Parent

Parenting Together Apart for the Non-Residential Parent

The Key to Your Custody Case: Win Over the Law Guardian or Guardian ad litem

Rebuild Your Financial Life After Divorce: Advice about Credit, Taxes, Mortgages, Retirement, Alimony, Child Support, and More Save Money On Your Divorce: Real Ways to Reduce The Costs

Web Sites and Organizations

Accountants

American Institute of Certified Public Accountants
www.aicpa.org

Alimony

Front-loaded alimony
www.divorceinfo.com/excessalimony.htm

State spousal support laws
family.findlaw.com/divorce/divorce-alimony/state-alimony-info
.html

Annulment

Catholic Annulment
www.americancatholic.org/Newsletters/CU/ac1002.asp

Jewish Annulment
www.beliefnet.com/story/75/story_7563_1.html

Attorneys

American Academy of Matrimonial Lawyers
www.aaml.org 312-263-6477

American Bar Association, Section of Family Law
www.abanet.org/family/home.html 312-988-5145

Sample Attorney Retainer Agreements:
www.michbar.org/pmrc/articles/0000086.doc
www.tedbondjrpc.com/pdf/fl_c.pdf
www.unbundledlaw.org/retainer_agreements/sample_retainer.htm

State Bar Association Finder
www.abanet.org/barserv/stlobar.html

Child Support
Federal Office of Child Support Enforcement
www.acf.dhhs.gov/programs/cse

Federal Parent Locator Service
www.acf.hhs.gov/programs/cse/newhire/index.html

Handbook on Child Support Enforcement
www.acf.hhs.gov/programs/cse/pubs/2005/handbook_on_cse.pdf

National Child Support Enforcement Agency
www.ncsea.org

State Child Support Calculators
www.alllaw.com/calculators/ChildSupport

State Child Enforcement Agencies
www.acf.hhs.gov/programs/cse/extinf.html

Wage Garnishment Law
www.dol.gov/esa/regs/compliance/whd/whdfs30.htm

Children and Parenting
Banana Splits
212-262-4562

Children's Rights Council
www.gocrc.org
301-559-3120

Choosing a child therapist
kidshealth.org/parent/emotions/feelings/finding_therapist.html

Parents without Partners
www.parentswithoutpartners.org
561-391-8833

Sample Visitation Plans
www.familymediationcouncil.com/publicreading.htm

Collaborative Law
International Academy of Collaborative Professionals
www.collaborativepractice.com
415-897-2398

Courts
Association of Family and Conciliation Courts
www.afccnet.org
608-664-3750

Credit
Free annual credit report
www.annualcreditreport.com

Domestic Violence
Justice for Children
www.jfcadvocacy.org

National Domestic Violence Hotline
  1-800-799-SAFE (7233)

Planning to leave
  www.ndvh.org/help/planning.html

Health Insurance
COBRA Coverage
  www.dol.gov/ebsa/faqs/faq_consumer_cobra.html

Military Continued Health Care Benefit Program
  www.humana-military.com/chcbp/main.htm

Laws
State laws
  www.findlaw.com

Uniform Child Custody Jurisdiction and Enforcement Act (UCCJEA)
  www.law.upenn.edu/bll/archives/ulc/fnact99/1990s/uccjea97.htm

Marriage Therapy
American Association for Marriage and Family Therapy
  www.aamft.org
  703-838-9808

American Counseling Association
  www.counseling.org
  800-347-6647

American Psychoanalytic Association
www.apsa.org

American Psychological Association
www.apahelpcenter.org
800-374-2721

American Psychiatric Association
www.healthyminds.org

Choosing a therapist
http://psychcentral.com/therapist.htm

National Association of Social Workers
www.naswdc.org

Mediation
American Bar Association, Section of Dispute Resolution
www.abanet.org/dispute
202-662-1680

Association for Conflict Resolution
www.acrnet.org
202-464-9700

Association of Attorney-Mediators
www.attorney-mediators.org
800-280-1368

Association of Independent Mediators
219-288-5100

Mediate.com
   www.mediate.com

Model Standards of Practice for Family and Divorce Mediation
   www.afccnet.org/docs/resources_model_mediation.htm

Military
Military Divorce Guide
   www.military-divorce-guide.com/former-spouse-benefits.htm

Health Insurance for Children: Defense Enrollment Eligibility Reporting
System (DEERS)
   www.tricare.osd.mil/deers/general.cfm

Name and Address Changes
Passport
   travel.state.gov/passport/get/correcting/correcting_2654.html

Post Office
   moversguide.usps.com

Social Security
   www.ssa.gov/pubs/10120.html

Separation
Sample Separation Agreement
   family.findlaw.com/divorce/divorce-forms/le22_3_1.html

Single Parenting
National Organization of Single Mothers
www.singlemothers.org

Parents without Partners
www.parentswithoutpartners.org

Responsible Single Fathers
www.singlefather.org

Single Parents Association
www.singleparents.org

Supervised Visitation
Supervised Visitation Network
www.svnetwork.net

Taxes
IRS
www.irs.gov
800-829-3676
(IRS publication #504 Divorced and Separated Individuals)

Valuation
Boat Valuation
www.buc.com/index.cfm

Business Valuation
www.bvresources.com

Home valuation
www.zillow.com

Vehicle Valuation
www.kbb.com/

State Bar Associations
Alabama
415 Dexter Avenue
Montgomery, Alabama 36104
(334) 269-1515
www.alabar.org

Alaska
PO Box 100279
Anchorage, AK 99510-0279
907-272-7469
www.alaskabar.org

Arizona
4201 N. 24th Street, Suite 200
Phoenix, AZ 85016-6288
602-252-4804
www.azbar.org

Arkansas
2224 Cottondale Lane
Little Rock, AR 72202
501-375-4606
www.arkbar.com

California
180 Howard Street
San Francisco, CA 94105
415-538-2000
www.calbar.ca.gov

Colorado
1900 Grand Street, Suite 900
Denver, CO 80203
303-860-1115
www.cobar.org

Connecticut
30 Bank Street
PO Box 350
New Britain, CT 06050-0350
(860) 223-4400
www.ctbar.org

Delaware
301 North Market Street
Wilmington, DE 19801
(302) 658-5279
www.dsba.org

District of Columbia
1250 H Street NW, sixth floor
Washington DC 20005-5937
202-737-4700
www.dcbar.org

Florida
> 651 E. Jefferson Street
> Tallahassee, FL 32399-2300
> (850) 561-5600
> www.floridabar.org

Georgia
> 104 Marietta St. NW, Suite 100
> Atlanta, Georgia 30303
> (404) 527-8700
> www.gabar.org

Hawaii
> 1132 Bishop Street, Suite 906
> Honolulu, HI 96813
> Phone (808) 537-1868
> www.hsba.org

Idaho
> P. O. Box 895
> Boise, Idaho 83701
> (208) 334-4500
> www2.state.id.us/isb/index.htm

Illinois
> 424 S. Second Street
> Springfield, IL 62701
> (217) 525-1760
> http://www.illinoisbar.org/

Indiana
> One Indiana Square
> Suite 530

Indianapolis, IN 46204
(317) 639-5465
http://www.inbar.org/

Iowa
521 East Locust
Des Moines, IA 50309-1939
(515) 243-3179
www.iowabar.org

Kansas
1200 SW Harrison
Topeka, KS 66612
785-234-5696
www.ksbar.org

Kentucky
514 W. Main Street
Frankfort KY 40601-1812
(502) 564-3795
www.kybar.org

Louisiana
601 St Charles Street
New Orleans, LA 70130
800-421-5722
www.lsba.org

Maine
PO Box 788
Augusta, ME 04332-0788
207-622-7523
www.mainebar.org

Maryland
> 520 W. Fayette St
> Baltimore, MD 21201
> 410-685-7878
> www.msba.org

Massachusetts
> 20 West St.
> Boston, MA 02111-1204
> 617-338-0500
> www.massbar.org

Michigan
> Michael Franck Building
> 306 Townsend Street
> Lansing, Michigan 48933-2012
> 517-346-6300
> www.michbar.org

Minnesota
> Niccollet Mall #380
> Minneapolis, MN 55402
> 800-882-6722
> www.mnbar.org

Mississippi
> Post Office Box 2168
> Jackson, Mississippi 39225-2168
> 601-948-4471
> www.msbar.org

Missouri
  PO Box 119
  Jefferson City, MO 65102
  573-635-4128
  www.mobar.org

Montana
  7 W. 6th Ave., Ste. 2B
  P.O. Box 577
  Helena MT 59624
  406-442-7660
  www.montanabar.org

Nebraska
  635 S.14th Street
  P.O. Box 81809
  Lincoln, NE 68501
  402-475-7091
  www.nebar.com

Nevada
  600 E. Charleston Blvd
  Las Vegas, NV 89104
  702-382-2200
  www.nvbar.org

New Hampshire
  2 Pillsbury Street, Suite 300,
  Concord NH 03301
  603-224-6942
  www.nhbar.org

New Jersey
    One Constitution Square
    New Brunswick, NJ 08901-1520
    732-249-5000
    www.njsba.com

New York
    1 Elk Street
    Albany, NY 12207
    518-463-3200
    www.nysba.org

North Carolina
    PO Box 3688
    Cary, NC 27519-3688
    800-662-7407
    www.ncbar.org

North Dakota
    504 N. Washington St
    Bismarck, ND 58501
    800-472-2685
    www.sband.org

Ohio
    1700 Lake Shore Drive
    Columbus OH, 43204
    800-282-6556
    www.ohiobar.org

Oklahoma
    P.O. Box 53036, 1901 N. Lincoln Blvd.,
    Oklahoma City, OK 73152-3036

405-416-7000
www.okbar.org

Oregon
5200 SW Meadows Road
Lake Oswego, OR 97035-0889
503-620-0222 or Inside Oregon: 800-452-8260
www.osbar.org

Pennsylvania
100 South Street
Harrisburg, PA 17101
800-932-0311
www.pabar.org

Rhode Island
115 Cedar Street
Providence, RI 02903
401-421-5740
www.ribar.com

South Carolina
950 Taylor Street
Columbia, SC 29202
803-799-6653
www.scbar.org

South Dakota
222 East Capitol Avenue
Pierre, SD 57501
605-224-7554
www.sdbar.org

Tennessee
    221 Fourth Avenue North, Suite 400
    Nashville, TN 37219-2198
    615-383-7421
    www.tba.org

Texas
    1414 Colorado St.
    Austin, TX 78701
    800-204-2222
    www.texasbar.com

Utah
    645 South 200
    East Salt Lake City, UT 84111
    801-531-9077
    www.utahbar.org

Vermont
    PO Box 100
    Montpelier, VT 05601-0100
    802.223.2020
    www.vtbar.org

Virginia
    707 East Main Street, Suite 1500
    Richmond, Virginia 23219-2800
    804-775-0500
    www.vsb.org

Washington
    1325 Fourth Ave., Ste. 600
    Seattle, WA 98101-2539
    800-945-9722

West Virginia
2006 Kanawha Boulevard, East
Charleston, WV 25311-2204
304-558-2456
www.wvbar.org

Wisconsin
5302 Eastpark Blvd.
Madison, WI 53718-2101
800-728-7788
www.wisbar.org

Wyoming
500 Randall Ave
PO Box 109
Cheyenne WY 82003
307-632-9061
www.wyomingbar.org

State Court Web Sites

Alabama
www.judicial.state.al.us

Alaska
www.state.ak.us/courts/home.htm

Arizona
www.supreme.state.az.us

Arkansas
courts.state.ar.us/index.cfm

California
www.courtinfo.ca.gov/index.htm

Colorado
www.courts.state.co.us/index.htm

Connecticut
www.jud.state.ct.us

Delaware
courts.delaware.gov

District of Columbia
www.dccourts.gov/dccourts/index.jsp

Florida
www.flcourts.org

Georgia
www.georgiacourts.org

Hawaii
www.courts.state.hi.us

Idaho
www.isc.idaho.gov

Illinois
www.state.il.us/court

Indiana
www.in.gov/judiciary

Iowa
   www.judicial.state.ia.us

Kansas
   www.kscourts.org

Kentucky
   courts.ky.gov

Louisiana
   www.lasc.org/judicial_admin/default.asp

Maine
   www.courts.state.me.us/index.html

Maryland
   www.courts.state.md.us/index.html

Massachusetts
   www.mass.gov/courts/index.html

Michigan
   courts.michigan.gov/index.htm

Minnesota
   www.mncourts.gov

Mississippi
   www.mssc.state.ms.us/StateJudiciary/default.asp

Missouri
   www.courts.mo.gov/

Montana
  courts.mt.gov/cao

Nebraska
  www.supremecourt.ne.gov

Nevada
  www.nvsupremecourt.us/aoc

New Hampshire
  www.courts.state.nh.us

New Jersey
  www.judiciary.state.nj.us

New Mexico
  www.nmcourts.com

New York
  www.courts.state.ny.us

North Carolina
  www.nccourts.org

North Dakota
  www.ndcourts.com/court/news/annualreport2001/administrator.htm

Ohio
  www.sconet.state.oh.us/default_highres.asp

Oklahoma
  www.oscn.net/oscn/schome/adminoffice.htm

Oregon
www.ojd.state.or.us

Pennsylvania
www.courts.state.pa.us

Rhode Island
www.courts.state.ri.us

South Carolina
www.judicial.state.sc.us

South Dakota
www.sdjudicial.com

Tennessee
www.tsc.state.tn.us

Texas
www.courts.state.tx.us/oca

Utah
www.utcourts.gov

Vermont
www.vermontjudiciary.org

Virginia
www.courts.state.va.us

Washington
www.courts.state.va.us

West Virginia
www.state.wv.us/wvsca/AO.htm

Wisconsin
www.wicourts.gov

Wyoming
www.courts.state.wy.us

State and Local Mediation Associations
Alabama
Alabama Center for Dispute Resolution
PO Box 671
Montgomery, AL 36101
334-269-0409
alabamaadr.org

Alaska
Alaska Dispute Settlement Association
P.O. Box 242922
Anchorage, AK 99524-2922
907-258-0624
www.adsa.ws

Arkansas
Arkansas Conflict Resolution Association
2024 Arkansas Valley Drive, Suite 305
Little Rock, AR 72212
501-224-0099

Arkansas Alternative Dispute Resolution Commission
625 Marshall Street
Justice Building
Little Rock, AR 72201-1020
501-682-9400
courts.state.ar.us/courts/adr.html

Arizona
Arizona State Alternative Dispute Resolution
www.superiorcourt.maricopa.gov/adr/Index.asp

Arizona Dispute Resolution Association (ADRA)
PO Box 7638
Phoenix, AZ 85011-7638
602-379-2372
www.azdra.org

California
Association for Conflict Resolution, Northern California
601 Van Ness Ave.
San Francisco, CA 94102-6300
650-745-3842
www.adrnc.org

California Association of Legal Mediators
PO Box 161321
Sacramento, CA 95816-1321
916-444-2295

California Bar Association, Family Law Section, ADR South Committee
1925 Century Park East, Suite 2000
Los Angeles, CA 90067
310-277-2236

California, Orange County Court Mediation
www.occourts.org/juvenile/mediation.asp

California Courts Self-Help Services Center
www.courtinfo.ca.gov/selfhelp/family/custody/programs.htm

California Dispute Resolution Council (CDRC)
PO Box 55020
Los Angeles, CA 90055
213-896-6540
www.cdrc.net

Northern California Mediation Association
Box 544
Corte Madera, CA 94976-0544
415-927-4308
www.mediators-ncma.org

Southern California Mediation Association
1405 Warner Avenue
Tustin, CA 92780
877-9MEDIAT
www.scmediation.org

Colorado
Colorado Council of Mediators
3100 South Sheridan Blvd
Denver, CO 80227
800-864-4317
www.coloradomediation.org

Connecticut
Connecticut Council for Divorce Mediation
888-236-CCDM
www.ctmediators.org/

Delaware
Delaware Federation for Dispute Resolution, Inc. (DFDR)
P.O. Box 358
Wilmington, DE 19899-0358
www.dfdr.org

Florida
Association of Broward County Mediators
224 SE 9th Street
Fort Lauderdale, FL 33316
954-524-8546
www.abcm.org

Florida Academy of Professional Mediators
800-808-8494
www.tfapm.org

Georgia
Family Mediation Association of Georgia
PO Box 2641
Decatur, GA 30031
404-373-4457
www.fmag.org

Georgia Commission on ADR
404-463-3788
www.ganet.org/gadr/

Georgia Council for Dispute Resolution
    3350 Cumberland Circle, Suite LL75
    Atlanta, GA 30339
    800-866-0160

Hawaii
Hawaii ADR
    www.courts.state.hi.us/page_server/Services/AlternativeDispute/4E3D89
    6DFE782019EB28F79FE3.html

Idaho
Idaho Mediation Association
    PO Box 2504
    Boise, ID 83701
    208-389-9211

Illinois
Mediation Association of Southern Illinois
    PO Box 1833,
    Marion, IL 62959
    618-453-3257
    www.mediatenow.org

The Mediation Council of Illinois
    3540 N. Southport #453
    Chicago, IL 60657
    312-641-3000
    www.mediationcouncilofillinois.org

Indiana
Indiana Association of Mediators
    6100 North Keystone
    Indianapolis, IN 46220

800-571-0260
www.mediation-indiana.org

Iowa
Iowa Association for Dispute Resolution (IADR)
   PO Box 3193
   Iowa City, Iowa 52244-3193
   319-358-6690
   www.friendlywork.com/iadr

Kansas
Heartland Mediators Association
   8826 Santa Fe Drive, Suite 208
   Overland Park, KS 66212
   913-381-4458
   www.idir.net/~mediaiton

Kentucky
Mediation Association of Kentucky
   PO Box 1641, Frankfort, KY 40602-1641
   Phone: (502) 875-5633
   www.kymediation.org

Louisiana
Family Mediation Council of Louisiana
   888-658-9080
   www.familymediationcoucil.com

Maine
Maine Association of Dispute Resolution Professionals (MADRP)
   PO Box 158
   Freeport, ME 04032
   207-865-9588
   www.madrp.org

Maine state ADR program
www.courts.state.me.us/courtservices/adr/index.html

Maryland
Maryland Society of Professional Family Mediators
211 Massbury Street
Gaithersburg, MD 20878
301-947-0500
www.familymediator.com/society.html

Maryland Mediation and Conflict Resolution Office
900 Commerce Road
Annapolis, MD 21401
410-841-2260
www.courts.state.md.us/macro/index.html

Massachusetts
Massachusetts Association of Mediation
Practitioners and Programs
10133 Federal Street, 11th Fl
Boston, MA 02110
617-451-2093

The Massachusetts Council on Family Mediation
23 Parker Road
Needham Heights, MA 02494
781-449-4430
www.divorcenet.com/ma-mediators.html

Massachusetts Office of Dispute Resolution
617-727-2224
www.mass.gov/modr/

New England Association for Conflict Resolution
1 Broadway, Suite 600
Cambridge, MA 02142
617-536-3227
www.neacr.org

Michigan
Michigan Council for Family and Divorce Mediation
489 Berrypatch Lane
White Lake, MI 48386
800-827-4390
www.familymediation.com

Minnesota
Minnesota Association of Custody Resolution Specialists
PO Box 1042
Willmar, MN 56201
320-732-4500

Minnesota Association for Conflict Resolution
www.mnacr.org/

Minnesota Association of Mediators
PO Box 11308
Minneapolis, MN 55411
612-879-4343
www.minnesotamediation.org

Montana
Montana Mediation Association
P.O. Box 6363
Great Falls, MT 59406

Phone: 406-727-8365
www.mtmediation.org

Nebraska
Mediation Association Network
8552 Cass Street
Omaha, NE 68114
402-397-0330

Nebraska Office of Dispute Resolution
521 S. 14th St., Suite 200
Lincoln, NE 68509
(402) 471-3148
court.nol.org/odr

Nevada
Mediators of Southern Nevada, Inc.
333 N. Rancho Drive, #144
Las Vegas, NV 89106
702-631-2790
www.mediatorsonv.com

New Hampshire
New Hampshire ADR
www.courts.state.nh.us/adrp/index.htm

New Hampshire Mediators Association
PO Box 7228
Concord, NH 03301-7228
800-783-9883
www.nhcra.org

New Jersey
New Jersey Association of Professional Mediators
203 Towne Center Drive
Hillsborough, NJ 08844-4693
800-981-4800
www.njapm.org

New Jersey Courts ADR program
www.judiciary.state.nj.us/services/medprogm.htm

New Mexico
New Mexico Center for Dispute Resolution
800 Park Avenue SW
Albuquerque, NM 87120
800-249-6884
www.nmcdr.org

New Mexico Mediation Association
PO Box 82384
Albuquerque, NM 87198
505-266-6560
www.city-pages.com/ergo/mediate.nmma.html

New York

Association for Conflict Resolution, Greater New York Chapter
250 West 57th Street, Suite 817
New York, NY 10107
212-946-1998
www.acrgny.org

Family and Divorce Mediation Council of Greater New York
114 West 47th Street, Suite 2200

New York, New York 10036
212-978-8590
www.DivorceMediationNY.org

Mediation Council of Central New York Family Mediation Center
7000 Genesee Street, Bldg. B
Fayetteville, NY 13066
315-446-5513

N.Y. State Council on Divorce Mediation
585 Stewart Avenue, Ste 610;
Garden City, NY 11530
800-894-2646
www.nysmediate.org

New York State Dispute Resolution Association, Inc.
182-A Washington Avenue
Albany, NY 12210
518-465-2500
www.nysdra.org

Rochester Association of Family Mediators
P.O. Box 10872
Rochester, NY 14610
585-234-2392
www.rafm.net

North Carolina
Mediation Network of North Carolina
4208 Six Forks Road
Raleigh, NC 27609
919-783-8483
www.mnnc.org

North Carolina Association of Professional Family Mediators
189 College Street
Asheville, NC 28801
704-251-6089
familymediators.org/index.html

North Carolina Dispute Resolution Commission
P.O. Box 2448
Raleigh, NC 2760
919-981-5077
www.nccourts.org/Courts/CRS/Councils/DRC/Default.asp

North Dakota
North Dakota ADR
www.court.state.nd.us/Court/ADR/

Ohio
Mediation Association of Northwest Ohio
331 Waet Clinton Street
Napoleon, OH 43535
419-592-9289
www.mediateohio.org

Ohio ADR Program
www.sconet.state.oh.us/dispute_resolution/

Oregon
Oregon Mediation Association
PO Box 2952
Portland, OR 97208
503-872-9775
www.mediate.com/oma

Oklahoma
Oklahoma Academy of Mediators and Arbitrators
   119 N. Robinson, Suite 1100
   Oklahoma City, OK 73102
   405-366-6100
   www.oama.org

Pennsylvania
Family Mediation Association of the Delaware Valley (FMADV)
   PO Box 15934
   Philadelphia, PA 19103
   215-545-4227

Pennsylvania Council of Mediators
   www.pamediation.org

Rhode Island
Newport County Association of Mediators
   580 Thames Street, Suite 207
   Newport, RI 02840-6741
   888-873-6226

Rhode Island Judiciary Mediation
   www.courts.state.ri.us/family/mediation.htm

South Carolina
Low Country Mediation Network
   PO Box 1404
   Charleston, SC 29402
   803-727-6613

South Carolina ADR Program
   www.scbar.org/member/adr/default.asp

Tennessee

Mediation Association of Tennessee, Inc.
118 29th Avenue, S.
PO Box 121541
Nashville, TN 37212
615-646-9363

Tennessee ADR Program
www.tsc.state.tn.us/geninfo/programs/adr/adrdir.asp

Tennessee Mediators Network
807 W. First North St
Morristown, TN 37814
www.tnmediators.com/

Texas

Austin Association of Mediators
1409 West 6th St.
Austin TX 78703
512-476-7226
www.austinmediators.org

College of Texas Mediators
1821 Stonegate
Denton, TX 76205
972-221-9333

Family Mediation Network of Greater Houston
Memorial City Plaza
800 Gessner, Suite 252
Houston, TX 77024-4256
Phone: 713-465-2347

Texas Association of Mediators
  PO Box 191208
  Dallas, TX 75219-1208
  713-629-1416
  www.txmediator.org

Texas State Bar ADR Section
  www.texasadr.org

Utah
Utah Association of Family Mediators
  6914 S. 3000 East, #205
  Salt Lake City, UT 84121
  801-944-5400

Vermont
Vermont Court Mediation
  www.vermontjudiciary.org/Mediation/default.htm

Vermont Mediators Association
  PO Box 1108
  Montpelier, VT 05601
  vma.freeyellow.com

Virginia
Central Virginia Mediation Network
  PO Box 814
  Richmond, VA 23218
  804-763-2788
  www.cvco.org/civic/organ/cvmednet/

Virginia Mediation Network
  2108 W. Laburnum Ave., STE 220
  Richmond, Virginia 23227

804-254-2666
www.vamediation.org

Virginia ADR Program
www.courts.state.va.us/drs/main.htm

Washington
Mediation Consortium of Washington State
1122 East Pike Street #1095
Seattle, WA 98122
206-833-3803

Washington State Dispute Resolution
Washington State Bar Association
2101 Fourth Ave., Fourth Floor
Seattle, WA 98121-2330
www.adr-wa.com

West Virginia
West Virginia ADR Program
www.state.wv.us/wvsca/familyct/cover.htm

West Virginia Center for Dispute Resolution
P.O. Box 828
Morgantown, WV 26507
304-296-2124
www.wvcdr.org

West Virginia Parent Education and Mediation Project
205 East King Street
Martinsburg, WV 25401
304-267-0038

Wisconsin

Wisconsin Association of Mediators
PO Box 44578
Madison, WI 53744-4578
608-848-1970
www.wamediators.org

State Collaborative Law Associations

Collaborative Practice California:
www.cpcal.org

Collaborative Law Institute of Michigan:
www.collaborativelawmichigan.com

Collaborative Law Institute of Minnesota:
www.collaborativelaw.org

Texas Collaborative Law Council:
www.collaborativelaw.us

Collaborative Family Law Council of Wisconsin:
www.collabdivorce.com

Appendix B

Sample Forms

In this appendix you will find the following sample divorce forms:

- Sample Separation Agreement
- Sample Summons
- Sample Affidavit of Service
- Sample Response or Answer
- Sample Request for Trial
- Sample Simplified Divorce Settlement
- Sample Judgment of Divorce
- Sample Agreement to Mediate

DO NOT use these forms. Each state has its own specific forms. These are included so that you can become familiar with what the forms may look like and the questions they ask. It is very important that you use only the forms designated by your specific state.

Sample Separation Agreement

Commonwealth of Massachusetts
The Trial Court
Probate and Family Court Department

Worcester Division, ss.

Docket No. _____

SEPARATION AGREEMENT
(APPLICABLE TO ALL DIVORCES)

_____
Party A

v.

_____
Party B

AGREEMENT made between _____
(Name of Party A)

of _____
(Street Address)   (City/Town, State, Zip)

(referred to as the Party A), and _____
(Name of Party B)

of . _____
(Street Address)   (City/Town, State, Zip)

(referred to as Party B)

The parties were married in: _____
(City/Town, State, Zip)

on_/___/____and last lived together at_____
(Date of Marriage)   (Street Address)

_____on_____   /____/____
(City/Town)   (State)   (Zip)

when an irretrievable breakdown of the marriage occurred.

Page 1 of 19

249

CHILDREN

o   No children were born of this marriage or were legally adopted by both parties.

o   The following children born of this marriage, or by legal adoption of both parties, are not yet emancipated because they are under the age of eighteen years OR are between the ages of 18 and 23 years and are dependent on the parties for support:

CHILD'S NAME   DATE OF BIRTH

_____   _____

_____   _____

_____   _____

_____   _____

D   The following children born of this marriage are over the age of eighteen years AND are emancipated, as he/she/they are no longer dependent on the parties for support.

CHILD'S NAME   DATE OF BIRTH

_____   _____

_____   _____

_____   _____

_____   _____

This Separation Agreement is made inorder to settle and determine:

a)   the property and support rights of Party A and Party B; and

b)   the care, custody, support, maintenance and education of the minor and/or dependent child(ren) of this marriage *(attach Schedule A)*; and

c)   all other rights and obligations arising from the marital relationship.

Inconsideration of the mutual promises contained in this Separation Agreement, Party A and Party B agree to the terms contained in this Agreement.

Page 2 of 19

PROPERTY DIVISION AND DEBTS

A. **Real Estate:**

    D   Neither party holds any interest in real estate.

    D   The parties have already divided their interest in the marital home located at:

    _____

                    (Street Address, Town, State, Zip Code)

    D   The parties agree to have the real estate appraised and listed for sale by ____/____/____. The expenses shall be paid by_____ and the proceeds from the sale shall be divided as follows: _____

    D   Said property is to be sold under the terms and conditions of a short sale. Both parties shall cooperate with all interested parties regarding the listing of the property and sale.

    D   Said property shall be refinanced by Party A/Party B on or before____/__/_____. In the event that Party A/Party B is unable to refinance, then the parties shall:

    _____

    D   Party A/Party B shall remain in the home until____/____/____., at which time:

    _____

B. **Personal Property** (including motor vehicle, excluding bank accounts): The parties hereby agree that:

    D   There has been a full and satisfactory division of all other personal property and each party shall hold full right, title and interest in all items of personal property now in their respective possession.

    D   The parties have personal property in the possession of the other or a third party. Retrieval of any and all personal property in the possession of the other, or any third party, shall be obtained by____/____/ at 5:00 P.M., unless otherwise agreed upon, in writing, by both parties to this agreement. Both parties hereby waive all rights, title and ownership, if any personal property is not claimed by said date and time.

Page 3 of 19

251

    D   **Party A** shall have full right, title and interest in the following items:

_____
_____
_____
_____
_____

    o   **Party B** shall have full right, title and interest in the following items:

_____
_____
_____
_____
_____

C.   **Pension / Retirement Benefits:**

    D   The parties have no retirement or pension benefits to be divided.

    D   Party A/Party B shall transfer _____ (amount or percentage), adjusted for gains or losses as of the date of transfer, of the _____ account (name of financial institution and last ___ digits of account #) to Party A/Party B on _____ (date) by a Qualified Domestic Relations Order. The parties shall cooperate with one another to prepare any and all necessary documents for this transfer. The parties shall equally share the cost of preparation and all other expenses associated with this transfer. Party A/Party B or third-party ▼_____
                           name
shall be responsible for the preparation of said Qualified Domestic Relations Order.

    D   Party A and Party B shall each keep their respective retirement accounts as listed in their financial statements dated _____

    D   The retirement or pension benefits of the parties shall be divided as follows:

_____
_____
_____
_____
_____
_____

D. **Stock /Bonds** (list values, shares, division)

- o   The parties have no interest in stocks or bonds.
- o   The stocks and bonds of the parties shall be divided as follows:

_____

_____

_____

_____

E. **Bank Accounts:**

The parties hereby agree that:

- o   **Party A** shall have full right, title and interest in the bank accounts and assets *(excluding retirement accounts)* in his/her name and listed on his/her financial statement dated_____/_____/_____or as follows:

_____

_____

- o   **Party B** shall have full right, title and interest in the bank accounts and assets *(excluding retirement accounts)* in his/her name and listed on his/her financial statement dated_____/_____/_____or as follows:

_____

_____

- D   The parties have no joint bank accounts.

F. **Debt:**

- o   **Party A** will be responsible for his individual debts and liabilities as listed on his financial statement dated_____/_____/ _____
- o   **Party B** will be responsible for her individual debts and liabilities as listed on her financial statement dated_____/_____/ _____
- o   The marital debts of the parties shall be paid as follows (creditor, amount owed, division):

_____

_____

_____

_____

Page 5 of 19

o   Each party hereby waives past and present alimony from the other. Both parties reserve the right to future alimony.

o   Each party hereby waives past, present, and future alimony from the other.

D   **Party A - Party B** shall pay to **Party A - Party B** the sum of $_____each and every week, beginning   /   /   ,as alimony.

Payments of alimony shall end:

D   on   /   /   (date)

D   when the following event(s) occur(s):

_____

_____

_____

_____

_____

HEALTH INSURANCE FOR PARTIES

Party A's health insurance coverage will be provided:

D   by **Party A**

o   by **Party B** for so long as it is available to him/her, and if there is any additional cost to continued coverage for the insurance:

     D   The additional out of pocket cost shall be paid by **Party A / Party B.** Payment of the additional cost shall be made on or before _____

     OR

     o   Party A shall have the option of choosing to provide his/her own health insurance coverage and shall notify **Party B in** writing if he/she elects to do so.

Party B's health insurance coverage will be provided:

D   by **Party B**

o   by **Party A** for so long as it is available to him/her, and if there is any additional cost to continued coverage for the insurance:

     o   The additional out of pocket cost shall be paid by **Party A / Party B.** Payment of the additional cost shall be made on or before_____."

     OR

     o   Party B shall have the option of choosing to provide his/her own health insurance coverage and shall notify **Party A** in writing if he/she elects to do so.

Page 6 of 19

UNINSURED MEDICAL EXPENSES FOR EACH PARTY

The cost of all reasonable uninsured and unreimbursed medical, dental, hospital, optical, prescription medication and therapeutic counseling services shall be paid:

D   By each party for himself/herself.

D   Party A shall pay to Party **B**_____% of said expenses or $_____for Party B.

D   Party B shall pay to Party A_____% of said expenses or $_____for Party A.

Copies of all invoices or bills shall be provided to the paying party within _____ days receipt. All payments to be made directly to the other party within _____ days of receipt of the bill(s).

LIFE INSURANCE

o   **Party** A shall maintain life insurance in the face amount of $_____ nammg_____as the beneficiary, and shall be required to keep the life insurance in effect until_____

o   **Party B** shall maintain life insurance in the face amount of $_____ nammg_____as the beneficiary, and shall be required to keep the life insurance in effect until_____

o   Neither party shall be required to maintain life insurance for the benefit of the other.

OTHER PROVISIONS

_____
_____
_____
_____
_____
_____

RESUMING FORMER NAME

D   As requested in the Complaint for Divorce, ——————————seeks to resume his/her former name, _____

GOVERNING LAW

This Separation Agreement shall be construed and governed according to the laws of the Commonwealth of Massachusetts.

FULL DISCLOSURE OF ASSETS AND LIABILITIES

Party A and Party B hereby represent that they have each made full disclosure to the other party of their individual assets. Each party repreents that Party A / Party B has provided the other with a current financial statement on the form promulgated pursuant to *Supplemental Probate Court Rules, Rule 401,* which discloses fully and completely all of Party A / Party B's income, expenses, assets and liabilities. By executing this Separation Agreement, the parties represent that the terms and provisions of this agreement are fair, just and reasonable and are not the product of fraud, coercion or undue influence, and that each signs this agreement freely and voluntarily.

SUBMISSION OF AGREEMENT TO COURT

Party A and Party B each agree that this Separation Agreement shall be submitted to the Worcester Division of the Probate & Family Court for a Judge's approval of the terms and entry of a Judgment of Divorce.

The parties further agree that the terms and provisions of this Separation Agreement shall be: *(Choose from the following)*

☐ incorporated and merged into the Judgment of Divorce Nisi of the Court.

☐ incorporated, but not merged, into the Judgment of Divorce Nisi, and shall remain as an independent contract between the parties.

☐ incorporated, but not merged, into the Court's Judgment, and shall survive and remain as an independent contract, except for the terms and provisions relating to the care, custody, support and education of the minor child(ren) (attach Schedule A) which terms nd provisions shall merge in said Judgment.

☐ incorporated, but not merged, into the Court's Judgment, and shall survive and remain as an independent contract, except for the terms and provisions relating to alimony and medical insurance (strike inapplicable term) which terms and provisions shall merge in said Judgment.

EXECUTION

Signed on_____

      (Date)

                             _____

                             Party A's Signature

                             _____

                             Party A's PRINT NAME

Signed on_____

      (Date)

                             _____

                             Party B's Signature

                             _____

                             Party B PRINT NAME

****

Commonwealth of Massachusetts

Worcester Division, ss.   Date: _____

Then personally appeared the above-named _____

                               (Name)

and acknowledged that HE / SHE signed the foregoing as HIS / HER free act and deed.

                             _____

                             Notary Public - My Commission

                             *Expires:*_____

****

Commonwealth of Massachusetts

Worcester Division, ss.   Date: _____

Then personally appeared the above-named _____

                               (Name)

and acknowledged that HE / SHE signed the foregoing as HIS / HER free act and deed.

                             _____

                             Notary Public - My Commission

                             Expires: _____

SCHEDULE A - CHILD RELATED MATTERS

LEGAL CUSTODY (which parent(s) make(s) major decisions for the child(ren) for health care, religion, education, etc.).

- o   The **Parties** shall have shared legal custody of the minor child(ren). The parties agree they are able to communicate and make joint decisions regarding their child(ren).

- o   **Party A** shall have sole legal custody of the minor child(ren).

- D   **Party B** shall have sole legal custody of the minor child(ren).

PHYSICAL CUSTODY (primary residence of the children and which parent makes the day-to-day decisions regarding the child(ren).

- D   **Party A** shall have sole physical custody of the minor child(ren).

- D   **Party B** shall have sole physical custody of the minor child(ren).

- o   The **Parties** shall have shared physical custody of the minor child(ren) in accordance with the PARENTING SCHEDULE specified below.*

- D   The **Parties** shall have split physical custody as follows:

- o   **Party B** will have physical custody of _____

       AND

- o   **Party A** will have physical custody of _____

- D   _____ shall have physical custody of

       (Name of Third Party)

_____

_____

*PARENTING SCHEDULE

The parties may agree to parenting time other than set forth below. However, in the event they cannot agree, the terms of this order/judgment shall apply.

Party A's parenting time with the children shall be as follows:

- D   Alternating weekends from _____ at _____ to _____ at _____

- D   The first weekend for Party A shall begin on _____ and shall be alternating thereafter.

D   When there is a Monday holiday, the weekend shall be extended until Monday at
_____

D   Other provisions (to include weekday parenting time)

_____

_____

_____

_____

_____

_____

_____

_____

Party B's parenting time with the child(ren) shall be as follows:

D   Alternating weekends from_____at_____A.M./P.M. to_____
_____ at _____M./P.M..

D   The first weekend for Party B shall begin on_____and shall be
alternating thereafter.

D   When there is a Monday holiday, the weekend shall be extended until Monday at
_____A.M./P.M.

D   Other provisions (to include weekday parenting time)

_____

_____

_____

_____

_____

The holiday and vacation schedule shall supercede the regular parenting schedule.

A week of summer or school vacation shall be seven days, to include a parent's regularly
scheduled weekend with the child(ren).

D   School vacations shall be shared as follows:

    D   At such time as the child(ren) are of school age, _____ shall have **February** school vacation in **odd** years. _____ shall have the **even** years.

    D   At such time as the child(ren) are of school age, _____ shall have **April** school vacation in **odd** years. _____ shall have the **even** years.

    D   _____

_____

_____

D   Summer vacation shall be as follows:

    D   _____ shall have first option for _____ weeks in the summer in **odd** years.

    D   _____ shall have first option for _____ weeks in the summer in **even** years.

The parties shall mutually agree/commit to summer vacation in writing by May 1 each year.

    D   Summer vacation weeks shall be taken consecutively, as follows:

_____

_____

    O   Summer vacation weeks shall be taken non-consecutively.

_____

_____

D   The child(ren)'s birthday shall be as follows:

_____

_____

D   The parties' birthdays shall be shared as follows:

_____

_____

_____

Page 12 of 19

260

D   Holidays to be as follows:

D   _____shall have Thanksgiving in odd years from_____

at_____A.M./P.M. to_____at_____A.M./P.M.

_____shall have Thanksgiving in even years from

_____at_____A.M./P.M. to_____at

_____A.M./P.M..

D   Other Holidays._____

_____

_____

_____

D   _____shall have Mother's Day from_____A.M./P.M. to_____
A.M./P.M..

D   _____shall have Father's Day from_____A.M./P.M. to_____
A.M./P.M..

D   The parties shall share the December Holiday(s)/vacation as follows:

_____

_____

_____

D   In even years, _____shall have December 24th from _____ to December
25th at_____, and _____shall have December 25th from___
to December 26th at_____. This schedule shall be reversed in odd years.

D   _____shall have Easter in odd years from _____ to
(Party A/Party B)
_____

D   ——————— shall have Easter in **even** years from _____ to

     (Party A/Party B)

     ———————

D   Any changes to the above parenting plan/vacation/holiday schedule may be mutually arranged between the parties upon_____advance notice.

D   The parties shall meet to exchange of the child(ren) at:

     _____

     _____

     _____

D   _____ shall transport the children at the beginning of the above parenting time.

D   _____ shall transport the children at the end of the above parenting time.

D   Additional provisions:_____

     _____

     _____

     _____

D   Neither party shall permanently relocate with the child(ren) from the Commonwealth of Massachusetts without written permission of the other or further order of the Court.

CHILD SUPPORT

D   Starting —"7'-_____7-_____, **Party A / Party B** shall pay child support as

     follows: The sum of $_____ each and every **week - two weeks - month,**

         (Amount)   *(Circle One)*

      D   Child support shall be payable directly to **Party A / Party B;**   **OR**

      D   Child support shall be payable by **Party A / Party B** through the **Department of Revenue (DOR)** *by wage assignment;*   **OR**

      D   Child support shall be payable by **Party A / Party B** through the **Department of Revenue (DOR),** *wage assignment being suspended.*

Page 14 of 19

D   Neither party shall pay child support to the other party for the following reasons:

_____

_____

_____

_____

D   The parties acknowledge that the child support order which would result from the application of the Child Support Guidelines is: per week.

o   The agreed amount of support is different than Guidelines amount because

_____

_____

_____

Child Support for a child(ren) over the age of eighteen who is/are principally domiciled with one parent and dependent upon the parents for support:

     o   Shall continue at the above amount until

     D   Shall continue at the above amount until emancipation, per Massachusetts General Law.

     D   Shall increase to $ ____ and terminate on ___

     D   Shall decrease to ____ and terminate on ___

     o   Shall be determined by the court at the hearing on a Compliant for Modification.

MEDICAL INSURANCE FOR CHILD(REN)

D   The Party A / Party B *(Circle One)* shall be responsible for providing health insurance for the minor child(ren):

     o   Through Party A's / Party B's employment OR

     o   By obtaining and maintaining a private health insurance policy OR

     D   Through current coverage under Mass Health. Either party shall obtain private health insurance, if and when it becomes available at a reasonable cost.

DENTAL

D   The **Party A / Party B** *(Circle One)* shall be responsible for providing **dental insurance** for the minor child(ren):

      o   Through **Party A's / Party B's** employment; **OR**

      D   By obtaining and maintaining a private health insurance policy; **OR**

      D   Through current coverage under Mass Health. Either party shall obtain private health insurance, if and when it becomes available at a reasonable cost.

UNINSURED MEDICAL AND DENTAL EXPENSES

The cost of all reasonable uninsured and unreimbursed medical, dental, hospital, orthodontic, optical, prescription medication and therapeutic counseling services for the minor child(ren) shall be as follows: *(Choose ONE of the following).*

      D   The first $250.00 per calendar year shall be paid by the custodial parent, who is, **Party A / Party B**, with the remainder to be paid equally by the parties.

      o   Shared and paid equally by the parties.

      D   Paid as follows: _____% by Party A _____% by **Party B.**

D   All uninsured medical, dental and pharmaceutical bills shall be presented by either _____ within _____ days of receipt of same. Each party shall reimburse his/her share of these costs to the other within _____ days from the date when these bills are received from the other parent.

Disputes regarding unpaid bills shall be filed in the Probate Court within one year of the date of treatment or collection shall be deemed waived.

Neither parent shall contract for orthodontic treatment for which the other is responsible without prior written approval from the other parent or further order of the Court.

LIFE INSURANCE

      D   **Party A** shall maintain life insurance in the face amount of: $_____, naming_____as the beneficiary, and shall be required to keep the life insurance in effect until _____.

      D   **Party B** shall maintain life insurance in the face amount of: $_____, naming _____ as the beneficiary, and shall be required to keep the life insurance in effect until _____.

      D   **Neither Party** shall be required to maintain life insurance for the benefit of the child(ren).

TAX DEPENDANTS

D   **Party B** shall claim the following child(ren) as her dependant(s) for state and federal income tax purposes:_____

_____

o   **Party A** shall claim the following child(ren) as his dependant(s) for state and federal income tax purposes:_____

_____

D   The   **Party A / Party B**   shall claim the child(ren) for **odd** years.·

D   The   **Party A / Party B**   shall claim the child(ren) for **even** years.

D   The **Parties** shall alternate years in claiming the children as dependants for state and federal income tax purposes as follows: ———————————————————

_____

_____

_____

_____

The parties shall cooperate with one another and the custodial parent shall sign all tax forms necessary to accomplish the tax provisions set forth herein.

EXHIBIT F EDUCATION

Party A and Party B agree that each child should receive the best education available in light of his or her aptitudes and interests, including education at the college level.

Party A and Party B, as he or she is financially able to do so, shall pay the cost of each child's educational expenses at such college, university or other educational institution a child(ren) may attend with the approval of the parties, which approval will not be unreasonably withheld.

As used in this exhibit, the term "educational expenses" shall include expenses in connection with applying to college, including, but not limited to application fees, testing fees, as well as tuition, board, room, books, usual and customary student activity fees and other, expenses normally charged on bursar's bills, as well as reasonable transportation costs and other costs agreed to by the Parties.

Party A and Party B agree that they will cooperate fully in seeking financial assistance for college expenses, including scholarships, grants, student loans and the like, which may be available in order to assist the parties in discharging this undertaking.

Party A and Party B agree that the choice of educational institutions for a child shall be made after joint consultation with due regard for the financial circumstances of each party, and the aptitudes, interests and desires of the child. Neither party shall make any commitment to any educational institution on behalf of the child without first notifying and obtaining the other party's written approval, which approval shall not be unreasonably withheld.

Neither parent shall commit to post secondary education expenses for which the other shall be responsible without prior written approval of the other or further order of the court.

EDUCATION (additional provisions):

_____
_____
_____
_____
_____
_____
_____

INCORPORATION of this SCHEDULE A into the SEPARATION AGREEMENT

The parties sign and date this Schedule A in the same manner as their Separation Agreement, to which it is attached, and the parties agree that the provisions of this Schedule A shall be considered to be fully incorporated into the Separation Agreement and incorporated and merged into any Judgment of Divorce that may be entered by the Worcester Division of the Probate and Family Court.

<u>EXECUTION</u>

Signed on_____

(Date)

_____

Party A 'sSignature

_____

Party A's PRINT NAME

Signed on_____

(Date)

_____

Party B's Signature

_____

Party B's PRINT NAME

****

Commonwealth of Massachusetts

Worcester Division, ss.

Date: _____

Then personally appeared the above-named_____

(Name)

and acknowledged that HE / SHE signed the foregoing as HIS / HER free act and

deed.

_____ ,Notary Public

My Commission Expires:_____

Commonwealth of Massachusetts

Worcester Division, ss.

Date: _____

Then personally appeared the above-named_____

(Name)

and acknowledged that HE / SHE signed the foregoing as HIS / HER free act and

deed.

_____ ,Notary Public

My Commission Expires:_____

Page 19 of 19

267

Sample Summons

SUPREME COURT OF THE STATE OF NEW YORK
COUNTY OF _____
--X

Index No.:_____
Date Summons filed:_____
Plaintiff designates _____
County as the place of trial
The basis of venue is:

_____

Plaintiff,

-against-

SUMMONS WITH NOTICE
Plaintiff/Defendant resides at:

_____
_____
_____

Defendant.
--X

ACTION FOR A DIVORCE

To the above named Defendant:

   YOU ARE HEREBY SUMMONED to serve a notice of appearance on the ❏ *Plaintiff* OR ❏ *Plaintiff's Attorney(s)* within twenty (20) days after the service of this summons, exclusive of the day of service (or within thirty (30) days after the service is complete if this summons is not personally delivered to you within the State of New York) and in case of your failure to appear, judgment will be taken against you by default for the relief demanded in the notice set forth below.

Dated _____

❏ *Plaintiff*
❏ *Attorney(s) for Plaintiff*
Phone No.:
Address:

NOTICE: The nature of this action is to dissolve the marriage between the parties, on the grounds **DRL §170 subd.____ - _____

The relief sought is a judgment of absolute divorce in favor of the Plaintiff dissolving the marriage between the parties to this action.
The nature of any ancillary or additional relief requested (see p.14 of Instructions) is:
_____

❏ Additional page describing ancillary relief requested is attached;
❏ Marital property to be distributed pursuant to separation agreement/stipulation;
❏ I waive distribution of Marital property;
For divorces commenced on or after 1/25/16 only:❏ *I am not seeking maintenance as payee as described in the Notice of Guideline Maintenance (the "Notice") other than what was already agreed to in a written agreement/stipulation* ; OR ❏ *I seek maintenance as payee, as described in the Notice*
❏ **NONE** - I am not requesting any ancillary relief;
AND any other relief the court deems fit and proper

**Read pp. 3-5 of Instructions and insert the grounds for the divorce:

DRL §170(1) - cruel and inhuman treatment	DRL §170(4) - adultery
DRL §170(2) - abandonment	DRL §170(5) - living apart one year after separation decree or judgment of separation
DRL §170(3) - confinement in prison	DRL §170(6) - living apart one year after execution of a separation agreement
	DRL §170(7) - irretrievable breakdown in relationship

(UD-1 Rev. 1/25/16)

Sample Affidavit of Service

AFFIDAVIT OF SERVICE

State of New York   }
County of _____ }

The undersigned being duly sworn, deposes and says:

_____ is not a party to the action, is over
(name of person serving papers)

18 years of age and resides at _____

_____
(complete address of person serving papers)

That on _____, deponent served the within
(date of service)

_____
(name of document[s] served)

upon _____ located at
(name of person/corporation served)

_____
(complete address where other party/corporation served)

(Select method of service)

_____ Personal Service: by delivering a true copy of the aforesaid documents personally;
deponent knew said person/corporation so served to be the person/corporation described.

_____ Service by Mail: by depositing a true copy of the aforesaid documents in a postpaid
properly addressed envelope in a post office or official depository under the exclusive care
and custody of the United States Postal Service.

_____
Signature of person serving papers

_____
Printed Name

Sworn to before me this _____

day of _____

_____
Notary Public

Sample Response or Answer

IN THE CIRCUIT COURT OF THE_____JUDICIAL CIRCUIT,
IN AND FOR_____COUNTY, FLORIDA

Case No.:_____
Division:_____

In re: the Marriage of:

_____
Husband,

and

_____
Wife.

ANSWER, WAIVER, AND REQUEST FOR COPY OF FINAL JUDGMENT OF DISSOLUTION OF MARRIAGE

I, {full legal name} _____, being sworn, certify that the following information is true:

1. I answer the Petition for Dissolution of Marriage filed in this action and admit all the allegations. By admitting all of the allegations in the petition, I agree to all relief requested in the petition including any requests regarding parenting and time-sharing, child support, alimony, distribution of marital assets and liabilities, and temporary relief.

2. I hereby waive notice of hearing as well as all future notices in connection with the Petition for Dissolution of Marriage, as filed and also waive my appearance at the final hearing.

3. I request that a copy of the Final Judgment of Dissolution of Marriage entered in this case be provided to me at the address below.

4. If this case involves minor child(ren), a completed Uniform Child Custody Jurisdiction and Enforcement Act (UCCJEA) Affidavit, Florida Supreme Court Approved Family Law Form 12.902(d), is filed with this answer.

5. A completed Notice of Social Security Number, Florida Supreme Court Approved Family Law Form 12.902(j), is filed with this answer.

6. A completed Family Law Financial Affidavit, Florida Family Law Rules of Procedure Form 12.902(b) or (c), _____ is filed with this answer or _____ will be timely filed.

Florida Supreme Court Approved Family Law Form 12.903(a), Answer, Waiver, and Request for Copy of Final Judgment of Dissolution of Marriage (11/15)

I certify that a copy of this document was ( ) mailed ( ) faxed and mailed ( ) e-mailed ( ) hand delivered to the person(s) listed below on {date} _____.

Other party or his/her attorney:
Name: _____
Address: _____
City, State, Zip: _____
Fax Number: _____
Designated E-mail Address(es): _____
_____

I understand that I am swearing or affirming under oath to the truthfulness of the claims made in this answer and that the punishment for knowingly making a false statement includes fines and/or imprisonment.

Dated: _____   _____
                                Signature Of ( ) HUSBAND ( ) WIFE

                                Printed Name: _____
                                Address: _____
                                City, State, Zip: _____
                                Telephone Number: _____
                                Fax Number: _____
                                Designated E-mail Address(es): _____
                                _____

STATE OF FLORIDA
COUNTY OF _____

Sworn to or affirmed and signed before me on _____ by _____.

                                _____
                                NOTARY PUBLIC or DEPUTY CLERK

                                _____
                                {Print, type, or stamp commissioned name of notary or deputy clerk.}

_____ Personally known
_____ Produced identification
       Type of identification produced _____

Florida Supreme Court Approved Family Law Form 12.903(a), Answer, Waiver, and Request for Copy of Final Judgment of Dissolution of Marriage (11/15)

IF A NONLAWYER HELPED YOU FILL OUT THIS FORM, HE/SHE MUST FILL IN THE BLANKS BELOW:
[fill in all blanks] This form was prepared for the: {*choose only one*} (   ) Husband (   ) Wife
This form was completed with the assistance of:
{name of individual} _____,
{name of business} _____,
{address} _____,
{city} _____,{state} _____,{zip code}_____,{telephone number} _____

SAMPLE FORM ONLY

Florida Supreme Court Approved Family Law Form 12.903(a), Answer, Waiver, and Request for Copy of
Final Judgment of Dissolution of Marriage (11/15)

Sample Request for Trial

Form 13

Commonwealth of Massachusetts

THE TRIAL COURT
THE PROBATE AND FAMILY COURT DEPARTMENT
_____ Division   Docket No. _____

REQUEST FOR TRIAL — PRE-TRIAL ASSIGNMENT

THIS FORM SHOULD **NOT** BE USED FOR MARK-UP OF TEMPORARY ORDERS AND MOTIONS
PLEASE PRINT OR TYPE

Please assign
for hearing: _____

                                              Plaintiff

                            v.

                   _____

                                              Defendant

TYPE OF CASE _____ TIME REQUIRED _____ HEARING AT _____

( ) Uncontested   The following papers must be on file before

( ) Contested   cases can be assigned for hearing:

    ( ) Merits   ( ) Summons or Return of Service

    ( ) Custody   ( ) Marriage Certificate

    ( ) Support   ( ) Statistical Form R408

    ( ) Visitation   ( ) Financial Statement (Supp. Rule 401)

    ( ) 208, § 34   ( ) Affidavits of Both Parties (1A Divorces)

    ( ) Other_____   ( ) Notarized Agreement (1A Divorces)

                                   ( )_____

Has Discovery Been Completed   ( ) Yes ( ) No

Has This Case Been Pre-Tried   ( ) Yes ( ) No

I hereby certify that, in my opinion, this case is ready for trial.

Requested by: Opposing Counsel:

_____   Name   _____

_____   Address and _____

_____   Phone No. _____

FOR REGISTER'S USE ONLY
ACTION

The above-entitled matter has been assigned for

_____ (Trial) _____ (Pre-Trial Conference)

at _____ on _____ 20 ____, at _____

_____ . Returned without action. Date Incomplete. See above.

                                   _____

                                   Clerk's Initials

SAMPLE FORM ONLY

Sample Simplified Divorce Settlement

IN THE CIRCUIT COURT OF THE _____ JUDICIAL CIRCUIT,
IN AND FOR _____ COUNTY, FLORIDA

Case No.: _____
Division: _____

In re: the Marriage of:

_____,
Petitioner,

and

_____,
Respondent.

MARITAL SETTLEMENT AGREEMENT FOR
SIMPLIFIED DISSOLUTION OF MARRIAGE

We, {Husband's full legal name}_____ and {Wife's full legal name}
_____ being sworn, certify that the following statements
are true:

1. We were married to each other on {date} _____.

2. Because of irreconcilable differences in our marriage (no chance of staying together), we have made this agreement to settle once and for all what we owe to each other and what we can expect to receive from each other. Each of us states that nothing has been held back, that we have honestly included everything we could think of in listing our assets (everything we own and that is owed to us) and our debts (everything we owe), and that we believe the other has been open and honest in writing this agreement.

3. We have both filed a Family Law Financial Affidavit, Florida Family Law Rules of Procedure Form 12.902(b) or (c). Because we have voluntarily made full and fair disclosure to each other of all our assets and debts, we waive any further disclosure under rule 12.285, Florida Family Law Rules of Procedure.

4. Each of us agrees to execute and exchange any papers that might be needed to complete this agreement, including deeds, title certificates, etc.

Florida Family Law Rules of Procedure Form 12.902(f)(3), Marital Settlement Agreement for Simplified Dissolution of Marriage (11/12)

SECTION I. MARITAL ASSETS AND LIABILITIES

A. **Division of Assets.** We divide our assets (everything we own and that is owed to us) as follows: Any personal item(s) not listed below is the property of the party currently in possession of the item(s).

   1. Wife shall receive as her own and Husband shall have no further rights or responsibilities regarding these assets:

ASSETS: DESCRIPTION OF ITEM(S) WIFE SHALL RECEIVE (To avoid confusion at a later date, describe each item as clearly as possible. You do not need to list account numbers Where applicable, include whether the name on any title/deed/account described below is wife's, husband's, or both.)	Current Fair Market Value
Cash (on hand)	
Cash (in banks/credit unions)	
Stocks/Bonds	
Notes (money owed to you in writing)	
Money owed to you (not evidenced by a note)	
Real estate: (Home)	
(Other)	
Business interests	
Automobiles	
Boats	
Other vehicles	
Retirement plans (Profit Sharing, Pension, IRA, 401(k)s, etc.)	

Florida Family Law Rules of Procedure Form 12.902(f)(3), Marital Settlement Agreement for Simplified Dissolution of Marriage (11/12)

Furniture & furnishings in home	
Furniture & furnishings elsewhere	
Collectibles	
Jewelry	
Life insurance (cash surrender value)	
Sporting and entertainment (T.V., stereo, etc.) equipment	
Other assets	
Total Assets to Wife	$

2. Husband shall receive as his own and Wife shall have no further rights or responsibilities regarding these assets:

ASSET: DESCRIPTION OF ITEM(S) HUSBAND SHALL RECEIVE (To avoid confusion at a later date, describe each item as clearly as possible. You do not need to list account numbers Where applicable, include whether the name on any title/deed/account described below is wife's, husband's or both.)	Current Fair Market Value
Cash (on hand)	$
Cash (in banks/credit unions)	
Stocks/Bonds	
Notes (money owed to you in writing)	

Florida Family Law Rules of Procedure Form 12.902(f)(3), Marital Settlement Agreement for Simplified Dissolution of Marriage (11/12)

Money owed to you (not evidenced by a note)	
Real estate: (Home)	
(Other)	
Business interests	
Automobiles	
Boats	
Other vehicles	
Retirement plans (Profit Sharing, Pension, IRA, 401(k)s, etc.)	
Furniture & furnishings in home	
Furniture & furnishings elsewhere	
Collectibles	
Jewelry	
Life insurance (cash surrender value)	
Sporting and entertainment (T.V., stereo, etc.) equipment	
Other assets	

SAMPLE FORM ONLY

Florida Family Law Rules of Procedure Form 12.902(f)(3), Marital Settlement Agreement for Simplified Dissolution of Marriage (11/12)

Total Assets to Husband		$

B. Division of Liabilities/Debts. We divide our liabilities (everything we owe) as follows:

1. Wife shall pay as her own the following and will not at any time ask Husband to pay these debts/bills:

LIABILITIES: DESCRIPTION OF DEBT(S) TO BE PAID BY WIFE (To avoid confusion at a later date, describe each item as clearly as possible. You do not need to list account numbers Where applicable, include whether the name on any mortgage, note, or account described below is wife's, husband's, or both.)	Monthly Payment	Current Amount Owed
Mortgages on real estate: (Home)	$	$
(Other)		
Charge/credit card accounts		
Auto loan		
Auto loan		
Bank/credit union loans		
Money you owe (not evidenced by a note)		
Judgments		
Other		
Total Debts to Be Paid by Wife	$	$

2. Husband shall pay as his own the following and will not at any time ask Wife to pay these debts/bills:

Florida Family Law Rules of Procedure Form 12.902(f)(3), Marital Settlement Agreement for Simplified Dissolution of Marriage (11/12)

LIABILITIES: DESCRIPTION OF DEBT(S) TO BE PAID BY HUSBAND (To avoid confusion at a later date, describe each item as clearly as possible. You do not need to list account numbers. Where applicable, include whether the name on any mortgage, note or account described below is wife's, husband's, or both.	Monthly Payment	Current Amount Owed
Mortgages on real estate: (Home)	$	$
(Other)		
Charge/credit card accounts		
Auto loan		
Auto loan		
Bank/credit union loans		
Money you owe (not evidenced by a note)		
Judgments		
Other		
Total Debts to Be Paid by Husband	$	$

C. Contingent Assets and Liabilities (listed in Section III of our Family Law Financial Affidavits) will be divided as follows:

_____
_____
_____
_____
_____

Florida Family Law Rules of Procedure Form 12.902(f)(3), Marital Settlement Agreement for Simplified Dissolution of Marriage (11/12)

279

SECTION II. SPOUSAL SUPPORT (ALIMONY) Each of us forever gives up any right to spousal support (alimony) that we may have.

SECTION III. OTHER

_____
_____
_____
_____

I certify that I have been open and honest in entering into this settlement agreement. I am satisfied with this agreement and intend to be bound by it.

Dated: _____

_____
Signature of Husband
Printed Name: _____
Address: _____
City, State, Zip: _____
Telephone Number: _____
Fax Number: _____
E-mail Address(es): _____

STATE OF FLORIDA
COUNTY OF _____

Sworn to or affirmed and signed before me on _____ by _____.

_____
NOTARY PUBLIC or DEPUTY CLERK

_____
[Print, type, or stamp commissioned name of notary or clerk.]

_____ Personally known
_____ Produced identification
Type of identification produced _____

IF A NONLAWYER HELPED YOU FILL OUT THIS FORM, HE/SHE MUST FILL IN THE BLANKS BELOW: [fill in all blanks]
This form was prepared for the Husband who is the {choose only one} (☐) Petitioner (☐) Respondent. This form was completed with the assistance of:
{name of individual} _____
{name of business} _____
{address} _____
{city} _____ {state} _____, {telephone number} _____ .

Florida Family Law Rules of Procedure Form 12.902(f)(3), Marital Settlement Agreement for Simplified Dissolution of Marriage (11/12)

I certify that I have been open and honest in entering into this settlement agreement. I am satisfied with this agreement and intend to be bound by it.

Dated: _____

_____
Signature of Wife
Printed name:_____
Address:_____
City, State, Zip:_____
Telephone number:_____
Fax number_____
E-mail Address(es):_____

STATE OF FLORIDA
COUNTY OF _____

Sworn to or affirmed and signed before me on _____ by _____.

_____
NOTARY PUBLIC or DEPUTY CLERK

_____
[Print, type, or stamp commissioned name of notary or clerk.]

☐ Personally known
☐ Produced identification
   Type of identification produced _____

IF A NONLAWYER HELPED YOU FILL OUT THIS FORM, HE/SHE MUST FILL IN THE BLANKS BELOW:
[fill in all blanks]
This form was prepared for the Wife who is the {choose only one} (☐) Petitioner (☐) Respondent.
This form was completed with the assistance of:
{name of individual}_____
{name of business}_____
{address}_____
{city}_____,{state} _____, {telephone number} _____

Florida Family Law Rules of Procedure Form 12.902(f)(3), Marital Settlement Agreement for Simplified Dissolution of Marriage (11/12)

Sample Judgment of Divorce

At the *Matrimonial/IAS* Part _____ of New York State Supreme Court at the Courthouse, _____ County, on _____ .

Present:
Hon.   *Justice/Referee*
--X

                          Plaintiff,
     -against-

                          Defendant.
--X

Index No.:
Calendar No.:
Social Security No.:

JUDGMENT OF DIVORCE

EACH PARTY HAS A RIGHT TO SEEK A MODIFICATION OF THE CHILD SUPPORT ORDER UPON A SHOWING OF: (I) A SUBSTANTIAL CHANGE IN CIRCUMSTANCES; OR (II) THAT THREE YEARS HAVE PASSED SINCE THE ORDER WAS ENTERED, LAST MODIFIED OR ADJUSTED; OR (III) THERE HAS BEEN A CHANGE IN EITHER PARTY'S GROSS INCOME BY FIFTEEN PERCENT OR MORE SINCE THE ORDER WAS ENTERED, LAST MODIFIED, OR ADJUSTED; HOWEVER, IF THE PARTIES HAVE SPECIFICALLY OPTED OUT OF SUBPARAGRAPH (II) OR (III) OF THIS PARAGRAPH IN A VALIDLY EXECUTED AGREEMENT OR STIPULATION, THEN THAT BASIS TO SEEK MODIFICATION DOES NOT APPLY.

THE FOLLOWING NOTICE IS ☐ *APPLICABLE* OR ☐ *NOT APPLICABLE*

NOTICE REQUIRED WHERE PAYMENTS THROUGH SUPPORT COLLECTION UNIT

NOTE:

(1)   THIS ORDER OF CHILD SUPPORT SHALL BE ADJUSTED BY THE APPLICATION OF A COST OF LIVING ADJUSTMENT AT THE DIRECTION OF THE SUPPORT COLLECTION UNIT NO EARLIER THAN TWENTY-FOUR MONTHS AFTER THIS ORDER IS ISSUED, LAST MODIFIED OR LAST ADJUSTED, UPON THE REQUEST OF ANY PARTY TO THE ORDER OR PURSUANT TO PARAGRAPH (2) BELOW. UPON APPLICATION OF A COST OF LIVING ADJUSTMENT AT THE DIRECTION OF THE SUPPORT COLLECTION UNIT, AN ADJUSTED ORDER SHALL BE SENT TO THE PARTIES WHO, IF THEY OBJECT TO THE COST OF LIVING ADJUSTMENT, SHALL HAVE THIRTY-FIVE (35) DAYS FROM THE DATE OF MAILING TO SUBMIT A WRITTEN OBJECTION TO THE COURT INDICATED ON SUCH ADJUSTED ORDER. UPON RECEIPT OF SUCH WRITTEN OBJECTION, THE

(UD-11 Rev.3/1/16)   -1-

COURT SHALL SCHEDULE A HEARING AT WHICH THE PARTIES MAY BE PRESENT TO OFFER EVIDENCE WHICH THE COURT WILL CONSIDER IN ADJUSTING THE CHILD SUPPORT ORDER IN ACCORDANCE WITH THE CHILD SUPPORT STANDARDS ACT.

(2) A RECIPIENT OF FAMILY ASSISTANCE SHALL HAVE THE CHILD SUPPORT ORDER REVIEWED AND ADJUSTED AT THE DIRECTION OF THE SUPPORT COLLECTION UNIT NO EARLIER THAN TWENTY-FOUR MONTHS AFTER SUCH ORDER IS ISSUED, LAST MODIFIED OR LAST ADJUSTED WITHOUT FURTHER APPLICATION BY ANY PARTY. ALL PARTIES WILL RECEIVE A COPY OF THE ADJUSTED ORDER.

(3) WHERE ANY PARTY FAILS TO PROVIDE, AND UPDATE UPON ANY CHANGE, THE SUPPORT COLLECTION UNIT WITH A CURRENT ADDRESS, AS REQUIRED BY SECTION TWO HUNDRED FORTY-B OF THE DOMESTIC RELATIONS LAW, TO WHICH AN ADJUSTED ORDER CAN BE SENT, THE SUPPORT OBLIGATION AMOUNT CONTAINED THEREIN SHALL BECOME DUE AND OWING ON THE DATE THE FIRST PAYMENT IS DUE UNDER THE TERMS OF THE ORDER OF SUPPORT WHICH WAS REVIEWED AND ADJUSTED OCCURRING ON OR AFTER THE EFFECTIVE DATE OF THE ADJUSTED ORDER, REGARDLESS OF WHETHER OR NOT THE PARTY HAS RECEIVED A COPY OF THE ADJUSTED ORDER.

This action was submitted to ❏ *the referee* OR ❏ *the court* for ❏ *consideration* this ____ day of

_____ OR for ❏ *inquest* on this ____ day of _____.

The Defendant was served ❏ *personally* OR ❏ pursuant *to court order dated* _____

❏ *within* OR ❏ *outside* the State of New York.

Plaintiff presented a ❏ *Verified Complaint and Affidavit of Plaintiff constituting the facts of the matter*

OR ❏ *Summons With Notice and Affidavit of Plaintiff constituting the facts of the matter.*

The Defendant has ❏ *not appeared and is in default* OR ❏ *appeared and waived his or her right*

to answer OR ❏ *filed an answer or amended answer withdrawing any prior pleadings and neither*

admitting nor denying the allegations in the complaint and consenting to the entry of judgment OR ❏

the parties settled the ancillary issues by ❏ *written stipulation* OR ❏ *oral stipulation on the record*

dated _____.

The Court accepted ❏ *written* OR ❏ *oral* proof of non-military status.

(UD-11 Rev.3/1/16)   -2-

The Plaintiff's address is _____, and social security number is _

_____. The Defendant's address is _____, and

social security number is _____.

Now on motion of _____, the ❑ *attorney for Plaintiff* OR ❑ *Plaintiff*, it is:

ORDERED AND ADJUDGED that the Referee's Report, if any, is hereby confirmed; and it further

ORDERED, ADJUDGED AND DECREED that the application of plaintiff is hereby granted to

dissolve the marriage between_____, plaintiff, and _____, defendant,

by reason of:

❑ (a) the cruel and inhuman treatment of ❑ *Plaintiff by Defendant* OR ❑ *Defendant by Plaintiff* pursuant to D.R.L. §170(1); and/or

❑ (b) the abandonment of ❑ *Plaintiff* OR ❑ *Defendant* by ❑ *Plaintiff* OR ❑ *Defendant,* for a period of one or more years pursuant to D.R.L. §170(2); and/or

❑ (c) the confinement of ❑ *Plaintiff* OR ❑ *Defendant* in prison for a period of three or more consecutive years after the marriage of Plaintiff and Defendant, pursuant to D.R.L. §170(3); and/or

❑ (d) the commission of an act of adultery by ❑ *Plaintiff* OR ❑ *Defendant,* pursuant to D.R.L. §170(4); and/or

❑ (e) the parties having lived separate and apart pursuant to a decree or judgment of separation dated _____ for a period of one or more years after the granting of such decree or judgment, pursuant to D.R.L. §170(5); and/or

❑ (f) the parties having lived separate and apart pursuant to a Separation Agreement dated _____ in compliance with the provisions of D.R.L. §170(6); and/or

❑ (g) the relationship between Plaintiff and Defendant has broken down irretrievably for a period of at least six months pursuant to D.R.L. §170(7); and

(UD-11 Rev.3/1/16)   -3-

284

The requirements of D.R.L. §240 1(a-1) have been met and the Court having considered the results of said inquiries, it is

      ORDERED AND ADJUDGED   that ❑ *Plaintiff* OR ❑ *Defendant* OR ❑ *third party,*

namely: _____ shall have custody of the minor child(ren) of the marriage, i.e.:

Name	Date of Birth	Social Security No.
_____	_____	_____
_____	_____	_____
_____	_____	_____
_____	_____	_____

OR ❑ *There are no minor children of the marriage;* and

The requirements of **D.R.L. §240 1 (a-1)** have been met and the Court having considered the results of said inquires, it is

      ORDERED AND ADJUDGED that ❑ *Plaintiff* OR ❑ *Defendant* shall have visitation with the minor child(ren) of the marriage ❑ *in accordance with the parties' settlement agreement* **OR** ❑ *according to the following schedule:* _____
_____
_____

OR ❑ *Visitation is not applicable;* and it is further

      ORDERED AND ADJUDGED that the existing _____ County, _____ Court order(s)

under ❑ *Index No.*._____ **OR** ❑ *Docket No.*_____ as to ❑ *custody* **OR** ❑

visitation   shall continue OR ❑ *There are no court orders with regard to custody or visitation to be continued;* and it is further

      ORDERED AND ADJUDGED that ❑ *Plaintiff* **OR** ❑ *Defendant*   shall pay

to ❑ *Plaintiff* **OR** ❑ *Defendant* **OR** ❑ *third party, namely:*_____,

as and for the support of the parties' unemancipated children of the marriage, the sum of $_____

___ per_____, pursuant to an existing order issued by the _____ County, _____ Court,

under ❑ *Index* **OR** ❑ *Docket* Number _____, the terms of which are hereby continued.

OR ❑ *There are no orders from other courts to be continued;* and it is further

(UD-11 Rev.3/1/16)   -4-

ORDERED AND ADJUDGED that:

A) ❑ Pursuant to the ❑ *agreement of the parties*
❑ *Court's decision*

the ❑ *Plaintiff* shall pay to ❑ *Plaintiff*
❑ *Defendant* ❑ *Defendant*

the sum of $_____ as ❑ *per week* and for maintenance:
❑ *bi-weekly*
❑ *semi-monthly*
❑ *monthly*

❑ *payments to be made as set forth in the agreement;*
❑ *commencing on the ____ day of _____ , ____ , and continuing until the ____ day of _____ , ____ ;*
            month   year   *month   year*

Payment shall be ❑ *a direct payment,*
❑ *by an Income Deduction Order issued simultaneously herewith;*

==OR==

B) ❑ *that there is no award of maintenance per the court's decision;*
❑ *that there is no request for maintenance;*
❑ *that the guideline award of maintenance under the Maintenance Guidelines Law (L.2015 c. 269), if applicable, was zero.*
  and it is further;

==OR==

C) Pursuant to the court's decision for cases commenced before 1/25/16
the ❑ *Plaintiff* ❑ *Defendant* shall pay to ❑ *Plaintiff* ❑ *Defendant*

the sum of ❑ $_____ *per week;* ❑ $_____ *bi-weekly;* ❑ $_____ *semi-monthly* ❑ $_____ *per month*

as and for maintenance

commencing on the ____ day of _____ , ____ , and continuing until the ____ day of _____ ; *month year*

Payment shall be ❑ *a direct payment,* ❑ *by an Income Deduction Order issued simultaneously herewith;*

==OR==

D) Pursuant to the court's decision for cases commenced on or after 1/25/16
the ❑ *Plaintiff* ❑ *Defendant* shall pay to
❑ *Plaintiff* ❑ *Defendant*
the sum of ❑ $_____ *per week;* ❑ $_____ *bi-weekly;* ❑ $_____ *semi-monthly* ❑ $_____ *per month*

as and for maintenance (the "Award") *commencing on the* ____ *day of* _____ , ____ , *and continuing until the* ____ *day of* _____ , ____ ; *month year*

Payment shall be ❑ a direct payment,
❑ by an Income Deduction Order issued simultaneously herewith;

The guideline award of maintenance under the Maintenance Guidelines Law is $ _____

For the reasons stated in the Findings of Fact and Conclusions of Law, which are incorporated here in by
reference: (Check the applicable boxes:)

❑ *The Award includes an award on income of maintenance payor up to $178,000 per year. In computing said award, the Court applied the Maintenance Guidelines Law (L.2015, c.269) ;* **OR**
❑ *the court adjusted the guideline award of maintenance due under the Maintenance Guidelines Law because it is unjust and inappropriate.*

❑ *The Award includes maintenance on income of maintenance payor in excess of $178,000 per year* **OR** ❑ *The Award does not include maintenance on income of maintenance payor in excess of $178,000 per year.*

ORDERED AND ADJUDGED that ❑ *Plaintiff* **OR** ❑ *Defendant* shall pay to ❑ *Plaintiff* **OR** ❑ *Defendant* **OR** ❑ *third party, namely:* _____, **OR** ❑ because a party is already receiving child support services or an application has been made for such services, through the NYS Child Support Processing Center, PO Box 15363, Albany, NY 12212-5363; as and for the support of the parties' unemancipated child(REN) of the marriage, namely:

Name	Date of Birth
_____	_____
_____	_____
_____	_____
_____	_____

the sum of $_____ ❑ *per week* **OR** ❑ *bi-weekly* **OR** ❑ *semi-monthly* ❑ *per month,* commencing on _____, and to be paid ❑ *directly to* ❑ *Plaintiff* **OR** ❑ *Defendant* **OR** ❑ *third party, namely:*_____, **OR** ❑ *through the NYS Child Support Processing Center, PO Box 15363, Albany, NY 12212-5363,* together with such dollar amounts or percentages for ❑ *child care* **OR** ❑ *education* **OR** ❑ *health care* as set forth below in accordance with ❑ *the Court's decision* **OR** ❑ *the parties' Settlement Agreement.* **OR** ❑ *This section is not applicable because there are no unemancipated children of the marriage;*

Such Settlement Agreement, if applicable, is in compliance with D.R.L. §240(1-b)(h) because:

The parties have been advised of the provisions of D.R.L. Sec. 240(1-b); the

unrepresented party, if any, has received a copy of the Child Support Standards

Chart promulgated by the Commissioner of Social Services pursuant to Social

Services Law Sec. 111-I;

(UD-11 Rev.3/1/16)   -6-

the basic child support obligation, as defined in D.R.L. Sec. 240(1-b),
presumptively results in the correct amount of child support to be awarded, and
the agreed upon amount substantially conforms to the basic support obligation
attributable to the non-custodial parent;

the amount awarded is neither unjust nor inappropriate, and the Court has
approved such award through the Findings of Fact and Conclusions of Law;

OR

The basic support obligation, as defined in DRL Sec. 240 (1-b), presumptively
results in the correct amount of child support to be awarded, and the amount
attributable to the non-custodial parent is $_____ per _____
the amount of child support agreed to in this action deviates from the amount
attributable to the non-custodial parent, and the Court has
approved of such agreed-upon amount based upon the reasons set
forth in the Findings of Fact and Conclusions of Law, which are incorporated
herein by reference;

OR ❑ *This provision is not applicable, and it is further*

ORDERED AND ADJUDGED that,
if maintenance is to be paid pursuant to this Judgment of Divorce, then, subject to
the terms of DRL 240(1-b), upon termination of the maintenance award, the amount
of child support payable shall be adjusted, without prejudice to either party's right to
seek a modification pursuant to DRL 236 (B)(9)(2); and it is further

ORDERED AND ADJUDGED that ❑ *Plaintiff* **OR** ❑ *Defendant*
shall pay to ❑ *Plaintiff* **OR** ❑ *Defendant* **OR** ❑ *third party, namely:*_____and
for reasonable child care expenses pursuant to ❑ *written agreement of the parties* **OR** ❑
the court's decision, the amount of $_____ *per year or*
_____ ❑ *per week* ❑ *bi-weekly* ❑*semi-monthly* ❑ *per month*.

OR ❑ *Not applicable*; and it is further

ORDERED AND ADJUDGED

1- that ❑ *Plaintiff* **OR** ❑ *Defendant* shall pay   to ❑ *Plaintiff* **OR** ❑

Defendant **OR** ❑ *third party, namely:* _____,**OR** ❑ *through the Support Collection
Unit (because a party is currently receiving child support services or an application has been made for
such services)* as and for non-custodial parent's pro rata share of future health care expenses not

(UD-11 Rev.3/1/16)   -7-

covered by insurance,_____% of such expenses pursuant to ❑ written agreement of the parties
OR ❑ the court's decision

OR ❑ *Not applicable;*

2- Check which box or boxes apply:

    a)   ❑ *if the custodial parent provides the health insurance for the children:*

        ❑ *Plaintiff* **OR** ❑ *Defendant* shall pay to ❑ *Plaintiff* **OR** *Defendant* **OR**
        ❑*third party, namely:* _____,**OR** ❑ *through the Support Collection Unit*
        (because a party is currently receiving child support services or an application has been
        *made for such services)*as and for ❑ *The non-custodial parent's pro rata share of*
        health insurance premiums for the children , $_____ *per year or* _____ ❑
        per week ❑ *bi-weekly* ❑*semi-monthly* ❑ *per month OR*

    b)   ❑ *if the non-custodial parent provides the health insurance for the children:*
        The custodial parent's pro rata share of health insurance premiums for the children,
        $_____ *per year or* _____ ❑ *per week* ❑ *bi-weekly* ❑*semi-monthly* ❑ *per*
        month will be deducted from the child support obligation.

3-   ❑ *Plaintiff* **OR** ❑ *Defendant* shall apply to the state sponsored health insurance
    plan for coverage for the unemancipated children of the marriage. The costs shall be
    allocated pursuant to ❑ written agreement of the parties **OR** ❑ the court's decision **OR**
    ❑ *Not applicable;* and it is further

    ORDERED AND ADJUDGED that ❑ *Plaintiff* **OR** ❑ *Defendant* shall pay
to ❑*Plaintiff* **OR** ❑ *Defendant* **OR** ❑*third party, namely:* _____**OR** ❑
*through the Support Collection Unit (because a party is currently receiving child support services or an
application has been made for such services)* ❑For education or extraordinary expenses of the children
$_____ *per year or* _____ ❑ *per week* ❑ *bi-weekly* ❑*semi-monthly* ❑ *per month or*
_____ *% of such expenses* pursuant to ❑ written agreement of the parties **OR** ❑ the court's
decision **OR** ❑ *Not applicable;* and it is further

    ORDERED AND ADJUDGED that ❑ *Plaintiff* **OR** ❑ *Defendant* is hereby awarded

exclusive occupancy of the marital residence located at_____

_____, together with its contents until further order of the court, **OR** ❑ as follows: _____

_____

_____; **OR** ❑ *Not applicable;* and it is further

ORDERED AND ADJUDGED that the Settlement Agreement entered into between the parties on the_____day of_____, ❏ *an original* **OR** ❏ *a transcript* of which is on file with this Court and incorporated herein by reference, shall survive and shall not be merged into this judgment, and the parties are hereby directed to comply with all legally enforceable terms and conditions of said agreement as if such terms and conditions were set forth in their entirety herein, and this Court retains jurisdiction of this matter concurrently with the Family Court for the purposes of specifically enforcing such of the provisions of said Agreement as are capable of specific enforcement to the extent permitted by law with regard to maintenance, child support, custody and/or visitation, and of making such further judgment as it finds appropriate under the circumstances existing at the time application for that purpose is made to it, or both; and it is further

ORDERED AND ADJUDGED that a separate Qualified Medical Child Support Order shall be issued simultaneously herewith **OR** ❏ Not applicable; and it is further

ORDERED AND ADJUDGED that, pursuant to the ❏ *parties' Settlement Agreement* **OR** ❏ *the court's decision*, a separate Qualified Domestic Relations Order shall be issued simultaneously herewith or as soon as practicable **OR** ❏ *Not applicable*; and it is further

ORDERED AND ADJUDGED that, ❏ *pursuant to the Court's decision* **OR** ❏ *pursuant to the parties' agreement*, the Court, Court or the Support Collection Unit (where a party is currently receiving child support services or an application has been made for such services) shall issue an income deduction order simultaneously herewith **OR** ❏ Not applicable because the Court has made a finding in the Findings of Fact and Conclusions of Law that alternative arrangements have been made between the parties, or that good cause exists not to require such an order; and it is further

ORDERED AND ADJUDGED that both parties are authorized to resume the use of any prior surname, and it is further

ORDERED AND ADJUDGED that ❏ *Plaintiff* **OR** ❏ *Defendant* is authorized to resume use of the prior surname _____; and it is further

(UD-11 Rev.3/1/16) -9-

ORDERED AND ADJUDGED that ❏ *Plaintiff* **OR** ❏ *Defendant* is hereby awarded counsel and/or expert's fees as follows:

_____

_____**OR** ❏ *Not applicable*; and it is further

ORDERED AND ADJUDGED that ❏ *Plaintiff* **OR** ❏ *Defendant* shall be served with a copy of this judgment, with notice of entry, by the ❏ *Plaintiff* **OR** ❏ *Defendant*, within _____ days of such entry.

Dated:

ENTER:

_____

J.S.C./Referee

SAMPLE FORM ONLY

Sample Agreement to Mediate

Purpose of Mediation

The purpose of mediation is to help you resolve the issues between you. Mediation provides a forum where an impartial mediator will lead you in a cooperative problem solving process so you can reach informed decisions on the matters that concern you. The understandings you reach will be included in your separation agreement or memorandum of understanding prepared by the mediator.

You agree that you are in mediation to decide separation or divorce issues and that the mediator will help you discuss and determine the best arrangements for you and your family regarding parenting, income needs, and all of the other arrangements needed for your separation or divorce.

Role of Mediator

The role of the mediator is to facilitate your communication, help you understand the decisions to be made, assist you in your discussion of the issues, and as needed, help you generate alternatives to consider. All decisions are yours and no settlement will be imposed upon you. It is understood that the mediator has no power or authority to decide issues for you. The parties understand that mediation is not a substitute for independent legal advice. You understand that the mediator cannot offer individual legal advice to either or both of you and will not provide therapy or arbitration. You understand that the mediator must remain completely impartial during the mediation process.

Role of Attorney and Advisors

The mediator recommends you each consult separate attorneys to obtain legal advice regarding your rights and obligations. Upon written request from both spouses, the mediator will discuss with your attorneys any matters involved in the mediation. Consultation with other advisors, such as accountant, financial planner, tax expert, or appraiser may also become necessary during the mediation and will be recommended to you when it seems appropriate. The actual selection of such advisors and payment of their fees will be made by you.

Voluntary Nature of Mediation

Mediation is a voluntary process and no agreement or resolution will be forced upon you. Either of you is free to terminate the process at any time, as is the mediator. You both agree that you will not initiate or pursue divorce, separation, custody, child support, or other related matter in court while this mediation is ongoing.

Disclosure

In order for you to make fair decisions, honest and full disclosure of the family's financial situation (including assets and debts) and all other factors pertinent to the issues is necessary. You will be asked to complete financial disclosure forms and to provide copies of your income tax returns for the prior three (3) years. It is also necessary that during the process no transfer or disposition of any property or securities be made by either of you without full disclosure to the other and no unusual debts be incurred without disclosure and agreements of the other.

Communication Guidelines

The most productive atmosphere for mediation is created when each person shows respect for the opinions and attitudes of the other even if there is disagreement between them. Each of you must refrain from telling the other what he or she needs, wants or thinks. You must also try to listen to the other and to present your statements in the most effective way to have them heard and understood by the other. Name calling, insults, and disparaging the other's opinion or requests does not encourage another to listen to you, and the mediator will help you avoid that.

Confidentiality

Certain financial documents you furnish may be submitted to the court and to your attorneys. Other than this, all information and records presented in the mediation are regarded as confidential by the mediator and it is expected you will do so as well. By signing this Agreement to Mediate, you agree not to subpoena or otherwise involve the mediator or any office staff or any records of this mediation in any court proceeding or lawsuit whatsoever. Mediation discussions and any drafts or unsigned agreements will not be admissible in any court or contested proceeding. You agree that the mediator may have caucus meeting with you individually and that all meetings and discussions will be confidential.

Fees

Fees for mediation sessions are $_____ per hour and are payable at the end of each session. Both parties are legally responsible for the payment of these fees. You may work any arrangement between yourselves as to how you will divide the cost. In addition, a deposit of $_____ is required at the first mediation session, which will be applied to time spent outside the mediation session drafting your separation agreement or other necessary work on your behalf such as conversations with your attorneys or other advisors which will be charged at the regular hourly rate. Any unused portion of the deposit will be refunded upon conclusion or termination of the mediation.

Agreement to Mediate

I agree to participate in the mediation process on the basis of the summary included herein which I have read and discussed with the mediator. I understand that the mediator is providing a forum for mediation and discussion and that he/she is not offering legal advice or psychological counseling. I also affirm that I have been advised to consult with my own attorney, so as to be adequately advised regarding my legal rights and responsibilities regarding the issues being mediated.

I understand that I hereby waive any right of action that I may have against the mediator, or his/her staff for any allegation of wrongdoing, absent gross negligence. I affirm, under penalty of damages, that I will not call upon the mediator or any member of his/her staff to act as a witness on my behalf in any court of record to testify to facts or conversations relating to any alleged deeds, wrongful acts, omissions or commissions of the parties associated with this mediation.

I further affirm that I will not seek the production of notes or records of any mediation session that the mediator may have in his/her possession.

I understand the mediation fees are $_____ per hour for time spent on my behalf, both in and outside of the mediation sessions, and I agree to pay in full for all services rendered.

_____ (printed name)

_____ (signature of party)

_____ Date

_____ (printed name)

_____ (signature of party)

_____ Date

_____ (printed name)

_____ (signature of mediator)

_____ Date

Appendix C

Frequently Asked Questions

These are frequently asked questions I've encountered in my work as an attorney and mediator and divorce expert for a Web site. Each situation is individual, so it is important that you consult an attorney about your own case and your specific questions.

Alimony

My husband quit his job so he won't have to pay alimony. How do I get him to pay?

If you do not yet have an order directing alimony, you can request it and make sure the court understands that your spouse is purposely reducing his income to avoid alimony. If you're entitled to alimony, you will get it, even though he quit his job. If you already have an order and your spouse isn't paying because he quit his job, you will have to take him back to court for violating the order and seek to have it enforced.

I think it is ridiculous that my wife wants alimony. Once I pay that and child support, I won't have enough to live on. How can I reduce it?

When the court determines alimony, present all of your information about how much you earn, what your expenses are, and how much child support you pay. The purpose of alimony is not to bankrupt you. Argue against alimony based on your financial situation and ask the court to set the payments at a reasonable amount if alimony is ordered.

Can I get my spouse to pay for my health insurance after the divorce?

Yes, this is one thing the court can order. You are able to continue health insurance through your spouse under COBRA, which allows you to get it at his or her employer's group rate, but you have to pay the premium. The court can decide that your spouse should pay that premium or reimburse you for it as part of the spousal support package.

Annulment

My spouse and I got married and we both now realize it was a mistake. Can we get an annulment?

No. Just deciding that you made a mistake is not grounds for an annulment. You must show that there was fraud or concealment, or that you were not legally able to marry.

I want an annulment, but my wife doesn't. Can I still get one?

If you are referring to a legal annulment, yes. As with a divorce, it is a judge who makes the decision whether or not to grant annulment. You can ask for it and your wife can oppose it. Ultimately, the judge will decide.

After we got married I found out my husband spends half the day watching TV and won't get up and do anything around the house. This is not what I thought marriage was going to be. Can I get an annulment?

No. Unless your spouse lied to you about important matters or there was fraud involved in the marriage, you need to get a divorce.

Do I have to get a legal annulment to be able to get a religious annulment?

No, these are two completely separate processes. Talk with your priest or rabbi about annulment procedures in your church or temple.

If we both agree to an annulment, can we get one?

If you meet the legal requirements for an annulment, you can get one. If not, the court will not approve your annulment.

I really want an annulment, but my attorney says I don't qualify. Somehow a divorce seems worse than an annulment. What can I do?

If you don't qualify for an annulment, your only option is a divorce. A lot of people decide their marriage is not working and want an annulment. In actuality, few people end up qualifying for an annulment. There is almost no difference between an annulment and a divorce. The court procedures are virtually the same. The same things happen—the court divides property and debt and determines custody and child support. The only difference is that an annulment says that legally no marriage ever existed. Having that piece of paper isn't going to change the fact that you really were married and together. You can't erase that.

We're getting an annulment. I want alimony. Can I get it?

No. Temporary alimony can be granted during the pendency of the case, but because an annulment says there was no legal marriage, there can be no permanent alimony after the decision.

Can I get an annulment if my spouse is abusive to me?

No. Things that happen after you are married do not qualify you for an annulment. An annulment is about whether the marriage was valid at the time it was entered into.

Appeals

I signed the settlement agreement but I shouldn't have. I feel as though my attorney pressured me into it and it's not what I wanted. What can I do?

If you did not willingly sign the settlement papers or stipulation, you can have them overturned. However, this is unlikely since you will need to prove you were coerced into signing them. Changing your mind afterwards is not enough. At the time you signed the settlement papers you have to have done so against your will.

The divorce is over and what the judge ordered is totally unfair. Can I appeal?

You always have the right to appeal. Your attorney can help you understand what your chances on appeal are. An appeal only examines if the judge followed the law. It does not reconsider the evidence or call new witnesses.

Assets

My spouse is in the military. Am I entitled to part of his military pension when he retires?

Payments to retired military are called retired pay. Up to 50 percent of this pay can be awarded in a divorce (up to 65percent including child support). The court can actually award more, but this will have to be paid personally by the retired service member. This is considered property and not a pension plan.

My spouse is not telling truth about her assets. What do I do?

If your spouse has provided false information to the court on a financial affidavit, you need to hire an investigator to find the real facts and present them to the court. If you cannot afford to hire an investigator, try to gather as much information on your own that will disprove what your spouse is telling the court.

When we bought our house we put it in my husband's name only. What am I entitled to?

If you bought the home while married, it is a marital asset and will be divided in the divorce. If it was purchased before marriage, a portion of the value will be considered a marital asset if you helped maintain the home, pay the mortgage, or made improvements.

My husband took all of our valuable antiques from the home and left them at his parents' house and now says they belong to them. Can he do this?
If the antiques are marital assets (bought with marital funds during the marriage or given as a gift to both of you), then they must be divided in the divorce. You can seek an injunction or restraining order requiring him to return them. You should create a list of what was taken and gather photos and bills of sale if you have them. A valuation guide will help you estimate the value.

My husband and I are separated. I want to use money from our joint checking account to pay the bills. Can I do this?
Most definitely. The account is a marital asset and belongs to both of you. You can use it to support yourself. You should think about seeking child or spousal support though, so that you will have a set amount of money coming in.

My spouse handles all of the money and all bank accounts are in his name. He says I'm not entitled to any of the money and that he is going to take it all. Is this true?
No. Unless your spouse has money that was his before marriage which he has kept separate as a separate asset, all bank accounts are marital property and belong to both of you. It doesn't matter whose name is on it. If it was acquired during the marriage, it belongs to both of you and must be divided in the divorce.

We are separated. My spouse is not paying me any child or spousal support even though I have custody of the children. Can I access a bank account that is in her name only to get money for support?
No. While this is probably marital property that will be divided in the divorce, a bank will not let you access the funds unless you are an account holder or have power of attorney. If you are in need of child or spousal support, go to family court and ask for it.

My spouse moved out. Can I change the locks on the house?

You need to check with your attorney about this. In some states you cannot change the locks just because your spouse moved out.

Attorneys

My spouse has an attorney. Do I have to have one?

You never have to have an attorney, but it is recommended often. If your spouse has an attorney, you may be best served to retain one, since it is difficult (although not impossible) to adequately protect your rights when you are up against a professional.

If my spouse and I agree about everything, do we have to have attorneys?

No. You can handle the divorce yourselves without attorneys. More and more people are choosing to go this route.

I don't like my attorney. Can I switch?

You can switch; however, if papers have already been filed in your case your current attorney technically needs the court's permission to withdraw. This shouldn't be a problem, except in cases where a party is changing lawyers constantly. At that point it can become too disruptive and the court may decide you have to just stick with what you've got.

My attorney never returns my calls. What do I do?

Call and leave a detailed message explaining what the problem is and why it is urgent. State how many times you have tried to reach him and say you expect a call back within twenty-four hours. If you do not get one, call your state attorney grievance committee (the local bar association can tell you whom to call) and talk with them about the situation. It is likely they will be able to get your attorney to respond.

I just got a bill from my attorney and there is no way I can pay this. I can't believe I was charged for phone calls and travel time to court. How he can get away with this?

You're entitled to ask for a detailed accounting of the time your attorney has spent on your case. However, it is likely you signed a retainer agreement that spelled out your attorney's rates and the fact that you would be paying not only for his or her time, but also for expenses relating to the case. If you can't pay the bill, call your attorney and ask about a payment plan. Many clients do not realize how much of their attorney's time they are actually taking up with phone calls until they get a bill.

I think my attorney has cheated me. He didn't use all of the retainer and won't refund it. I think he signed papers I did not agree to. What can I do?
Contact your state bar grievance committee to file a complaint against your attorney.

I saw my attorney laughing and joking with my wife's attorney. I'm worried they're working together somehow and I'm going to get cheated. Should I fire him?
What you need to understand is that attorneys are colleagues. They work together on different cases, see each other at bar association meetings, refer clients to each other, and are part of a law community. Depending on the size of your city or town, it's likely they all know each other. The fact that they are friendly with each other can be a good sign. It means they are able to work together and can suggest compromises or settlements to each other. It does not mean they working against you in any way. Your attorney's job is to represent you and work for your interests. He can still do that while being pleasant to the other attorney on the case. If this really bothers you and is an ongoing problem, mention it to him. Let him know it makes you uncomfortable.

I told my attorney some very specific things I want. I told her to file a motion for temporary custody and told her I had to have a big alimony award. She's ignoring everything I say and has not filed any motions. Any advice?
In this situation, it would be a good idea to sit down with your attorney and have a talk. In most cases, the attorney is the one who plots the strategy of the case. She might have a very good reason for not filing any motions.

Then again, it's also possible she's not the right lawyer for you. Talking with her about what her plan is, how she intends to ask for what you want, and what the strategy is will help answer your questions. It is also important to realize that cases do not happen overnight. You can't ask your attorney to do something on Monday and be upset that it is not done by Wednesday.

Child Support

My spouse is supposed to provide health insurance for our children. She just lost her job and says she can't afford insurance. What do I do?

If she has been ordered to provide health insurance, she is responsible for it. If she has no job though this may be like getting water out of a stone. Every state now has child health insurance programs that offer free or low cost programs based on income. This is an option to consider if there are no other choices.

If I remarry will it affect the child support I receive?

It could. An increase in your household income could impact what you are entitled to.

If I remarry will it increase the amount of child support I owe?

Yes, if your new spouse has income. An increase in household income can be justification for an increase in the support you pay.

Why can't I buy food and clothes and other things for the kids instead of having to give money to the other parent for child support?

If this is something the two of you agree to, you could do so. You need to get it approved by the court (which frankly is unlikely) or have a child support order in place that you both decide not to honor (not a good idea since your ex could take you back to court anytime for failure to pay, even if you agreed otherwise). Despite this, there are parents who work out this kind of arrangement on their own. As far as the court is concerned, it is much simpler to police and quantify a regular weekly payment. If you don't pay the full amount, there is no question. There is too much wiggle room in any other type of agreement (how much food is enough? How much clothing is sufficient?).

My spouse is in the military. Can child support be withheld from his pay for child support?

Yes. Members of the military can have their wages garnished to pay child support. Your state child support enforcement agency will do so through the Defense Finance and Accounting Service (DFAS) Center in Cleveland, Ohio.

My spouse is in the military. Can my child be covered under her health insurance plan?

Yes. Health insurance for children of parents in the military is handled through the Defense Enrollment Eligibility Reporting System (DEERS). There is information available at: http://www.tricare.osd.mil/deers/general.cfm

My spouse's employer is refusing to garnish his wages for child support. What do I do?

Employers are required to comply with garnishment requests and have no choice. If your spouse's employer is not responding appropriately, let your attorney know. A simple phone call often will solve the problem. If you do not have an attorney, you may need to go back to court and have the court enforce the order with the employer.

My spouse is supposed to take out a life insurance policy naming the children as beneficiaries. He hasn't done it and says he is not going to. What can I do?

You have to go back to court to have the order enforced by the court.

I receive child support. I just got a new job that pays more. Is my child support going to be reduced?

It could be if the other parent asks for a modification based on a change in circumstances. However, if your new job means an increase in expenses such as child care, you may end up netting about the same, which could mean there would be no change.

Does child support include the cost of college?

It can. In some states, child support continues until the child is twenty-one if she is in school. College costs are one expense that can be included in a child support order. You can also wait until your child is ready to go to college and modify the child support order then.

My son is seventeen. I pay child support to his mother. He recently moved out and moved in with his girlfriend and their new baby. My wife says I have to continue paying her the child support. He says I should pay him. Who's right?

Neither of them. If a child becomes emancipated—lives independently on his own—child support no longer applies. It's wise to check with an attorney to make sure your situation fits the criteria set out by your state law. In this kind of situation, it might be worth considering how you can help your son. Even though you have no legal obligation, you do have a moral obligation to help your child. That doesn't mean you have to hand him cash, but you could help out by bringing groceries or offering to pay for him to get his GED or go to college.

I have children from a previous marriage that did not live with me before. Now they do. Does that affect the child support I have to pay for the children of my current marriage?

Yes, any increase in household expenses, or decrease in household income can affect child support.

My husband moved in with his girlfriend. Is her income considered when child support is set for our children?

In many cases it is, if they are sharing household expenses and incomes. An increase in income may mean he can pay more in child support.

My ex is far behind on child support. Can I stop visitation until he pays up?

No. Child support and visitation are two entirely separate issues. Withholding visitation can be grounds for a change in custody. Visitation is set up to benefit your child—so that he has two parents. Stopping visitation adversely affects your child. It can be tempting to want to pull the plug on visitation if child support is not being paid, but it's not legally permitted.

Children

My sixteen-year-old refuses to visit her father. Am I going to be in contempt of court if I don't make her go?

Most likely, no. The older the child, the more likely the court is to take her opinion into consideration when creating parenting plans. Your role is to encourage her to go and to encourage her to maintain contact with her father. Let your ex know you are doing so and are on his side. If you work together, he shouldn't contemplate taking you back to court, which will mostly be a waste of everyone's time.

My spouse does not use the visitation that has been set up on a temporary basis by the court. What do I do?

Your spouse's failure to use visitation will be a consideration when the court makes its final custody determination. In the meantime, I suggest you talk to her about why visitation is not being exercised. Try to be encouraging and welcoming. Sometimes parents feel uncomfortable with formal visitation and have no idea what to do with the kids during it. You might consider inviting the other parent to stop by for a few hours to watch a DVD with your child, or to attend your child's sporting event. Don't pressure him, just make the offer. Try not to micromanage the relationship between parent and child. They have to figure it out on their own at some point.

My spouse is a complete jerk and I don't think he should be able to spend time with my kids. I think he's a bad influence and is just going to end up hurting them. What can I do?

You should discuss your concerns with your attorney, or if you do not have an attorney, you need to present your concerns to the court. Almost everyone in a contested divorce believes his or her spouse is a jerk, but the fact of the matter is that being a jerk to your spouse does not make you a bad parent.

Unless you can prove that your spouse is in fact a bad parent, he is going to have a legal role in your child's life. If in fact your spouse is simply a jerk, this is something you have to allow your child to find out on his own. If you step in and tell your child "your father is a jerk and I don't want you to see him," at some point later in his life, your child is going to blame you for keeping him from his father. Make sure your child is going to be safe and well cared for and then take a deep breath and let go. They have to be able to manage their relationship on their own and your child has a right to know his father, with all the faults.

I don't like what my spouse is doing while the kids are at his house. He has really strict rules about making them eat all their vegetables and not leaving the table before their milk is gone. He also will not let them use the phone after 8 o'clock. I think he is being unreasonable and the kids hate it. Can I make him change what he's doing?

In short, no. Each parent has the right to parent in their own individual ways. You don't have the authority to tell him what to do in his house, just as he has no right to tell you want to do in your house. It's time to learn to step back and let him live his own life. He and the kids will figure it out on their own.

My wife has two kids from a previous marriage. I love them as if they were my own, but she is now saying she won't let me see. What can I do?

Unfortunately, in most states, step-parents do not have an absolute right to visitation. There are some situations in which the law looks at this differently. If you were the children's primary caretaker, you could have the right to seek custody. Because the laws in this area are so complicated and vary from state to state, it is a good idea to talk to an attorney so you can understand what your rights are. It is also a good idea to try to find a way to work this out with your ex on your own, because if you have no legal recourse, the only way you will be able to be a part of their lives is if she lets you. Try to frame the discussion around what is best for the children. Being suddenly ripped away from a parental figure is not good for them. Ongoing contact would allow them to adjust to the divorce more easily.

My spouse never uses his visitation. The kids are ready and waiting and he doesn't come and doesn't return my calls. Can the court force him to come?

Unfortunately, no. The court can strongly urge him to use his time, but if he chooses not to, there is nothing you can do about it legally. It is very hard for children to be in this situation. It may be a good idea to get them into a therapist who can help you find a way to deal with the sudden absence of their father. Going to court to have his visitation taken away from him is counter-productive. Try talking to him if you can to find out why he doesn't use his visitation. Suggest using another person as the intermediary if it is the problems between the two of you that is causing this.

We're getting a divorce because my wife has admitted she's a lesbian. I don't think it is a good idea for the kids to be around her. Can I stop visitation?

Being gay does not make anyone a bad parent and there is no court that (openly at least) will penalize a parent for being gay. Gay parents have just as much a right to custody or visitation as other parents. Being gay does not "rub off" on your children or in any way set a bad example.

My spouse has a girlfriend and whenever he has visitation, the girlfriend is there. She even sleeps over. I want this to stop. What do I do?

It's true that visitation is meant to be a time for parent and children to be to-gether, but there is no rule that excludes other people from being around. If you're concerned about the situation, try to pinpoint why. It is common to be jealous or uncomfortable, but this does not mean your child is in danger or is being ne-glected. I usually suggest talking to the other parent when there is a problem, but usually in a situation like this, there is no way to have a civilized conversation about this. You will come off as jealous and controlling and he will come off as stubborn and selfish. The best plan is to learn to accept the fact that the other parent is not going to do things your way and that is ok. Your kids will adjust.

I don't think my ex is a good parent. What can do I get supervised visitation set up?

Supervised visitation is used only in situations where the parent has been proven to be a poor parent and failed to give the children proper care. You will need to present a strong case that convinces the court that your child is not safe alone with your ex.

My children were born in one state and I now live in another and want to file for divorce here. Can I, or do I have to file where they were born?

You file for divorce in your state of residency, unless you meet residency requirements elsewhere. Place of birth has nothing to do with where custody or divorces are handled.

Counseling

I don't want a divorce. Can the court force my spouse to go to marital counseling with me?

Yes, a judge can order a couple to attempt counseling before proceeding with the divorce. Note, however, that counseling achieves its best results when both parties are there willingly and participating with interest.

The judge has ordered us to go to co-parent counseling. I think this is stupid. How do I get out of it?

You can't. If the judge ordered you to do it, failing to do so places you in contempt of court. If you go to counseling with an open mind and a cooperative attitude you will probably find you will learn some things and may find ways to work together with your spouse.

I saw a counselor during marriage and told her a lot of personal details. Can she be forced to testify against me in the divorce?

It is unlikely since there is a therapist-patient privilege.

Debts

I took out a personal loan to pay for our kitchen remodel. My wife has bad credit, so I did the loan in my name only. Am I now responsible for this?

No. A loan taken out during marriage is a marital debt and both of you are responsible for it.

My husband took out a student loan while we were married. Am I responsible for this?
Yes. Student loans taken out during marriage are marital debts.

Grounds
I don't want a divorce at all. Shouldn't that matter to the court?

Yes, your opinion matters; however, if you live in a no-fault state, your spouse doesn't have to prove anything to get a divorce. If you live a in a state that requires grounds for divorce, your spouse will have to prove them in a grounds trial. The final decision is up to the judge.

My wife had an affair while we were married. Can I sue the other man for causing our divorce?

In some states you can do this, by suing for alienation of affection or tortuous interference. You must be able to show the affair happened before you separated or agreed to divorce. You also need to show the affair is what caused the divorce. It's a good idea to consider what you're going to gain from this kind of lawsuit. If you don't win, it will be expensive, not to mention potentially embarrassing.

We have a covenant marriage. Does this mean I can't get a divorce?

A covenant marriage does not make divorce impossible; however, it makes divorce harder to qualify for. You are required to attend marriage counseling, remain separated for a longer period of time, and use a fault grounds in order to be eligible for a divorce in a covenant marriage.

Household Expenses
My husband moved out and refuses to help pay the mortgage or utility bills. I don't have a job and can't make the payments. What do I do?

You can go to court and ask for a temporary order requiring your spouse to pay all or some of the household expenses. If you are planning on divorcing, you would do this as part of your divorce case. If you are not sure about getting a divorce, you can go to family court and seek spousal support while still married.

Jurisdiction

My wife and I live in different states and neither is the state in which we were married. Where do I file for divorce?

You can probably file in the state in which you currently live, if you meet your state's residency requirements. These require that you have lived there for a certain period of time or that the reason for divorce arose in that state.

We got married in Mexico. Will a U.S. divorce end our marriage?

Yes. Most countries recognize each other's marriages and divorces.

Procedure

I started a divorce case a year ago but haven't done anything with it. How do I get it going again?

Call the court clerk and ask. You may have to start over, or you may be able to pick up where you left off. Be sure to have your case number when you call.

I filed for divorce, but I've changed my mind. Is it too late to stop it?

As long as a divorce decree or judgment has not been issued, it is not too late. You can simply withdraw the case. If you aren't sure if you want to go through with it or not, it is possible to put the case on hold while you and your spouse go to counseling or try to work out your problems on your own. The court would rather see you stay married than rush you through a divorce. In some states there are procedural rules that require the court to complete a divorce case within a certain period of time, so if you are close to that, you may have to withdraw your case even if you are unsure. There's nothing wrong with taking some time to reevaluate what you are doing so that you can make the right decision.

My spouse lied to the court. What can I do?

The only thing you can do is try to prove it was a lie. One thing people often lie about in divorce is their financial situation. Your attorney can subpoena records, or even hire an investigator to provide evidence about untruths in a financial statement. If your spouse is lying about other things, such as how well you've taken care of the kids, you need witnesses to show that this is untrue. Those kinds of statements can be hard to disprove since they are based in opinion. What you should do is try to present as many facts as possible which back up your side of the story.

We've been married only a few months. We don't qualify for an annulment. Can we get a divorce?

Yes. There is no required length of time you must be married to be eligible for a divorce.

I got a notice for a case management conference. What is this?

The terminology varies by state. A case management conference is a settlement conference. It's also sometimes called a pre-trial hearing. It's an opportunity for the parties to meet with a court official and determine what is agreed on and what is still being disputed.

How do I file an answer?

You need to use your state form for this. Call the clerk or check the state court Web site to locate one. Using an attorney is the best bet, because she will help make sure all of your rights are protected and that you do not agree to something you should not.

I got served with divorce papers but did nothing. The date to respond has passed. Is there anything I can do?

You should consult with an attorney who will help determine if you can still enter the proceeding.

I found out my spouse divorced me, but I was never served with any papers. What can I do?

Get an attorney. He will help determine if service was legally performed. If it was, there is nothing you can do. However, it is possible that your spouse failed to perform service correctly.

Separation

Am I legally separated if I move out?

No. A legal separation only occurs when a court issues a judgment of separation. A separation occurs anytime you live apart, but it is not the same thing as a legal separation.

Can I get married again if I am legally separated?

No. If you are legally separated, you are still married. You cannot remarry until your divorce is final.

If we get separated, do we have to get divorced?

No. You can remain married but separated forever if you want.

My husband and I are legally separated. Can my boyfriend move in?

Letting your boyfriend move in is your choice. In some states, this can have repercussions on your divorce. Your spouse may decide to use adultery as grounds for divorce. Having someone move in while you are still married can cause bad feelings with your spouse, who may decide to make things difficult for you. In the end, you are the one who can decide what is best for you.

Service

I have no idea where to find my husband to serve him papers. Can I still get a divorce?

Yes. You have to make reasonable effort to find your spouse, but if you are unable to locate him, then you can ask the court to allow you to give notice by publication. You'll publish a notice in a newspaper. If your spouse doesn't respond you are able to go forward with the divorce on an uncontested basis.

I sent my wife divorce papers and she refuses to sign them. Can she do that?

Your spouse does not have to consent to the divorce or agree to the terms that you are seeking. If he refuses to sign papers, you will need to have her formally served and proceed with the divorce on a contested basis.

My spouse has moved to another country. How do I serve him with divorce papers?

You need to consult an attorney who can arrange for service abroad. Many countries are signatories to the Hague Convention on Service Abroad of Judicial and Extrajudicial Documents, which sets out how service must be performed. Not all countries are members though, so you need an attorney who can determine what the requirements are in the other country and how best to work within them.

My spouse is in the military. How do I have her served?

Your attorney will need to comply with the Uniformed Services Former Spouse Protection Act (USFSPA) and serve her according to that.

I got the divorce papers but I signed them after the deadline. What happens now?

If you sent in the signed papers and agreed with everything, the court may choose to proceed as if they were on time. If, however, you did not agree with everything in the papers and were indicating this, you may need to appear at the next scheduled court date to make your position known. Consult an attorney, or at the very least, call the court clerk for some information about what is scheduled next.

I was served with the divorce papers, but I lost them. What do I do?

You can call your spouse's attorney and ask that another copy be mailed to you. If your state requires that papers be filed first, then served, they will be on record in the court clerk's office and you can get a copy there. At the very least, you can find out when the scheduled court appearance is, and appear there.

Other

What happens if I find a new partner before the divorce is final?

Most of the time, nothing. Technically, this is adultery and your spouse could seek to change the grounds for divorce, or seek an adjustment in alimony. In most cases, though, this does not happen. If you move in with someone else it can affect your eligibility for alimony and child support since your household income may go up. You're not free to remarry until the divorce is final.

What do I do if I think the judge is biased against me?

This is a difficult situation. You can appeal, but the appellate court will consider only points of law. If there is a clear bias, you can ask the judge to recuse herself, but if the judge doesn't agree, it's likely she will dislike you even more. The best solution is to get an attorney who can present a strong case for you.

Index

Accountant, 91
Adultery, 6
Alimony. *See* Spousal support
Anger, 192
Annulment
    reasons for, 23
    religious, 24, 204
    vs divorce, 22–24
Appeal, 196
Appraiser, 91
Arbitration, 100–101
Assets
    finding, 136–137
    hidden, 149
    household and personal, 139–140
    investments, 144–145
    marital, 133–134
    non-concrete, 147–148
    protecting before divorce, 48–52
    real estate, 140–142
    retirement, 143–144
    separate, 133–134
    valuation, 137–138
Attorney
    affording, 59–60
    evaluate, 57–59
    finding, 57

Bank accounts, 49
Bankruptcy, 168–169, 178–179
Behavior in court, 76–78
Best interests rule, 111
Bills, 51–52
Budget, 52–56
    single, 187–189
Business, dividing, 143

Career impact, 17, 193–194
Cash, 49

safety, 187
thinking about, 186

Mediation, 30, 80–99
    and attorney, 90–91
    attorney-assisted, 104–105
    benefits of, 83–85
    checklist, 94–97
    co-mediation, 103–104
    cost, 87–88
    court-ordered, 92–93
    deciding on, 82–83
    drawbacks of, 85–87
    how it works, 81–82
    long-distance, 105–106
    mediator qualifications, 88–89
    moving it along, 97–98
    and other professions, 91–92
    preparation, 93–94
    result of, 98–99
    shuttle mediation, 104
    unsuccessful, 99
Memorandum of understanding, 98
Mortgage, 142
Moving on, 207–208

Name change, 79, 201–203
Negotiating, 106–107
No-fault divorce, 36–37, 70–72

Opposing divorce, 25–26

Paralegal, 60
Parenting
    classes, 112
    divorce, 16–17
    uncooperative parent, 121
Parenting plan
    changes to, 206–207

Made in the USA
Monee, IL
14 March 2020